AN ANVIL ORIGINAL
Under the general editorship of Louis L. Snyder

THE TARIFF IN
AMERICAN HISTORY

SIDNEY RATNER
Professor of History
Rutgers University

D. VAN NOSTRAND COMPANY
New York   Cincinnati   Toronto   London   Melbourne

To
Jonathan and Ronnie Ratner

D. Van Nostrand Company Regional Offices:
New York, Cincinnati, Millbrae

D. Van Nostrand Company International Offices:
London, Toronto, Melbourne

Copyright © 1972 by Sidney Ratner
Library of Congress Card Number: 72-7968

Published by D. Van Nostrand Company
450 West 33rd Street, New York. N. Y. 10001

Published simultaneously in Canada by
Van Nostrand Reinhold Ltd.

10 9 8 7 6 5 4 3 2 1

Preface

From the first tariff measure of 1789 to the present, no generation of Americans has escaped the tariff controversy. Few other issues have aroused such intense debate. The reciprocal trade agreements that were developed after 1930 as a means of reducing or eliminating undesirable effects of tariffs have been no less productive of controversy. As the events of August, 1971 demonstrate, problems of foreign trade and the tariff are still with the American people and will persist for some time to come.

Although a large number of monographs on the passage and effects of different tariff acts and reciprocal trade agreements have been published, no full-scale history of the tariff has been written since the early classic by F. W. Taussig, and no single volume synthesizes the findings on reciprocal trade agreements. Nor has any general collection of significant documents on tariff controversies been published since Taussig's in 1921. Hence, a need exists for an overall view of the history of the tariff in the United States from colonial times to the present. In the present volume, the main contours of a very complex story have been carved out and highlighted. The focus of attention has been on the legislative struggles, the pressures exerted by economic and political groups, and relevant economic analysis and theory.

Chapter 1 presents a theoretical prelude to the historical narrative. The final chapter weighs the implications of the tariff for the past and future economic growth and welfare of the United States. The readings in Part II have been chosen to help the student understand in greater depth the arguments of historic figures and the circumstantial detail of major statutes and executive messages. The bibliography presents a selective list of factual and theoretical studies that supplement the data and analyses of the text. For the benefit of the general reader, an "Explanation of Some Key Economic Terms" has been included.

I am conscious of my debt to others who have done research in this field, but I have also drawn extensively upon my own research over many years. I am indebted to Professor Louise M. Rosenblatt of New York University and Professor Robert Hessen of Columbia University for their helpful suggestions, to Professor Louis Snyder for involving me in this project, and to Mrs. Carolyn Kappes for her skillful secretarial assistance. The U. S. Tariff Commission, the Treasury Department, the Council of Economic Advisers, and the Office of the Assistant to the President for International Economic Affairs supplied needed documents. The Rutgers University Research Council made possible special research on the period since 1933.

SIDNEY RATNER

Princeton, New Jersey

Contents

PREFACE   iii

PART I—THE TARIFF IN AMERICAN HISTORY

1. ECONOMIC GROWTH, TRADE, AND
   TARIFFS   3
   - The Benefits of Trade   3
   - The United States in World Trade   4
   - Tariffs: The Reasons Why   5

2. INDEPENDENCE, ECONOMIC EXPANSION,
   AND SECTIONAL CONFLICT   9
   - Colonial, Revolutionary Background   9
   - The Constitution of 1787   10
   - The Tariff Act of 1789   10
   - The Young Republic: 1790–1815   11
   - Nationalism and the Tariff Act of 1816   12
   - The Tariff, 1818–1827   14
   - The Tariff Act of 1828   15
   - Jackson and the 1832 Tariff Act   18
   - Nullification and the Compromise Tariff   19
   - The Whigs, John Tyler, and the "Black" Tariff
     Act of 1842   21
   - Manifest Destiny, Polk, and the Tariff Act of
     1846   23
   - Commercial Expansion, Slavery, and the Tariff
     Act of 1857   25
   - 1854 Reciprocity Treaty with Canada   26

3. THE CIVIL WAR, ECONOMIC CHANGE, AND
   POLITICAL CONFLICT   28

   The Republicans, War, and the Morrill Tariffs of
     1861   28
   Civil War Finance and the 1862–1864 Tariff
     Acts   29
   Republican Cleavages on Tariff Policy 1865–
     1871   31
   Republican Finance and the Tariff, 1872–1882   32
   Treasury Surpluses and the Tariff Act of 1883   33
   Grover Cleveland and the Democratic Thrust for
     Tariff Reform   35
   Big Business and the McKinley Tariff Act of
     1890   36
   The Democratic Return to Power and the
     Wilson-Gorman Tariff Act of 1894   38
   Republican Fiscal Conservatism and the 1897
     Dingley Tariff Act   39
   Insurgency and the Payne-Aldrich Tariff Act of
     1909   41
   Taft and Reciprocity with Canada, 1911   43
   Wilson, the Democrats, and the Underwood-
     Simmons Tariff Act of 1913   44
   Impact of World War I on Tariff, 1913–1921   46
   Republicans, Normalcy, and the Emergency
     Tariff Act of 1921   46
   Economic Nationalism and the Fordney-
     McCumber Tariff Act of 1922   47

4. THE DEPRESSION, THE NEW DEAL, AND
   WORLD WAR II   50

   Hoover and the Hawley-Smoot Tariff of 1930   50
   World Reaction Against the 1930 Tariff   53
   The 1932 Election, F.D.R., and the Tariff   54
   F.D.R., Hull, and Reciprocal Trade   55

5. AMERICA'S NEW ROLE IN THE WORLD ECONOMY, 1945–1970   58

International Trade Organization   58
Geneva Agreement of 1947 on Tariffs and Trade   60
The Temporary Status of GATT   61
Restrictions on Tariff Negotiating   62
European Common Market   65
European Free-Trade Association   66
Far Eastern Textiles   66
The United States and the Alliance for Progress   67
The Soviet Bloc: Aid and Trade   67
Kennedy and the Trade Expansion Act of 1962   68
Johnson and the Kennedy Round   70
Nixon and Foreign-Trade Policy   72
The Crisis in the U. S. Balance of Payments   73
The 1971–1972 Crisis in Foreign Trade   77
East-West Trade   78
Less Developed Countries   78
Continuing Problems   79

6. RETROSPECT AND PROSPECT   80

Political and Economic Nationalism   80
Internal Free Trade and External Protectionism   81
The Conditions of Economic Growth and the
    Tariff   82
Methods of Protection   83
The Effects of Tariffs on Recent Output and
    Employment   83
America's Stake in Foreign Trade: the Future
    Prospects   84

PART II—READINGS

1. The Tariff Act of July 4, 1789   91
2. Hamilton's Report on Manufactures, 1791   95

3. Clay's Speech of 1824 on American Industry   106
4. Webster's Speech of 1824 upon the Tariff   109
5. The Morrill Tariff Act of 1861   112
6. Cleveland's Message of 1887   118
7. McKinley's Speech on the Mills Tariff Bill   125
8. Reed's Speech on the Mills Tariff, 1888   133
9. Wilson's Tariff-Reform Message of 1913   139
10. The Protests of Economists Against the Hawley-
    Smoot Tariff   142
11. Roosevelt's Request for Authority to Enter into
    Reciprocal Trade Agreements, March 2, 1934   145
12. Reciprocal Trade Agreements Act of June 12,
    1934   147
13. Roosevelt's Request for Strengthening the Trade
    Agreements Act, March 26, 1945   150
14. Extension of Trade Agreements Act, July 5, 1945   155
15. General Agreement on Tariffs and Trade: Objec-
    tives and General Most-Favored-Nation Treatment   157
16. Truman's Executive Order for Escape Clauses from
    Concessions in Trade Agreements, February 25,
    1947   159
17. The Marshall Plan   162
18. Kennedy's Special Message on Foreign-Trade
    Policy, January 25, 1962   166
19. The Trade Expansion Act of 1962   179
20. The Kennedy Round, Geneva, 1964-1967   180
21. Johnson's Message on the Proposed Trade-Expan-
    sion Act of 1968   182
22. Nixon's Message on U. S. Trade Policy, November
    18, 1969   188
23. The Smithsonian Accord of December 18, 1971   196
SELECT BIBLIOGRAPHY   198
APPENDIX: EXPLANATION OF SOME KEY
    ECONOMIC TERMS   205
INDEX   207
LIST OF ANVIL BOOKS   216

Part I

THE TARIFF
IN AMERICAN HISTORY

CHAPTER 1

Economic Growth, Trade, and Tariffs

The Benefits of Trade. We all know that if each individual had to supply all his own requirements for food, clothing, shelter, heat, transportation, etc., he would be reduced to bare subsistence living. On the other hand, when each worker becomes a specialist at the job he does best and his products are exchanged with those produced by other workers, everyone is better off.

The advantages of specialization and higher output per worker hold true for geographical regions also. When people in different regions of a country specialize in the production of commodities that are best suited to their human and natural resources and interchange their regional specialties, the people in each region obtain more goods than they otherwise could have produced for themselves within their single region. American farmers, for example, buy automobiles from Detroit, petroleum from Texas, and clothing from the Northeast with the wheat, fruit, or cotton they grow in the Midwest, California, or the South. All Americans, whatever their occupation or geographical location, benefit in terms of the greater quantity and higher quality of food, clothing, and other consumer or producer goods achieved through this specialization in production.

International trade, like interregional trade, is based upon the varying geographical distribution of natural and human resources. Each country has a special combination of land, minerals, fauna, flora, labor supply, management skills, and machinery that enables it to produce certain commodities and services at lower production costs than other countries. When each country concentrates production on those goods and services it can produce relatively cheaply, international trade then permits each country to diversify its consumption. The goods each country produces in excess of its own domestic requirements can then be exchanged for a variety of goods

3

from elsewhere. This "division of labor" among nations tends to increase general economic welfare through the greater efficiency it permits in the use of the world's limited resources.

It is easy to see the common benefits of trade between a country
in the tropics and another in a temperate zone, or between two nations where one is more efficient in the production of one commodity, say steel, and the other nation is making another commodity, say
cloth, more efficiently than the first. It takes great economic sophisti-
cation, however, to realize that international trade is beneficial to
two countries even though one country may be absolutely more
efficient in the production of the goods or services it is importing
from the other country. A simple example of the economic principle
involved is the case of a highly gifted author who happens also to be
a better typist than anyone in his locality. Should he give up the time
he has for writing original fiction in order to do typing in which he is
efficient, but which pays him far less than his writing does? It is
worth his while to devote all of his energy to doing those things in
which he has a *relative* or *comparative* advantage, and to avoid doing
those things for which he is at a relative disadvantage. On the other
hand, the typist, although less efficient than the author in these two
activities, is at the least relative disadvantage in typing. From the
economist's point of view, he or she has a comparative advantage in
typing.

A similar logic applies to countries that are trading partners. Suppose that the United States produces coal with only one-fifth the
labor that Japan does and produces motorcycles with nine-tenths
the labor. The United States then has a comparative advantage in
coal and a comparative disadvantage in motorcycles. This situation
prevails even though the United States is in absolute terms more
efficient in both these industries. The logical converse of this is that
Japan has a comparative advantage in motorcycles. The important
conclusion that the economists draw from this analysis of the principle of comparative advantage is that Americans stand to benefit
most from specializing in their most efficient industries, and then
trading the products from these industries for goods in which another nation has a comparative advantage on its side.

The United States in World Trade. The United States is the
world's greatest exporter and importer of commodities. Until World
War II, it was second to Great Britain in the value of its imports;
since the war, however, it has become the top importing country.

During the colonial period and the first hundred years of its existence as an independent nation, the United States depended greatly on foreign markets both for imports of needed manufactured goods and raw materials and for exporting its agricultural products, especially cotton and grains. In 1800 the value of U. S. imports equalled 13.1 percent of the national income. But as the territory of the United States expanded to include the unexploited resources of the West beyond the Mississippi, and the manufacturing industries of the country became more developed, American exports began to exceed American imports. The ratio of imports to the national income fell to 9.5 percent in 1900, to 3.7 percent in 1950, and to about 3.6 percent in the mid-1960's. The corresponding percentage of the national income for U. S. exports was 10.2 in 1800, 5.5 in 1900, 4.3 in 1950, and 5.2 in the mid-1960's.*

Although small in relation to the national income, the total value of American trade is the largest in the world. U. S. exports in the last decade have amounted to about 15 percent of the world trade, and U. S. imports in the same period to about 12 percent of the world trade. The exports and imports of the United States have nearly equalled the combined exports and imports of West Germany and the United Kingdom, the next two biggest trading countries.

Hence, American trade, especially imports, is economically of great importance to the American economy—especially in terms of strategic materials—and of vital importance to countries that look to the United States for markets for their main exports. The smaller these countries are, even relatively large ones such as Japan, West Germany, France, and the United Kingdom, the more important their foreign trade, especially with the United States, is to their prosperity and welfare.

Tariffs: The Reasons Why. From time immemorial the merchants who have engaged in international trade have had to pay duties upon commodities crossing a political frontier. In modern times the term "tariff" has been defined as a schedule of rates of import or export duties upon different articles of merchandise to be paid to a government for their importation or exportation. The term "tariff" is

---

* For some purposes it is useful to know that if the components of national income or GNP are measured in 1913 dollars instead of in current dollars, then over the period between 1880 and 1960 foreign trade grew as rapidly as national output.

also used for a duty levied on one class of articles, e.g. the tariff on silk. Finally, "tariff" is also used to mean laws regulating such import or export duties.

In ancient and medieval times tariffs were used only for revenue purposes. With the growth of mercantilism and nationalism in the sixteenth and seventeenth centuries, however, they were put to new uses: to protect domestic industries against foreign competition, to promote a favorable balance of trade, and to punish and decrease the power of rival countries. Export duties, which at first were of major importance, were gradually abolished, and tariffs came to consist mainly or entirely of import duties, except in tropical and subtropical countries.

From the viewpoint of citizens of the world interested in general world welfare, there is no doubt that free trade is best for the great majority of people. The reason is that free trade helps to maximize the world's output of goods and services and is to that extent a substitute for the perhaps more inconvenient movements of productive factors such as people and machinery. Nevertheless, any one country may be induced to impose restrictions on international trade through tariffs or import duties for a variety of reasons, good or bad, valid or invalid. One reason may be the need for a national government to get revenue easily. This was true in the United States until the Federal Income Tax became a permanent part of the national revenue system in 1913. At the outbreak of the Civil War, about 95 percent of the total national Government revenue came from tariffs on imports. By 1913 customs made up less than half of the Federal revenues, and in 1970 it was less than 1 percent.

One argument in defense of tariffs is that it may promote industries needed for national security or defense. This had some validity until the invention of the atom bomb and the hydrogen bomb. Since then, the nature of warfare has changed so drastically that this argument no longer is as important as it was previously.

Another argument is one that had considerable influence in the United States immediately after the War of 1812 and also during and after the Civil War. Its contention is that infant industries such as the textile and iron and steel industries in the United States might require tariff protection against the competition of more mature industrial nations such as Great Britain so that these industries might gradually build up skilled managers, labor, and reliable suppliers of raw materials. The danger here is that in many cases, once an industry gets a special subsidy through a protective tariff, it is difficult for the Government to then take away the protective tariff after the so-called young industry has become mature. Some economists have argued that when infant industries justify special subsidies, these should be given in the form of outright grants from the national Government rather than as tariffs; then the direct costs upon the rest of the nation can be seen. A halt can also be imposed more easily on that special subsidy than when a tariff is used for such purposes.

The third powerful argument for tariffs is that they may help to combat unemployment created by a decline in domestic demand during a depression in the business cycle. Tariffs can also be used to decrease unemployment that may be high in certain industries that compete unsuccessfully with imports during a period of otherwise general prosperity. Nevertheless, even here the tariffs are relatively inefficient tools. They do not expand employment in the more efficient export industries, but in the relatively less efficient import-competing industries. This is not the wisest economic policy for a country to follow. There are other alternatives, such as creating greater flexibility in wage-rates or altering a country's exchange rate until the high-cost countries' prices are aligned with the prices of the competing nations. Similarly, a depression can be better fought by using Keynesian government-spending policies and expanding its money supply rather than by resorting to protective tariffs.

One very popular argument for the protective tariff is that it acts as a protection for the high wages and high living standards of American workers against the competition coming from cheap foreign labor. This ignores the fact that there is a vital connection between high wages and high efficiency. When wages are higher in an American industry than in a foreign industry, this usually occurs when the American labor in that industry is more productive than the foreign labor. As each nation specializes in producing those commodities and services in which it has a comparative advantage and imports those where another country has a comparative advantage, the real wages and the living standards in all nations are increased.

There are other arguments that have won large support in the United States at different times but which the economist has reason to question. One is the appeal to farmers to support a tariff for industry on the ground that this will bring them a large home market for their products. This argument, however, ignores the fact that cutting down industrial imports causes Americans to lose out on a corresponding amount of farm exports. It is claimed that this loss will be counterbalanced by the extra home market for farm produce, but the total domestic demand for farm products would be at a lower level of real income than would have existed if the foreign trade of the country were maintained at a high level.

In 1970 many of the above arguments were revived with great force and emotional intensity by groups interested in renewing or extending the protective tariff. The tariff history of the United States thus demonstrates how different pressure groups have used arguments for achieving sectional, class, or national objectives, based sometimes on fact and logic, sometimes on fantasy and illogic. The study of tariff history can teach us much about how national policies have been made, under the pressure of different economic and political groups, with consequences for the American people and the outside world often far greater or different from those originally envisaged.

CHAPTER 2

Independence, Economic Expansion, and Sectional Conflict

Colonial, Revolutionary Background. Custom duties were important sources of revenue for the British colonies in America. Nearly every colonial legislature imposed import duties for its own treasury, in addition to those duties levied by England in the execution of the Navigation Acts. The main purpose was fiscal, but sometimes the motive for framing these laws was the protection of home industries; sometimes a check against the importing of articles, the consumption of which was regarded as injurious or useless; and in certain cases, retaliation against rival colonies or European nations other than England. Low or moderate duties were levied, mainly on slaves and articles considered luxuries such as sugar, tea and coffee, rum, spirits, and wine. Duties on exports, generally imposed only for revenue, were also common, and the range of commodities selected was wide, extending from tobacco to furs, wool, iron, and timber.

These colonial customs continued after the Colonies declared their independence of England in 1776. During the following decade the Northern states increased their import duties in order to protect local business against interstate and international competition. From 1774 to 1781 the Continental Congress acted as a revolutionary, extra-legal but *de facto* national coordinating and directing government. The Congress assumed the power to contract debts, but it could only apportion the amounts it needed among the colonies and ask them to remit. When in 1781 the Articles of Confederation went into effect, they did not confer upon the Congress any right to levy taxes. Moreover, the Articles provided "that no treaty of commerce shall be made whereby the legislative power of the respective States shall be restrained from imposing such imposts and duties on for-

eigners as their own people are subjected to, or from prohibiting the
exportation of any species of goods or commodities whatsoever."
This provision left the making of tariffs to the states. The financial
problem of Congress led it to propose, first in 1781 and then in 1783,
that it be granted power to levy specific customs duties upon certain
classes of imports. But these proposals were blocked by Rhode
Island in the first instance, by New York in the second.

The Constitution of 1787. Although the achievements of the
Confederation were greater than many of its past critics have allowed, the Confederation Government never managed to obtain
enough revenue from its requisitions on the states to cover its expenditures between 1781 and September, 1789; it depended upon
foreign and domestic loans to meet most of its current expenses.
When the framers of the new Constitution of 1787 met in Philadelphia, they strengthened the national Government by empowering
Congress to "lay and collect taxes, duties, imposts, and excises, to
pay the debts and to provide for the common defense and general
welfare of the United States." Certain limits, however, were imposed
upon Congress: All duties, imposts, and excises were to be (geographically) uniform throughout the United States; no duties were
to be imposed by Congress upon articles exported from any state.
On the other hand, no export or import duties were to be imposed
by any state without the consent of Congress. The new Constitution,
hence, put an end to state tariffs and made the regulation of commerce with foreign nations the responsibility of the national Government.

The Tariff Act of 1789. When Congress met in the spring of
1789, it was faced with the urgent need to provide revenue for the
new government. James Madison opened the tariff debate in the
House by offering a simple proposal to levy duties on imports,
mainly for the sake of revenue. He recommended special duties on
eight noncompetitive imports, e.g. tea, coffee, sugar, and taxes on all
other articles at a single low rate. But at once a demand for protection arose that divided Southerners against sponsors of manufacturing in the North. A Pennsylvania Congressman, Thomas Hartley,
pleaded for tariff protection of infant industries against foreign competition. After an extended congressional debate, President Washington signed the first tariff act on July 4, 1789. (*See Reading No. 1.*)

This statute proclaimed as its objectives "the support of the government, the discharge of the debts of the United States, and the en-

couragement and protection of manufactures." It was protectionist in intent, but primarily a revenue measure in effect. Specific duties were imposed on more than thirty kinds of commodities; ad valorem duties, varying from 7½ percent to 15 percent, on a few specified articles; and a 5-percent duty on all goods not otherwise enumerated. The average rate of duty, under this tariff, when reduced to an ad valorem basis, was 8½ percent.

In the debate in Congress, there was little fiscal generalization. Madison was the only person to treat the subject broadly, and he preferred to limit the tariff bill to the object of revenue exclusively. He argued that if industry and labor were left to take their own course, they would generally be directed to the most productive objects. Nevertheless, he allowed some exceptions to the general rule of free trade: Established manufactures within the United States ought not to be ruined; prohibition of imports for sumptuary reasons should be allowed; and protective duties might be justified when they contributed to national defense and security.

The first tariff act was limited to seven years; Congress did not seem yet to care to adopt a high tariff as a permanent system. The statute also provided for such important administrative matters as the use of both ad valorem and specific duties, the granting of drawbacks (return of import duties) on the exportation of goods solely for the purpose of transfer from one country to another, and the principle of discrimination against the shipping of foreign countries as a whole and against particular countries. Consideration was shown for the trade with the Far East; the specific duties placed upon teas were doubled if the importations were made in foreign vessels; and on all other goods imported from China or India in foreign ships there was a higher ad valorem rate of 12½ percent. On goods imported in vessels built or owned entirely in the United States, there was a discount of 10 percent on the duties.

Shortly after the passage of this law, a measure was adopted for regulating the collection of import duties. The United States was divided into collection districts; ports of entry and delivery were enumerated; and provision was made for the appointment of customs officers. The administration of the customs was simple at first, and much was left to the discretion of the collectors. Ten years later new legislation was enacted that carefully prescribed forms, bonds, schedules, and oaths.

The Young Republic: 1790–1815. In 1790 additional revenue was needed, and the tariff was increased slightly. Congress then directed the Secretary of the Treasury to draw up a report on how to encourage and promote such manufactures as would help to render the United States independent of other nations for essential, particularly for military, supplies. On December 5, 1791, Alexander Hamilton submitted his brilliant "Report on Manufactures," with its powerful argument for the protective tariff as a means of developing manufacturing and a more diversified economy. (*See Reading No. 2.*) Although this essay became a storehouse of arguments for American and European protectionists, it had little, if any, effect on the legislation of its day. The moderate policy of 1789 was retained. Between 1792 and 1816, some twenty-five acts were passed affecting tariff duties, but the changes were usually for the purpose of revenue, or to continue previous laws of temporary duration. In 1812 Congress doubled the duties on imports in order to obtain additional revenue for the war that had broken out with Great Britain. The rates continued one year after the establishment of peace.

During the war, exports from England to the United States were almost discontinued, and American manufacturing, which had been thrown on its own resources as far back as 1806 when the Non-Importation Act had been passed, expanded greatly. When peace was established in 1815, foreign goods poured into the American market in such large volume that by 1816 imports were almost double those of any year before the war. The great influx of foreign goods was said by champions of the manufacturing interests to threaten ruin to the newly developed industries. Moreover, increased revenue was necessary to meet the debts resulting from the War of 1812.

Nationalism and the Tariff Act of 1816. The War of 1812 had evoked a patriotic fervor throughout the South and the West that led President Madison, Thomas Jefferson, and other Jeffersonian Republicans to give up their earlier opposition to the protective tariff. They championed the protective tariff as the bulwark for industries that were indispensable to the preservation of national independence. The control of congressional policy at the end of the War of 1812 was still in the hands of a group of young men who had brought about the War of 1812. They had a strong feeling that the manufacturing establishments that had grown up during the war should be assisted. But there was little sentiment either in Congress or among the people in favor of a permanent strong protective tariff policy.

Madison's Secretary of the Treasury, Alexander Dallas, was called upon to prepare a tariff bill, which he later submitted in February, 1816, with the principles upon which he had framed the measure. The interests of agriculture, manufactures, trade, and navigation were to be conciliated, and the collection of revenue was to be made both equitable and certain. Articles of importation were to be arranged in three classes. The first class included commodities manufactured in adequate supply at home, on which it was proposed to place duties sufficiently high to exclude foreign competition; the second class embraced articles partially supplied in the United States, which were to receive less protection; the third, articles not produced at home and therefore subject to purely revenue duties.

The tariff bill finally introduced (not by a Congressman representing northern industry, but by William Lowndes of South Carolina) carried rates somewhat less than those recommended by Secretary of the Treasury Dallas. These new rates, though generally less than those prevailing during the war, were higher than the previous peacetime levels. In its final form the 1816 act provided for a general level of rates on dutiable goods of about 20 percent. Cotton and woolen goods paid a duty of 25 percent, which was reduced after three years to 20 percent. All cotton cloths that originally cost less than twenty-five cents per square yard were deemed to have cost that sum and were to pay duties accordingly. This was the introduction of the minimum-value principle. The statute also levied a 30-percent ad valorem duty on such other goods as hats, cabinet wares, manufactures of wood, carriages, leather and its manufactures, and paper. Specific duties from three to twelve cents per pound were laid upon sugar.

The 1816 Tariff Act made protection for the first time the primary principle of the tariff system and treated revenue as secondary to industrial needs. The debate over this bill introduced the first in a series of nationwide discussions of the relative advantages of free trade and protection. One of the outstanding congressional champions of the protective principle at that time was John C. Calhoun of South Carolina; another was Henry Clay of Kentucky. Among its leading opponents was the brilliant, eccentric Congressman from Virginia, John Randolph of Roanoke, who forcibly expounded free-trade principles. Another impressive opponent was Daniel Webster, who represented the commercial, but not the industrial, interests of New England at this time. He voted against the measure, although he admitted that in so doing he was opposing the wishes of a very large majority of the country.

The Tariff, 1818–1827. The tariff of 1816 did not protect American iron products against competition from England, Sweden, and Russia. The English cut their iron costs through a process using coke, Russia and Sweden through their cheap and abundant labor and wood supplies. In 1818, Congress passed a special tariff act that raised the duties on iron; at the same time it postponed the reduction of the 1816 duties on cotton and woolens until 1826. Considerable industrial and financial distress in 1819 and 1820 was made the occasion by champions of cotton, woolen, and iron manufactures for an unsuccessful attempt to raise tariff duties on these products.

In 1824 pressure from industrialists in the Northeast, the wool, hemp, and flax growers of Ohio, Kentucky, and Tennessee, and the Louisiana sugar planters led to a general revision of the tariff. The most important changes in the new tariff were in the higher duties on iron, lead, wool, hemp, cotton bagging, and other articles whose protection was urged mainly by the Middle Atlantic and western states. The duties on textile fabrics were also increased. Those on cotton and woolen goods rose from 25 to $33\frac{1}{3}$ percent. This increase, however, was counterbalanced, so far as woolens were concerned, by a duty of 30 percent imposed on raw wool, which had before been admitted at 15 percent. Wool growers for the first time became an important pressure group in the drafting of American tariffs. The principle of minimum value was extended from cotton to woolen goods. Hemp manufactures were taxed 25 percent. On cotton goods, the minimum valuation was raised in order to protect some finer grades of fabric.

One consequence of the 1824 Tariff Act was that the manufacturers of woolen goods were in about the same position as in 1816, owing to the higher cost of raw wool. On the other hand, the heavier duties on iron and hemp resulted in a financial setback to the New England shipbuilders.

The conflict of sectional interests was clearly revealed in the congressional debates upon this measure. In general, support for the bill came from a combination of Middle Atlantic and western states. The opposition represented the planting interests of the South and the commercial-shipping interests of the Northeast. The producers of iron, wool, hemp, glass, and lead were united against the importers and the owners of the merchant marine. Henry Clay of Kentucky, the sponsor of the "American System," spoke eloquently about the high protective tariff creating a great home market for American raw materials and agricultural produce. He hoped to build up American iron, hemp, textiles, and shipbuilding industries to the point of independence of foreign competition. (*See Reading No. 3.*)

Daniel Webster, representing Massachusetts, spoke with at least equal eloquence against these arguments for the protective tariff and argued effectively that the prosperity of the United States did not require any excessive subsidies granted to special interests under the 1824 Tariff Act. At this time Webster was a champion of free trade, especially as it benefited the commercial and shipping interests of New England. He was willing to support a "moderate," but not a "prohibitive" protective tariff. (*See Reading No. 4.*)

The Tariff Act of 1828. The general average of the 1824 Tariff Act was a little over 30 percent, but the gains thereby secured failed to satisfy the beneficiaries for long. Parliament in 1824 had reduced drastically the duty of raw wool imported into England from twelve pence to a penny a pound. This enabled the English manufacturers of woolen goods to sell their products more cheaply in America. Consequently, the American woolen manufacturers, especially in Massachusetts, pressed for higher tariff duties. In January, 1827, the Mallary Bill was drafted to protect American woolen goods and wool from English competition by extending the minimum principle of valuation. Although this bill passed the House, it was lost in the Senate by one vote, that of the Vice-President, John C. Calhoun.

This defeat by such a narrow margin inspired the champions of higher protection to launch a national campaign for a higher protective tariff. During the summer of 1827 a tariff convention was held in Harrisburg, Pennsylvania. A program for higher duties on wool and woolens and on manufactures of cotton, hemp, flax, iron, and glass was proposed to Congress and to the American voting public. Two economists who supported this policy were Matthew Carey of Philadelphia, an influential and original American economic theorist, and the German economist, Friedrich List, then a newspaper editor in Reading, Pennsylvania.

At this point Presidential politics became an important factor in the development of the 1828 tariff. John Quincy Adams, who had been elected President in 1824 through the aid of Henry Clay, was committed to building a National Republican party, based on a coalition of the Northeast and the Ohio Valley and dedicated to promoting the protective tariff, the Second Bank of United States, and internal improvements. Adams' and Clay's program was opposed by the supporters of Andrew Jackson for the Presidency in what was then called the Democratic Republican party. But the Democratic party was hopelessly divided along sectional and class lines on the protective tariff issue. Most Southerners were against the protective tariff, most northern Democrats were for it.

The managers of Jackson's 1828 Presidential campaign thought that they could escape the horns of their dilemma by fabricating a tariff bill that would hurt New England by imposing such heavy duties on raw materials that the bill would be repudiated by the New England manufacturing interests. The Jacksonian strategists' idea was to force the bill to a vote without amendment, and then to unite with the disaffected interests in its defeat. The proposed duty on raw wool was high; on finished woolens, low. Duties were increased on the iron and hemp required by New England shipbuilders, and on the molasses so profitably made into rum in various New England towns. The belief of Martin Van Buren and the other Jacksonian manipulators of Congress was that on such a tariff, the Democrats would vote according to the interests of their geographical sections. On the other hand, the New England supporters of the Adams Administration were thought to be in a position where they would be forced to defeat the measure in order to protect their own constituents. The result, as the Van Buren group saw it, would be that the South would be pleased, the Adams-Clay coalition damaged, and Jackson would emerge on both sides of the tariff issue, uncommitted but with his popularity untouched.

This cunning scheme misfired, however. The bill was odious, but the protective tariff interests were so strong that the measure was accepted by both houses of Congress. Democrats from the Middle Atlantic and western states wanted duties raised, no matter what their southern friends thought, and were not prepared to support a bill only to bring about its final defeat. New England had become by 1828 a dominantly manufacturing rather than commercial economy; many there wished to have the tariff duties raised. Although the bill in its original form was damaging to the New Englanders' interests, it passed the House by a vote of 105 to 94, with the support of the Administration Congressmen from the Northeast. A sharp conflict developed in the Senate on a number of key items in the House bill but once certain modifications were made, the Senate passed the measure 26 to 21. The unanimity of the Senators from the Middle Atlantic and western states was a decisive factor in the bill's passage, along with Daniel Webster's winning six out of eleven New England Senators to his side.

The Tariff Act of 1828 represented the height of protective legislation before the Civil War. It was generally condemned and derisively called the "Black Tariff" and the "Tariff of Abominations." Its predominant feature was the protection given to the woolen manufacturers; hence, the measure was often referred to as the "Woolen Tariff." Raw wool also received further protection. Under the 1824 act imported raw wool had been taxed 30 percent ad valorem, but in the 1828 statute it was subject to both an ultimate ad valorem duty of 50 percent and to a specific duty of four cents a pound, one of the first compound duties in the tariffs of the United States. Woolen goods were protected by an ad valorem duty of 45 percent, to be raised to 50 percent the following year. Another innovation was a series of minimum valuations according to which woolen cloths costing not to exceed fifty cents were valued at that sum, cloths costing between fifty cents and $1.00 were valued at $1.00, those costing $1.00 up to $2.50 were valued at $2.50, etc. This was practically an extension of the minimum-value principle first applied to cottons in 1816. The insertion of a minimum at $1.00 was regarded by many protectionists as a blow at their system. It offered a great temptation to undervalue goods that cost above the $1.00 limit so as to secure the advantages of the lower rate, and the results were shown quickly by fraudulent undervaluations.

Another important change was the considerable increase in the duties on most iron products, e.g. the duty on rolled iron bars was raised to $37.00 a ton, and the rate on hammered bars to a cent a pound, a tax that was to be especially felt by the farmer. Some advances were also made for cotton goods and the manufactures of glass. The duties on hemp, flax, and molasses were made very high, and those on indigo, distilled liquors, and slate were noticeably increased. The fiscal impact of this tariff soon appeared in the statistics of 1830 and showed the average ad valorem rates on dutiable imports to be nearly 49 percent and on free and dutiable together to be over 45 percent.

An analysis of congressional voting on the 1828 tariff reveals strong opposition to the tariff from nearly the entire South. Yet in the Senate, Thomas Benton of Missouri, R. M. Johnson of Kentucky, and John H. Eaton of Tennessee (Jackson's close friend) voted in its favor. It also obtained the support of such northern Democrats as Martin Van Buren of New York, James Buchanan of Pennsylvania, and Silas Wright of New York. In the House, the entire Kentucky delegation (led by Henry Clay) voted in its favor, but Tennessee (Jackson's home state) was completely against it. Massachusetts, with its manufacturing interests gaining on the commercial, was divided. Most of its representatives in the House voted against it. On the other hand, Daniel Webster (the state's key Senator), spoke powerfully in its support and declared his conversion to the protective tariff doctrine.

Although the 1828 Tariff Act aroused violent southern opposition, and elicited threats of nullification and secession from South Carolina, the Democratic leaders in the South controlled the hotheads and bided their time. They hoped that the election of Andrew Jackson in the fall of 1828 would make everything right once more.

Jackson and the 1832 Tariff Act. Jackson, after defeating John Quincy Adams for the Presidency, declined to make tariff reform an Administration policy. Henry Clay and the more extreme champions of protective tariff wished to retain the major high duties in the 1828 Tariff Act intact. They tried to meet the problem of revenue surpluses coming from the 1828 tariff duties by abolishing the duties on most of the imports that did not compete with American products. But most of the protectionists, led by John Quincy Adams, now a representative in the House, took a more moderate course and approved the gradual removal of the abominations of 1828. In 1830 the duty on molasses was cut in half, and the drawback on the exportation of rum, which had been stopped in 1828, was restored. Another statute reduced the duties on tea, coffee, and cocoa, as one means of reducing the Federal revenue.

Finally, out of a maze of conflicting sectional proposals made in Congress, came the Tariff Act of July 14, 1832, closely based on a moderate protectionist report written by John Quincy Adams, as Chairman of the House Committee on Manufactures. The system of minimum valuation was abolished. Woolen goods were subjected to a simple ad valorem duty of 50 percent. The duties on hemp, pig iron, and bar iron were reduced. Flax and cheap wool, costing less than eight cents a pound, were admitted free of duty.

The protective tariff system was restored to what it had been in

1824. When the tariff was cleared of the objectionable additions imposed in 1828, the champions of protection could advocate its permanent retention more effectively than before. But the reduction of duties in 1832 was not based on any theory of free trade. Revenue was still to be obtained chiefly from duties on articles requiring protection. In fact, the duty on woolens was raised, and woolen yarn was taxed for the first time. On articles not produced in the United States, either low duties were imposed, as on silks, or no duties at all, as on tea and coffee. But the average rate on dutiable articles was about 33 percent.

A careful scrutiny of the votes in the House of Representatives on the Tariff Act of 1832 indicates that it was favored almost unanimously by the West and Southwest and predominantly by the Middle Atlantic States. New England and the Southeast were split evenly on the tariff, and in the South, while Virginia and North Carolina strongly supported the tariff, South Carolina and Georgia were intensely opposed to it.

Nullification and the Compromise Tariff. One consequence of the deep cleavage was that South Carolina passed in November, 1832, a nullification ordinance providing "that the tariff law of 1828, and the amendment to the same of 1832, are null and void." It also declared that no collection of the tariff duties of 1832 would be permitted in the state of South Carolina after February 1, 1833. When Congress met in December, President Jackson called for reduction of the tariff to the lowest possible point consistent with the protection of those American products that might be harmed by foreign competition. At the same time he issued a proclamation announcing his determination to enforce all national laws throughout the United States, by military force if necessary.

In an effort to conciliate South Carolina, Jackson's Secretary of the Treasury, Louis McLane, made recommendations on the tariff; they became the basis of a congressional measure called, after a New York Congressman, the Verplanck Bill. This provided for reducing tariff duties immediately, without giving adequate time to the manufacturers for adjustment. To the champions of the "American system" of protection of industrial production, it seemed an economic disaster. An alternative emerged, however, when Henry Clay introduced two months later a new bill that became known as the Compromise Tariff of 1833. It recognized the principle of the horizontal rate that the southern champions of nullification considered necessary to tariff revision, but it was to be so gradual in its effects as to give the industrialists the time they needed to adjust their business to the tariff changes.

Although the political desirability of a settlement through concessions was generally recognized, the new measure did not pass easily. New England and the Middle Atlantic States were committed to protection so much as to be unwilling to compromise, and the West divided about evenly. But the South and Southwest were almost unanimously in favor of the compromise tariff. Here Henry Clay and John Calhoun acted as allies. Clay probably thought that the opposition majority in succeeding Congresses might overthrow the whole protective tariff system, and if it were to be changed, it should be done gradually instead of hastily. He also quite likely wanted to avoid a serious break with South Carolina.

Calhoun accepted the compromise measure in part because he was persuaded of the futility of struggling any longer against Jackson, in part because the bill affirmed the principle for which South Carolina and the rest of the South had been contending. On the other hand, Daniel Webster opposed this tariff on the ground that the protective principle required discrimination between various classes of imports and this discrimination would be impossible, if one accepted a horizontal regulation. He also held it unwise and unconstitutional for Congress to commit itself for a term of years, and he was strongly opposed to the states-rights philosophy urged by the South. Any compromise with the South while nullification was widespread seemed to him a destruction of the constitutional principles of national unity and sovereignty.

The compromise statute provided for the retention of a considerable degree of protection for almost nine years, and thereafter for a rapid reduction to a uniform 20 percent rate, with the tariff of 1832 as the starting point. Between 1834 and 1842 duties were to be lowered by a biennial reduction of one-tenth of the excess over 20 percent; and in January and July, 1842, the remaining excess was to be removed. The law also enlarged the free list.

Whatever the political merits of this measure, it was badly drafted. One error was the failure to provide for methods of lowering specific duties in the contemplated reductions. This caused considerable difficulties for the Treasury. The scheme adopted for these cases resulted in irregular duty reductions in different items. Nevertheless, the tariff changes provided in 1833 had brought the average rate on dutiable goods down to 30 percent by 1840, and on free and dutiable goods together to 15 percent. But the lowered rate remained in effect only two months in 1842, when it was replaced by a new tariff act.

The Whigs, John Tyler, and the "Black" Tariff Act of 1842. During the depression of 1837–1842, there was a serious decrease in Government revenues from the customs. Although Government receipts were insufficient to meet expenses, further reductions were in sight, owing to the provisions of the 1833 tariff statute. These circumstances led champions of the protective tariff to argue that the tariff duties were both too low to offer adequate protection to business and also not productive enough to support the national treasury. But the political managers of the Whig party did not deem it wise to force the tariff question before the people in the 1840 Presidential campaign. Hence, Henry Clay and Daniel Webster, the most competent candidates for the Whig Presidential nomination, were passed over in favor of General William Henry Harrison. John Tyler of Virginia, an ex-Jacksonian Democrat and a Calhoun nullifier, was nominated for Vice-President in order to win southern votes. The short-term consequence of a strategy and campaign based completely on political showmanship was a decisive Whig victory over the Democratic candidate, Martin Van Buren, and the Liberty party candidate, J. G. Birney.

Once in control of Congress, the Whig party leaders planned to put over a protective tariff by sacrificing the income from the sale of public land through distribution among the states of the proceeds from these sales. This policy would aid the protectionists in their argument that high protective duties were needed to keep the Treasury supplied. It also found many supporters among those who wanted the states to engage in costly internal improvements. But this program did not satisfy John Tyler, who had become President upon the death of Harrison a month after his inauguration in March, 1841. In order to win the new President's approval of the 1841 distribution act, the Whig party chiefs were forced to include in the statute a provision that if at any time the duties from the compromise tariff were raised, the distribution of revenue should be suspended. This restriction was strongly opposed by Henry Clay and his followers. In two tariff bills passed by Congress in 1842, Clay's provision for distribution was attached. Tyler speedily interposed his vetoes.

This gave the Whigs an opportunity to frame a third tariff bill, without the former provision as to distribution tacked on. Tyler then gave his approval to the Tariff Act of August 30, 1842.

This new statute was highly protective. Duties were raised, but not uniformly, to the height of the 1832 tariff. The average rate on dutiable articles over the next four years was 32 percent. Specific duties, wherever practicable, were imposed, with special consideration being given to iron products. On some individual commodities the rates were exceedingly high, ranging from 51 percent ad valorem on molasses to 77 percent on railroad iron, 100 percent on refined sugar, and from 62 to 165 percent on window glass. An innovation was made in the method of collecting customs duties. The credit system for the payment of duties was abolished. Previously credit had been granted to importers if they gave bonds to cover the payment of the duties within a certain period. This was now discontinued, and the payment of duties was placed upon a cash basis. In 1846 the merchants succeeded in getting it modified by the establishment of a system of government warehouses.

The 1842 tariff was called "the Black Tariff" by southern cotton planters. As one historian has written, it was a political dagger thrust into John Tyler's back by Henry Clay. Clay had control of the Whig majority in both houses of Congress and used them to get through a tariff bill that Tyler felt compelled to accept only because of the persisting hard times and the desperate condition of the Treasury. But Congress had some strong divisions on this subject. Some southern Whigs refused to approve the 1842 tariff; the western Whigs did so reluctantly. The northern Whigs were joined by two important Democratic Senators, James Buchanan of Pennsylvania and Silas Wright of New York. The latter thereby committed the northern wing of the Democratic party to a protective tariff and helped to bring about the dissolution of the alliance between the North and South in the Democratic party.

Students of pressure politics believe that this tariff, despite its Whig champions, did not have as strong popular feeling behind it as had been displayed in favor of the 1824, 1828, and 1832 protective tariffs. In the agricultural states the support for Clay's home-market idea had decreased perceptibly. In the industrial states the pressure came more from the manufacturers directly concerned than from the public at large. Calhoun rightfully said that the 1842 tariff was passed largely because the politicians needed an issue and the "moneyed men," the fiscal conservatives, wanted the Treasury filled.

Manifest Destiny, Polk, and the Tariff Act of 1846. The 1842 Tariff Act remained in force for only four years. By 1844 prosperous times had returned, and the tariff became a distinct party issue in the campaign. Yet each of the parties in the 1844 electoral competition was cautious and even vague on its exact intention or position. The Democratic Presidential candidate, James K. Polk of Tennessee, was elected over Henry Clay, the Whig candidate, primarily on the issue of the re-annexation of Texas and the re-occupation of Oregon. But shortly after the Democrats entered office in the spring of 1845, they attacked the existing tariff law. The excess in the national Treasury encouraged them to attempt a downward tariff revision. Robert J. Walker, Polk's Secretary of the Treasury, was an outstanding advocate of free trade and presented a notable downward revision of import duties before Congress in December, 1845. He advocated that no duty be imposed on any article above the lowest rate that would yield the largest amount of revenue. Below such a rate, discrimination might be made, descending in the scale of duties, or for imperative reasons the article might be placed on the free list. The maximum duty should be imposed on luxuries, and all minimums and all specific duties should be abolished and ad valorem duties substituted. Congress accepted nearly all of Walker's proposals, but failed to impose any duties on tea and coffee because of popular disapproval of any tax on these articles.

The new tariff bill, although in effect moderately protectionist, in its time was judged the nearest approach to free trade the United States had known since Jefferson's Presidency. On many occasions during its dangerous legislative journey through Congress, it was challenged, modified, and vehemently attacked; but finally it passed. To many Americans and Englishmen, the Walker tariff was dependent upon the repeal of the Corn Laws by the British Parliament, and its passage was deliberately delayed in Congress until word came from England that the British part of the tacit bargain had been fulfilled. The tariff bill was then passed by a combination of southern and western votes—easily in the House but with greater difficulty in the Senate, where the party machine had to exert pressure on recalcitrant Democrats. Even there the Vice-President, George M. Dallas of Pennsylvania, had to cast his vote in order to break a final tie and thereby to destroy the high protective tariff policy so dear to his own state.

Under the Tariff Act of July 30, 1846, articles of import were divided into various schedules designated by letters of the alphabet from A, B, C, D to G, H, I. All the articles classed in Schedule A paid duties of 100 percent; all in Schedule B, 40 percent; all in Schedule C, 30 percent; and the items in Schedules D to H, correspondingly lower duties. Schedule C, with the 30-percent duty, included most of the articles with which the debate on protective tariff was concerned: iron and metals in general, manufactures of metals, wool and woolens, manufactures of leather, paper, glass, and wood. Cottons were in Schedule D and paid 25 percent, but tea and coffee, along with copper ore and a few other commodities, were exempt from duties.

The average rates under the 1846 act during its last eight years (to 1857) were 26 percent on dutiable goods, and 23 percent on free and dutiable goods. A change from specific to ad valorem duties was another feature of this tariff. Until 1816 both methods were in use; after that time the tendency was toward the substitution of specific duties wherever practicable, and by 1846 the reversal was complete. In theory the system was ideal; in practice it admitted of grave injustices: frauds from undervaluation; unequal appraisals of goods at different ports.

The method of appraisement of goods was also changed and defined more precisely by an 1851 amendment, which provided that the evaluation be placed on the actual market value or wholesale price at the time of its exportation to the United States, and that to this value be added the cost of packing or covering, the commission of the broker who sold the goods, the export duties if there were any, wharf duties, and the cost of putting the goods on board.

A system of Government warehouses was also established in which goods imported might lie under the custody of the national Government with duty unpaid for a certain length of time and then be re-packed, re-assorted, and re-exported. This innovation eased the burden upon the importer by enabling him to postpone the actual payment of the duties upon imported merchandise until such time as the goods were required for use. It also facilitated the re-export trade by freeing such commerce from customs duties; the trader was permitted to store the imported goods without payment of duty until such time as he found it convenient to export them, at the consummation of which obligation for payment of customs upon them ceased. The system quickly justified itself and has continued until the present time. The 1846 tariff did not produce the dire results that the Whigs predicted, was a success as a revenue producer, and was accompanied by prosperity for nine out of the eleven years during which it was in force.

Commercial Expansion, Slavery, and the Tariff Act of 1857. The period from 1846 to 1857 was one of great prosperity. New territorial and economic frontiers opened up for the American people with the extension of railroads into the trans-Mississippi West, the discovery of gold in California, and the increased demand by Europe for American agricultural products in part owing to the famine in Ireland and the abortive revolutions in Europe during the mid-1840's. Another factor in the increased exports from the United States was the reduction and abolition of import duties in England that began in 1842. The acquisition of territory from Mexico in 1848 also increased the volume of imports into the United States and the revenue therefrom.

Even though national Governmental expenditures reached much higher levels after than before the Mexican War, there was such an excess of receipts over expenditures that during the ten years between 1846 and 1856 the protectionists could not make the tariff question an important issue in politics. In the party platforms of 1848, 1852, and 1856, the Whigs were the only ones to make a reference to the tariff when they mildly referred in 1852 to the wisdom of tariff discrimination by specific duties as a means of encouraging American industries. Congress and the American people during this period focused their attention mainly on the slavery issue in the congressional debates of 1847–1850, the Kansas-Nebraska Act of 1854, and the Dred Scott decision of 1857.

In fact, there was a national trend toward free trade, and some even proposed that all tariffs be repealed. James Guthrie, Secretary of the Treasury under President Pierce from 1855 to 1857, would not go as far as this, but he did suggest further reductions in the customs duties. He also advised that the free list be extended and championed the admission of raw materials used in manufactures free of duty. Although James Buchanan of Pennsylvania, the Democratic candidate for President, was elected in 1856 over the Republican candidate, John C. Frémont of California, Congress felt there was such an urgent need to reduce its revenue that it enacted a new low tariff on March 3, 1857, one day before Buchanan's inauguration. The vote in the House of Representatives on this measure did not show any sharp party cleavage. Geographically, most of New England joined with the South, Southwest, and California in support of the new tariff while the Middle Atlantic States, led by Pennsylvania, joined with a large part of the Northwest and West in opposition.

The 1857 statute lowered many duties and enlarged the free list. The 1846 schedules and the ad valorem duties were used as a basis for systematic duty reduction. The duty on the important protective articles in Schedule C was lowered from 30 to 24 percent; cottons were transferred to that schedule. The rates upon articles in Schedules A and B were reduced from 100 and 40 percent respectively to 30 percent; in Schedule D, from 25 to 19 percent; in Schedule E, from 20 to 15 percent; in Schedule F, from 15 to 12 percent; in Schedule G, from 10 to 8 percent; in Schedule H, from 5 to 4 percent; and on articles not specifically provided for, from 20 to 15 percent. Many drugs and certain raw materials, such as raw silk, tin, and wood, were placed upon the free list or else transferred to lower rate schedules. Cotton manufactures, however, were given special consideration by cotton duties nearly as high as those established by the 1846 tariff. The average ad valorem rates during approximately four years of the 1857 Tariff Act were about 20 percent on dutiable goods and 16 percent on free and dutiable goods (the lowest in the century between 1812 and 1913). A few months after the passage of the 1857 Tariff Act a commercial and banking panic developed. This lasted for almost two years. By 1860 prosperity had definitely returned.

1854 Reciprocity Treaty with Canada. In 1854 the first reciprocity treaty between the United States and any other country was concluded with Canada and became effective in 1855. This treaty virtually established free trade in natural products between the United States and Canada. Arrangements were also made for the joint sharing of the Atlantic Coast fisheries and both countries' canal systems, as well as for the use by Americans of the St. Lawrence River and by British vessels of Lake Michigan. Although the reciprocity treaty proved to be of greater advantage to Canada in its exports to the United States than to the U. S. in its exports to Canada, the total trade between the two countries over eleven years increased about threefold, and the United States' trade with Canada became second in importance to its commerce with Great Britain. Unfortunately the treaty was abrogated as the result of Canada adopting protectionism; the resentment aroused in the United States by the Canadian attitude during the Civil War; and the need for increased revenues in both countries. In addition, Congress responded to the pressure of groups with competing interests in fish, lumber, and coal in the United States. The United States denounced the treaty in March, 1865, with the termination of the treaty becoming effective the next year. This resulted in a substantial loss in trade to both the United States and Canada, but especially the United States.

CHAPTER 3

The Civil War, Economic Change, and Political Conflict

The Republicans, War, and the Morrill Tariffs of 1861. Although the Tariff Act of 1857 had been passed almost without debate and without arousing any popular feeling, once the depression of 1857 began, various pressure groups—led by iron, cotton, and woolen manufacturers—started a vigorous campaign for a higher protective tariff. As Allan Nevins put it, "The sleeping tiger of tariff controversy awakened, to ramp and roar his way through the next three generations of history." * During the winter of 1859–1860, an astute Vermont Republican, Justin S. Morrill, Chairman of the Ways and Means Committee, introduced a tariff designed to stimulate the metal, textiles, and other industries by a return to specific duties on many commodities, such as carpets, cotton bagging, and raw wool, and by raising ad valorem duties back to the level of the 1846 duties. The measure passed the House on May 10, 1860, by a vote of 105 to 64; the majority consisted of Republican and (pro-Union southern) Opposition party members, with half-a-dozen Democrats concurring. In the Senate, however, it was blocked by the South and northern supporters of the Democratic low-tariff tradition.

Nevertheless, this partial success inspired delegates from Pennsylvania and New Jersey to the Chicago convention of the Republican party a few weeks later to press for a strong protectionist plank in the Republican platform. But the opposition of Western and New England delegates led to a compromise plank, calling for a revenue tariff together with "such an adjustment of those imposts as to en-

* *The Emergence of Lincoln,* 2 vols. (New York, London: Scribner's, 1951), I, 220.

28

courage the development of the industrial interests of the whole country." Lincoln would have preferred no tariff plank at all. Yet this compromise protectionist plank of the Republicans proved to be influential in winning Pennsylvania and other northeastern states, as well as the Northwest, for Lincoln in November, 1860. Although Lincoln did not win a majority of the popular vote, the secession of the southern states that began in December allowed the Morrill Bill of the previous spring to pass by the Senate that winter, with the aid of Democratic votes from Pennsylvania, New Jersey, and New York. President Buchanan signed it on March 2, 1861, two days before Lincoln was inaugurated. (*See Reading No. 5.*)

The supporters of the new tariff act declared they simply wanted to restore the rates of 1846. They proposed to do this by substituting specific for ad valorem duties. But this proved to be a pretext upon their part because they established specific duties that were in many cases considerably higher than the 1846 ad valorem duties. The most significant direct changes in this 1861 statute were in the increased duties on iron and wool, made in the hope that Pennsylvania and some western states would be won over to the Republican party.

Shortly after the first Morrill Tariff Act was passed, the Civil War began with the Confederate firing on Fort Sumter. The need for additional revenue was felt at once. When Congress met in special session on July 4, 1861, Lincoln's Secretary of the Treasury, Salmon P. Chase, proposed that duties be levied on tea and coffee, then admitted free, and on sugar, which was lightly taxed; in addition, he suggested a slight increase on the general list of dutiable articles. He put his main reliance for war finance upon Government loans, the tariff, and internal taxes. In response, Congress passed the Tariff Act of August 5, 1861, levying duties on sugar, tea and coffee, and increasing those on hemp, hides, rubber, molasses, silk, lead, salt, fruit, drugs, spices, and a few other articles. Four months later Congress passed the Tariff Act of December 24, 1861, raising the duties on sugar, tea, and coffee. From that time on until the end of the Civil War, no congressional session passed in which some increase of duties on imports was not made.

Civil War Finance and the 1862–1864 Tariff Acts. Congress, in working out its complex war-finance system, was induced by different pressure groups to change the tariff again and again, motivated by the need for additional revenue and by the principle of so-called "compensatory" duties—high tariff rates that were supposed to protect American manufacturers from foreign competition while they were subjected to heavy internal taxes during the Civil War. The Tariff Act of July 14, 1862, was passed on this principle. As J. S. Morrill said: "it will be indispensable for us . . . to make proper reparation; otherwise we shall destroy the goose that lays the golden egg. If we bleed manufacturers, we must see to it that the proper tonic is administered at the same time." Considerable increases were made in the duties on iron and steel products, woolen manufactures, and salt. The free list in the 1861 Morrill Tariff Act was cut by nearly half. The average ad valorem rate mounted from 19 percent on dutiable goods in 1861 (under the law of 1857) to an average of 35 percent during the three years between 1862 and 1865.

There seems to be no doubt that the increases in protective duties would not have been tolerated if there had not been enacted on July 1, 1862, an internal revenue act that established a comprehensive and weighty system of excise taxation. Specific taxes had been imposed upon the manufactures of iron and steel, coal-oil, paper, and leather. A general ad valorem tax was also levied on other manufactures. A general income tax had been imposed, as well as license fees in many callings. These internal taxes made the pleas of protectionists more acceptable than they otherwise would have been.

As the Civil War went on, the need for revenue constantly increased. Congress made a notable expansion of its internal-revenue system on June 30, 1864. As one economist saw it, the principle underlying these new general-revenue taxes seemed to be that of the Irishman at Donnybrook Fair: "Whenever you see a head, hit it; whenever you find an article, tax it." The increases in income taxes and in taxes on manufactured goods gave J. S. Morrill, Thaddeus Stevens, and other protectionists from New England, Pennsylvania, and Ohio an opportunity to raise the protective tariff even higher than it had gone in 1862. The average ad valorem rate on dutiable commodities was raised from 37.3 percent under the act of 1862 to 49 percent. The bill was pushed through Congress with only five days of debate in both the House and the Senate. Pressure groups such as the National Associations of Wool Manufacturers and Woolgrowers, the New England Cotton Manufacturers Association, the American Iron and Steel Association, and the National Manufacturers' Association had been organized during the Civil War expressly to influence Congress on the tariff. They succeeded in their aim.

As one tariff historian, Edward Stanwood, wrote, American manufacturers found their opportunity in the necessity of the Government. They had only to state what rate of duty they deemed essential, and that rate was accorded to them. Unfortunately, what was
put through as an emergency war measure remained virtually unchanged for twenty years or more. When changes finally were made,
they were undertaken on the assumption that the 1864 rates were the
normal results of an established policy rather than the exceptional
measure that Congressmen in 1864 believed they were. Authorities
agree that the 1864 tariff was crude and ill considered in many respects and was more extreme in its protective duties than any previous tariff act in American history. It also contained flagrant abuses
in the shape of duties whose chief effect was to create fortunes for
various private individuals and corporations.

Republican Cleavages on Tariff Policy 1865–1871. After the
Civil War ended in the spring of 1865, it became evident that the
revenue exceeded the needs of the national Government. A strong
demand arose for relief from the heavy taxes imposed during the
Civil War. By 1872 most of the internal taxes, including the income
tax, had been abolished except for some excises on spirits, tobacco,
fermented liquor, adhesive stamps, banks and bankers, and a few
other products. With the removal of these internal taxes, a reduction
of import duties should have taken place. Opposition, however,
came from the vested interests that had benefited from the high war
tariff and from those who believed in foreign-trade restriction and
tariff protection as permanent national policies.

Although most Democrats favored a tariff for revenue, the Republicans were in control of Congress and the Presidency throughout
most of the post-Civil War period. Some groups within the Republican party, especially from the West and from New England, were in
favor of tariff reduction. Other groups, notably those from the wool-
growing Midwest and from the iron industry in Pennsylvania, were
strongly for either retention of, or increases in, the Civil War tariff
duties. The failure of Congress to pass any tariff legislation of major
importance during the Reconstruction period from 1865 to 1877 is a
reflection of the conflict between the supporters and foes of the protective tariff. As neither interest group was able to triumph, tariff
rates, on the whole, underwent relatively minor changes.

Nevertheless, keen battles over tariff proposals and legislation
took place during this period. In 1866 Justin S. Morrill persuaded

the House to pass a highly protective tariff bill, but failed to get it through the Senate. On the other hand, early in 1867 the Senate passed a tariff bill revising downward the duties on raw materials and slightly lowering the duties on most manufactured goods. But the bill's sponsors in the House, although they had a majority, could not get the two-thirds majority required to suspend the rules and bring the bill before the House. With the defeat of this bill, framed by David A. Wells, Special Commissioner of the Revenue, the cause of tariff reform was set back critically. Soon two tariff acts were passed that greatly strengthened the protective tariff. One was the Woolens Act of March 2, 1867; this raised the duties on raw wool and manufactures of wool to a much higher level than ever before. The other was the Copper Act of February 24, 1869.

But the steadily increasing Government revenue made some kind of general tariff revision desirable, especially as strong dissatisfaction was expressed in the West by Republicans like James A. Garfield, then a Congressman from Ohio, and by Senator John Sherman. Congress responded in a characteristic half-hearted manner by passing the Tariff Act of July 14, 1870. Reductions were made almost without exception on purely revenue articles, such as tea, coffee, wines, sugar, molasses, and spices. An important reduction in the duty on pig iron from nine dollars to seven dollars a ton was counterbalanced by increases in duties on steel rails, marble, nickel and other protected articles.

Republican Finance and the Tariff, 1872–1882. In 1872 high Government revenue and increased public pressure from Republican taxpayers, especially in the West, induced Congress to take some action on tariff revision. A bill was introduced into the House that provided for an appreciable and permanent reduction of the Civil War tariff duties, especially those on wool and woolens, cottons, pig iron, coal, salt, and lumber. But meanwhile the Senate had passed a much weaker bill that simply proposed to reduce all protective duties by 10 percent. Although some champions of high protection in the Senate and the House opposed even this mild horizontal reduction, they were persuaded by such strategists as John L. Hayes, the Washington lobbyist for the wool manufacturers, James G. Blaine, Speaker of the House, William D. Kelley, Henry L. Dawes, and John Sherman to accept this 10-percent cut as preferable to the larger reductions in the House bill. As a consequence, the highly organized and unified protectionist forces succeeded in getting the

Senate bill through Congress with some concessions to the reform group.

The Tariff Act of June 6, 1872, had as its major feature the 10-percent reduction in the duties on all manufactures of cotton, wool, iron, steel, metals in general, paper, glass, and leather—in short, the products of all the great domestic protected industries. But it also contained a number of small, yet important, changes of duty. The rate on salt was reduced by half, and that on coal almost as much. Many other specific rates were lowered and certain raw materials, notably hides and paper stock, were admitted free of duty, as well as some minor articles used by manufacturers. On May 1, 1872, tea and coffee had been placed on the free list. The ostensible liberality of Congress on the extension of the free list actually was put through in order to prevent a more extended reduction of the protective duty on the products regarded as important to domestic manufactures. Unfortunately, this tariff reform did not last long. After the panic of 1873, Government revenue fell drastically, caused in part by the reduction of duties, in part by the reduction in domestic demand due to the depression. As a result, the 10 percent horizontal reduction was repealed by Congress in 1875. The repeal attracted comparatively little attention and was accomplished without any great opposition.

The average ad valorem rate of the 1872 tariff was 39 percent on dutiable goods, and 28 percent on free and dutiable goods together during the three fiscal years of 1873 to 1875. From 1876 to 1883 (eight fiscal years) almost a third of the imports consisted of goods on the free list. The average ad valorem rate was 43 percent on dutiable goods and 30 percent on free and dutiable goods.

Treasury Surpluses and the Tariff Act of 1883. The great depression that began in 1873 ended in 1879. With the return of prosperity, there was a great increase in imports and customs revenue. From 1880 onward, the surplus revenue in the Treasury was on the average about a hundred million dollars annually. As a result, by 1882 key Republicans came to fear they might lose power if they did not make some concessions to the growing public pressure for reduction of high protective tariff duties and of the Federal revenue. Hence, Congress authorized the appointment of a Tariff Commission whose duty was to report on "the establishment of a judicious tariff, or the revision of the existing tariff, upon a scale of justice to all interests." President Chester A. Arthur appointed nine commissioners the ma-

jority of whom were advocates of high protection; their chairman
was John L. Hayes, the secretary of the Wool Manufacturers' Association. After conducting hearings in twenty-nine different places
and examining 604 witnesses, the commission issued its report in
which it stated its conclusion "that a substantial reduction of tariff
duties was demanded, not by a mere indiscriminate popular clamor,
but by the best conservative opinion of the country, including that
which has in former times been most strenuous for the preservation
of our national industrial defenses." The commission proposed an
average reduction of from 20 to 25 percent, applying to commodities
of necessary general consumption, such as sugar and molasses,
rather than to luxuries, and to raw rather than to manufactured materials.

But these moderate protectionist recommendations did not succeed in winning the approval of Congress. The Senate tacked a tariff
bill, based in the main on the recommendations of the Tariff Commission, onto a House bill for the reduction of internal taxes. The
protectionists in the House, however, managed by an adroit ma-
noeuvre to have the Senate bill revert to a conference committee.
After abolishing various internal taxes—e.g. on bank checks and
savings-bank deposits—the radical protectionists were able to secure
changes along lines of high and even increased protection. The result
was that the tariff act, as finally passed, contained much less reduction than the original Senate bill; and it was passed in the Senate
only by a strict party vote of 32 to 31 as against the original Senate
bill being passed by a vote of 42 to 19.

The Tariff Act of March 3, 1883, made some reductions in the duties on raw wool, cheap cotton goods, pig iron, steel rails, copper,
marble, nickel, and barley. Duties, however, were raised on protected articles, importations of which had continued in large volume,
especially on iron ore, certain manufactures of steel, and the better
classes of woolen and cotton goods. The increase in rates was by no
means universal, but it was made in so large a number of important
cases as to make the Act distinctively protectionist in its trend. Although its sponsors made a half-hearted attempt to make some concessions to the demand for a more moderate tariff system, the Act
kept, with minor changes, the high level of the Civil War tariff duties. The average ad valorem rates for the next seven years, 1884–
1890, were 45 percent on dutiable goods (an increase of nearly 2 per-

cent) and 30 percent on free and dutiable goods (unchanged as compared with the period ending in 1883).

Grover Cleveland and the Democratic Thrust for Tariff Reform. During the succeeding five years the Democrats were powerful enough to secure the consideration by Congress of two general tariff bills, but not strong enough to enact any new legislation. In 1884 William R. Morrison of Illinois, the Democratic Chairman of the House Ways and Means Committee, proposed an average all-round tariff reduction of 20 percent, with such important additions to the free list as iron ore, coal, and lumber. Unfortunately, his bill aroused the objection that its principle of uniform reduction might cause expected injuries and might introduce new inequities as objectionable as those created by the 1883 Tariff Act. Within the Democratic party a strong protectionist group, led by Samuel J. Randall of Pennsylvania, joined with the Republicans on May 6, 1884, in voting down Morrison's bill by a vote of 156 to 151 in the House.

The bitter, scandalous, and dramatically close election of 1884, with James G. Blaine pitted against Grover Cleveland, put the Democratic party in power for the first time since the Civil War. President Cleveland in the spring of 1886 advocated a radical overhauling of the tariff and by his vigorous demands helped to unite the Democratic party on this question. But the second attempt by William R. Morrison to have the tariff revised downward was defeated on June 17, 1886, by a vote of 157 to 140 through a coalition of 122 Republicans and 35 Democrats, the latter headed again by S. J. Randall of Pennsylvania. The tariff issue consequently was carried over into the congressional campaign of 1886, but the results of the election were indecisive on this point. Cleveland pleaded again for tariff reduction in his December, 1886 message to Congress, but shortly thereafter Morrison's renewed thrust at opening the tariff issue was voted down in the House by 154 to 149, a narrower margin of defeat than that of the previous spring.

The next year Cleveland broke all precedents by devoting his entire annual message to Congress in December, 1887, to an attack on the high protective tariff as a "vicious, unequitable, and illogical source of unnecessary taxation" that "ought to be at once revised and amended." Without championing free trade, he advocated the reduction of the surplus revenue through general reduction of tariff duties and the removal of the duties on imported raw materials. He also objected to the tax imposed upon the consumer for the profit of the manufacturer and claimed it aided the growth of industrial trusts and their ability to charge high prices. (*See Reading No. 6.*)

Eloquent high tariff pleas were made by William McKinley and Thomas Reed, but the power of Cleveland's message induced the Democratic House to vote for the strong reform bill introduced in the spring of 1888 by Roger Q. Mills, the free-trade chairman of the Ways and Means Committee. (*See Readings Nos. 7 and 8.*) The Republicans countered this move, however, by preparing in the Senate, where they controlled a majority, a high protectionist tariff bill. The consequence was a stalemate, but the tariff position of both parties was sharply defined and squarely presented to the American people in the Presidential campaign of 1888. In the popular vote, Cleveland received a larger plurality in 1888 than he had obtained four years before, but the bigger campaign chest and greater unity of the Republicans enabled Benjamin Harrison, their Presidential candidate, to win the larger vote in the electoral college. As a result the Republican party, with its high protective tariff position, came into power.

Big Business and the McKinley Tariff Act of 1890. With the election of 1888, the Republicans acquired a majority in both Houses of Congress. The Harrison Administration proceeded to enact some legislation that represented concessions to the small businessman, farmers, miners, and Civil War veterans. But these measures were counterbalanced by its pro-big industry program centered especially on the tariff. Under the leadership of William McKinley in the House and Nelson W. Aldrich in the Senate, the Republicans felt committed to a drastic extension of high protection. They revised a bill that had passed the Senate, but not the House, in the fall of 1886. As McKinley was the Chairman of the House Ways and Means Committee, the revised bill was given his name. After extended debates and hundreds of amendments, the bill passed both Houses and became law on October 1, 1890.

The McKinley Tariff Act represented a general extension of the principle of protection. Increased duties were imposed upon wool, woolen goods (especially the finer grades), and dress goods; upon the finer cottons, lawns, laces, and embroideries; upon linens, silk laces, and plush goods; and upon cutlery and tin-plate. Protection was given to such agricultural products as barley, wheat, corn, hemp, and flax in order to counteract the dissatisfaction of western farmers who might be turning toward the rival Democratic and Populist parties. In certain cases, e.g. woolen goods, the customs duties were prohibitory in effect and thereby reduced the Government revenue. The minimum-value principle was extended to groups or classes of cotton stockings, velvets, and plushes, boiler and plate iron, penknives, shotguns, pistols, and table knives. The same specific duty was laid on all goods of the same class.

On the other hand, there was a repeal of the raw sugar duty, which was counterbalanced by a bounty of two cents a pound for fourteen years on the production of sugar within the United States. Duties were reduced on steel rails, on structural iron and steel, and on copper. The duties on steel rails and copper were allowed to remain, however, at a prohibitive rate. The rates on iron, already highly protective, were hardly changed except by an increase in the duty on tinplate. There was an extension of the free list that embraced a number of articles of no great economic importance. During the next three fiscal years, 1892–1894, the average customs rate proved to be over 49 percent, or a 4-percent increase, on dutiable articles, and 22 percent on free and dutiable articles. The remission of sugar duties accounted for most of the fall of 8 percent from the average under the preceding law. It should be noted that there was an increase in the percentage of goods entering free from about 33 percent in 1884–1890 to nearly 55 percent of all merchandise.

One significant new feature of the McKinley tariff was the recognition of commercial reciprocity. The President was empowered to impose duties by proclamation on sugar, molasses, tea, coffee, and hides if he thought that any country, exporting these commodities to the United States, imposed duties on agricultural and other products of the United States, which in view of the free admission of sugar, molasses, tea, coffee and hides into the United States, he might judge to be reciprocally unjust and unwarranted. This policy was drafted so as to apply particularly to Central and South America and was adopted mainly through the influence of James G. Blaine who favored a wider measure of Pan-American commercial union. Through this procedure the Administration was relieved from submitting to the Senate special reciprocity treaties. Under this provision commercial agreements bearing on reciprocal trade were made with Brazil, Guatemala, Salvador, Nicaragua, the Dominican Republic, and Honduras; with Spain for Cuba and Puerto Rico, with Great Britain for Jamaica, Trinidad, Barbados, and British Guinea; as well as with Germany, Austria, and Hungary. Only three nations became subjected to the proclamation duties: Colombia, Haiti, and Venezuela. The 1890 reciprocity provisions had a short life because the Tariff Act of 1894 restored the duty on sugar and admitted tea and coffee free, thereby removing the reciprocity weapon.

The Democratic Return to Power and the Wilson-Gorman Tariff Act of 1894. A month after the McKinley Bill became law, the congressional elections resulted in an overwhelming Democratic majority in the House, even though this was a period of business prosperity, a fact that usually aided the party in power. Two years later Grover Cleveland was elected President over both Benjamin Harrison and the Populist party candidate, General James B. Weaver.

A panic developed in May, 1893. This and fear of gold losses necessitated a repeal of the Sherman Silver Purchase Act on October 30, 1893. The depression lasted until the end of 1897 and gave the Republicans an excuse for opposing tariff reform. The repeal of the Sherman Silver Purchase Act divided the Democratic party and prevented effective unity on many questions. Nevertheless, the Democratic party went ahead with its program of tariff reform. William L. Wilson, Chairman of the Ways and Means Committee, introduced into the House a tariff bill that made sweeping reductions in the duties of manufactured goods and put raw materials on the free list. After a sharp debate on this tariff reduction and on a provision for a moderate income tax, the House finally passed the new Wilson Bill, on February 1, 1894, by a vote of 204 to 140. The greatest support for the bill came from the agricultural South and Middle West, the strongest opposition from the industrial Northeast and some of the states of the extreme Far West.

The Senate, however, was dominated by an unofficial coalition of protectionist Republicans and Democrats. Although there were 44 Democrats, and 3 Populists vs. 38 Republicans, various Democratic Senators from New York, Louisiana, West Virginia, Maryland, Alabama, New Jersey, and Ohio were opposed to the Wilson Bill. Moreover, high-tariff lobbyists had been putting pressure for months on Democratic Senators they thought they could influence. The upshot was that after an extended debate, on July 3, 1894, the Senate passed by a vote of 39 to 34 a tariff bill with 634 amendments, which was far removed from the Wilson Tariff Bill and was re-named the Wilson-Gorman Tariff Bill. The House violently disagreed with the Senate revision, and President Cleveland called the Senate's abandonment of tariff reform "party perfidy and party dishonor." Nevertheless, the Senate protectionist Democrats were able to insist upon their amendments being accepted by the House in the special conference committee that was supposed to work out a compromise between the two houses of Congress. The consequence was that the bill became law on August 27, 1894, without President Cleveland's signature, because he disapproved of the Senate revision, yet wanted to keep the tariff reductions that were made.

The changes made by this statute were not very great, but nearly all of them were in the direction of lowering the tariff. Raw wool was placed on the free list, and some rates on woolens were reduced, although hardly more than enough to offset the effects upon manufacturers' costs of the abolition of the tariff on raw wool. Small reductions were made on cotton and silk goods, pig iron, steel rails, and many other articles. Larger reductions were put through on coal, iron ore, chinaware, and tin-plate. To make up for the expected reduction in revenue, a duty was again laid upon raw sugar; this benefited the sugar growers of Louisiana. In addition, a moderate income tax was levied, but the Supreme Court declared this unconstitutional the next year.

Under this law, for the three fiscal years of 1894 to 1897, the average ad valorem rates were 41 percent on dutiable goods and 21 percent on free and dutiable goods, compared with 49 and 22 percent respectively under the McKinley tariff for 1892–1894. The percentage of imports entering free under this statute proved to be less than under the McKinley Act, as a result of the sugar duty and depressed business conditions.

Republican Fiscal Conservatism and the 1897 Dingley Tariff Act. The Presidential campaign of 1896 was waged on the free silver-versus-gold issue and on the need for reform in taxation, the tariff, and the controls over railroads and monopolistic corporations. Despite William Jennings Bryan's support from the Democrats and Populists, William McKinley and the financially powerful Republican party won the election, partly because of the fears among large groups of the middle class of an "unsound" currency, but also because of the four years of depression that the country had endured under the Cleveland Administration. It seems quite likely that large numbers of voters supported McKinley in spite of, rather than because of, his high protectionist beliefs. But his inauguration was soon followed by a special session of Congress to deal with the problem of raising additional revenue. Nelson Dingley, Jr., of Maine,

Chairman of the Ways and Means Committee, introduced a tariff bill into the House on March 15, 1897. Under the pressure of the Republican party machine, headed by Thomas B. Reed, the Speaker of the House, the tariff bill was passed on March 31, after only four days of general debate, by a vote of 205 to 122, almost entirely on strict party lines. Dingley's bill then went to the Senate, which imposed some 872 amendments and then passed the bill on July 7 by a vote of 38 to 28. About four-fifths of these amendments were agreed to by both Houses, and the Dingley bill became law on July 24, 1897.

The new act embodied a marked increase in protective rates. On some commodities the duties of 1890 were restored; on others, compromises between the rates of 1890 and 1894 were accepted; and in a few instances, the lower rates of the Wilson-Gorman tariff were permitted to stand. Duties were re-imposed on wool, and on hides, which had been untaxed since 1872. Duties were increased on flax, cotton bagging, woolens, silks, linens, chinaware, and certain manufactures of iron and steel. On coal, there was a compromise; on iron and steel, duties were left almost unchanged. On sugar, which played an important role in Federal finances, there was a major revision: In place of the ad valorem rate of 40 percent on raw sugar, the duty was increased and made specific. The policy of free raw sugar, which the Republican party had adopted in 1890, was definitely abandoned, as the need for revenue was urgent, and the slowly developing beet-sugar industry was demanding protection. The Sugar Trust was allowed to retain the protection of one eighth of a cent a pound on refined sugar that the 1894 tariff had granted it, but the spokesmen for the Sugar Trust in the Senate were unsuccessful in gaining any increase.

The principle of reciprocity authorized by the McKinley tariff was again incorporated into the tariff system, but was to be put into effect through treaties executed by the Senate, instead of by Executive proclamation as provided in the act of 1890.

The Dingley Tariff had the longest life of any tariff act in our history because other issues absorbed public attention until the next tariff revision in 1907—e.g., the Spanish-American War, imperialism, railway-rate regulation, and monopoly control. The average rate on dutiable goods under the first full fiscal year of operation of the Dingley Tariff, 1899, was the second highest in American history, 52 percent, while it was almost 30 percent on free and dutiable goods. In practical operation, however, owing to the numerous specific duties, the average rate was steadily moderated by the rapid rise of the general price level. This rise came to 35 percent during the period between 1897 and 1909. Also, a treaty with Cuba, effective December 27, 1903, reduced by 20 percent the duty on sugar of Cuban origin. Steadily increasing quantities came in at this lower rate. The average rate of duties collected for the period of twelve years was 46 percent on dutiable goods and 26 percent on free and dutiable goods, compared with 41 and 21 percent respectively under the Wilson-Gorman tariff.

Insurgency and the Payne-Aldrich Tariff Act of 1909. During the twelve years that the Dingley Tariff Act was in operation, public opinion gradually grew stronger throughout the United States in favor of further revision downward of the tariff. This arose partly from the discontent with steadily rising general prices, which were not fully matched by the increases in wages. In part this movement accompanied concern and agitation against the growth of great industrial trusts and great fortunes, both of which it was widely believed the protective tariff had greatly aided. During the political campaign of 1908 both the Democratic and the Republican parties promised to revise the protective tariff. The national Republican platform of 1908 declared that "the true principle of protection is best maintained by the imposition of such duties as will equal the difference between the cost of production at home and abroad, together with a reasonable degree of profit." This was interpreted by many Republicans, especially in the West, as a basis of tariff revision, and this conviction was strengthened by statements by William Howard Taft, the Republican candidate for President, who often spoke with approval of "revision downward."

After Taft defeated Bryan in the 1908 election and took office in March, 1909, he called a special session of Congress for the exclusive purpose of framing a new tariff. At once a struggle of the industrial and agricultural interests took place. On March 17, 1909, Sereno Payne, Chairman of the House Ways and Means Committee, introduced his tariff bill. When passed by the House, it was protectionist, but made significant reductions in the duties on lumber, iron and steel, and a few manufactured products. The free list was extended to include raw materials used by manufacturers, such as wood pulp, hides, petroleum and its products, iron ore, and raw flax. On the other hand, the bill gave increased protection to mercerized fabrics, women's gloves, hosiery, plate glass, and fruits competing with California's. New duties were imposed on tea and crude cocoa, solely to provide revenue. The wool and woolen rates on the Schedule K in the Dingley tariff were not revised although there had been strong protests from consumers and manufacturers who used carded wool and wished lower rates on the raw material.

The Payne Bill met with an unfavorable reception in the Senate. At this time the Senate consisted of 59 Republicans and 33 Democrats. Most of the Republicans were strong champions of high protection, and they were led by Nelson W. Aldrich of Rhode Island, a millionaire in his own right, allied to the Rockefeller family by marriage, and the undisputed leader of the Senate since the 1890's. Ten insurgent Republicans from the Midwest, led by Robert M. La Follette of Wisconsin, defied Aldrich and attempted to prevent him and his allies from imposing some 847 amendments to the House bill. Although the insurgents were not able to effect any important changes in the tariff schedule, they won public admiration and helped build up the Progressive movement in 1912. The tariff bill that passed the Senate on July 8, 1909, by a vote of 45 to 34 imposed duties on iron ore, coal, and hides and raised the rates on lumber and the cotton and hosiery schedules.

President Taft was disappointed by the Senate tariff revision, yet had refrained from trying to influence the tariff legislation during the debates in Congress. But he did exert some pressure on the House-Senate conference committee that made the final adjustments. One result of this Executive pressure was the putting of hides on the free list. Another was the reduction of duties on gloves, hosiery, lumber, coal, iron ore, pig iron, steel rails, leather, and shoes. Although the insurgent Republicans and Democrats in the House were dissatisfied with the conference committee's compromises, the Republican majority succeeded in getting it approved for the conference report on August 5 by a vote of 47 to 31, with seven of the ten insurgent Republicans standing firm in their opposition despite all the pressure that Senator Aldrich could exert.

The tariff bill signed by Taft that same day preserved the extremely high rate structure and hostile attitude toward foreign trade embodied in the McKinley and Dingley Tariff Acts. The abolition of a duty on hides was one change that many considered important. It was estimated that the 1909 statute reduced rates in 584 instances affecting 20 percent of the imports. On the other hand, rates were increased in three hundred instances, including certain grades of cotton hosiery, zinc ore, silk, and a number of items in the cotton schedule. The wool and woolen duties were left unchanged, except for reductions in duty on wool tops and a slight reduction on yarn and dress goods. Similarly, the duties on sugar were left virtually untouched. But it was provided that raw sugar not exceeding three hundred thousand tons per annum should be admitted free of duty from the Philippine Islands. In regard to its general effect, the first two full years of the Payne-Aldrich tariff showed, as compared with the last years (1908–1909) of the Dingley tariff, a decline of 2.38 percent on dutiable articles, and of 4 percent on free and dutiable articles.

This act abandoned the principle of reciprocity and adopted the maximum-and-minimum-value principle. According to this, the enacted tariff rates were the minimum rates, to which rates of 25 percent ad valorem could be added on goods coming from countries that "unduly" discriminated against the United States. But by April 1, 1910, the President had ordered the minimum rate to be in effect for all countries. To carry out the maximum and minimum clause provisions, the President was authorized to establish a Tariff Board, which was to collect data on the cost of production at home and abroad in an effort to provide a scientific basis for carrying out the maximum and minimum laws. This board was a concession to the insurgent Republicans, who had demanded a strong, independent tariff commission as an objective counteragent to the protectionists' propaganda. Although this board made several valuable reports, it was denied further support and went out of existence in June, 1912.

Taft and Reciprocity with Canada, 1911. Although the 1909 Tariff Act slighted reciprocity, President Taft showed an intense interest in securing reciprocity with Canada. He was inspired to do this as a means of restoring the prestige of the Republican party that had been damaged by the revolt of progressive Republicans in the House against the dictatorship of the Speaker, Joseph G. Cannon, and the scandal over alleged favoritism by the Secretary of the Interior, Richard A. Ballinger, to banker interests in Alaska. Taft also had hopes that the reciprocity agreement would help the Republican party to win the 1910 congressional elections and block the movement for drastic tariff reform by the insurgent Republicans and the Democrats.

The preliminary agreement between Canada and the United

States was signed on January 21, 1911. It provided for free trade of certain food products, decreased the rates on others, and reduced duties on manufactured goods. Republican protectionists and north-western farmers brought pressure on Congress against the agreement, but the bill passed the House by a vote of 221 to 93, despite a majority of the Republicans voting against it. In the Senate, although the struggle was renewed, the bill passed on July 22, 1911. It never went into effect, however, except on the free importation of print paper and wood pulp, because the Liberal administration of Sir Wilfred Laurier was defeated in Canada in the general elections of September 21, 1911, owing to the influence of certain manufacturing interests that were fearful of American competition and appealed to the Canadian antipathy to American annexation. Not until 1936 was a reciprocity treaty between the two countries negotiated, and the opposing interests brought into harmony.

Wilson, the Democrats, and the Underwood-Simmons Tariff Act of 1913. The Payne-Aldrich tariff aroused as much widespread criticism as the 1828 "Tariff of Abominations," and the tariff became a leading issue in the 1910 and 1912 campaigns. The Republicans lost the congressional election of 1910, and the new Democratic House passed several tariff bills that reduced rates, especially on cotton and woolens, and enlarged the free list. Some of these bills were approved by the Senate, but vetoed by President Taft on the ground that the bills were loosely drafted and action should be postponed until the Tariff Board completed its investigations.

The Democrats in 1912 achieved a decisive victory over both the Progressive and Republican parties, owing to the conflict between supporters of Theodore Roosevelt and William H. Taft. Woodrow Wilson called a special session of Congress for April 7, 1913, to revise the tariff and to consider other related problems. (*See Reading No. 9.*) Shortly afterward, on April 22, Oscar W. Underwood of Alabama, Chairman of the House Ways and Means Committee, presented to the House a bill that contained the most drastic downward revision of the tariff for the past five decades. Strong hostility to these changes was expressed by wool and sugar producers, cotton manufacturers, paper makers, fruit raisers in California, millers in Minnesota, and cattlemen from Texas. Nevertheless, Wilson, with the support of Underwood, Cordell Hull, and the powerful Democratic leaders, succeeded in getting the House to approve the Underwood tariff bill on May 8, 1913, by a vote of 281 to 139.

The Democrats in the Senate outnumbered the Republicans 51 to 45, yet the Senate's independence of the President, and powerful pressure by lobbyists for the different vested interests caused a battle of four months over the tariff bill. After receiving it from the House, the Senate Finance Committee, headed by Furnifold McLendel Simmons of North Carolina, revised it even further downward. Although a strong conservative, Simmons led the struggle for these tariff changes because Wilson had backed his election as Chairman of the Senate Finance Committee. Wilson also aided his Senate supporters through an unprecedented public attack on the tariff lobbyists in Washington. His skillful leadership and the joint action of the Democratic majority and two Progressive Republicans, La Follette and Poindexter, enabled the Senate to pass the Underwood-Simmons tariff bill on September 9 by a vote of 44 to 37. When the differences between the House and the Senate were harmonized by a conference committee, the bill became law on October 3, 1913.

The new law attempted to lower the cost of living for the consuming masses and to end exorbitant profits to giant industries. Yet at the same time it gave a moderate protection to "legitimate" domestic industries through a "competitive tariff": one by which rates would be fixed at a point where foreign competition might be effective. Among the innovations in the 1913 tariff act was a great expansion of the free list through the inclusion of raw wool, iron ore, pig and scrap iron, steel rails, coal, lumber, many farm products (wheat, flour, cattle, meats, eggs, milk, flax, tea, and hemp), and various manufactures such as leather boots, shoes, gunpowder, wood pulp, and print paper. Moderate reductions were made in the rates on many manufactured products, e.g. woolens, cottons, linens, jute goods, earthenware, glassware, bar iron, steel bars, and tin-plate. Schedules that were left almost unchanged included tobacco, spirits and wines, and silks (already very high). The rates on various luxuries were either unchanged or raised. Raw sugar was to be admitted free after May 1, 1916, but in 1915 Congress decided to retain the duty of $1\frac{1}{2}$ cents a pound.

Ad valorem duties replaced many specific duties. The provisions for maximum and minimum duties established in 1909 were dropped entirely. Regulations governing customs administration were made more effective against fraud than they had been previously. A new feature was the provision for lower duties for goods imported in American ships when existing commercial treaties did not prohibit such discrimination. This attempt to aid the Merchant Marine revived the policy that had prevailed in the period between 1789 and 1815. The general prevalence of commercial treaties, however, made it inoperative. Finally, since the Government was in need of revenue to take the place of the anticipated reduction in receipts from customs duties, the Underwood Tariff Act included a provision for an income tax that had been made possible by the Sixteenth Amendment to the Constitution. This combination of a return to moderate protection in the tariff and a shift in the burden of taxation from the low-income to the high-income classes were two significant features of the 1913 Tariff Act.

Impact of World War I on Tariff, 1913-1921. The new tariff was in operation for less than a year when World War I erupted in August, 1914. The first eight months that the 1913 tariff was in effect, the ad valorem rate on dutiable goods proved to be 36 percent (about 4 percent less than in the previous year), and the rate on free and dutiable goods together, about 14 percent (over 3 percent less than in the preceding year). But international commerce was so disturbed during the war that it is difficult to make valid comparisons for this period.

The reduction in the average ad valorem rate was less than anticipated. Many of the reductions had little effect because the former rate had been much higher than was needed to cut off imports. In other cases, the old rates were only nominal and of no effect because they were on goods regularly exported, not imported, e.g. farm products and cotton goods. Yet it seems likely that some of the 1913 tariff reductions would have forced less efficient plants in some industries either to increase their efficiency or to go out of business. In any normal peace-time situation, time is needed for such adjustments, but an adjustment of a most unusual or atypical kind was going on during the war. Although imports from Europe fell to some extent, total imports after 1915 increased, and American exports grew tremendously. Old industrial plants became converted for a time to different wartime uses. The comparatively low duties of 1913 had no effects injurious to domestic American industry, and actually stimulated American international trade to adapt itself far more speedily to international conditions and to profit more from the war opportunities than would have been possible with a high tariff.

Republicans, Normalcy, and the Emergency Tariff Act of 1921. With the ending of World War I in November, 1918, the agitation for higher duties began to be heard again. The war had increased the demand for national preparedness; numerous "war babies" had been born—particularly in the chemical and metallurgical industries—and felt they needed protection against the resumption of European, especially German, imports. The unprecedented drop in prices in 1920–1921 induced farmers, notably in the West, to press for agricultural tariff protection. Congress responded by passing the Fordney Emergency Tariff Bill, which levied high duties on imported agricultural products. Although President Wilson vetoed this bill on March 3, 1921, after Harding's inauguration, Congress met in special session and passed the revised Emergency Tariff Act of May 27, 1921. This attempted to protect farm products from foreign competition by imposing high duties on wheat, corn, meat, wool, and sugar. The new agricultural duties were stipulated for only a six-month period, but they were re-enacted until the final passage of the 1922 Tariff Act. Although they failed to halt the decline in farm prices, they served to prepare the way for the protectionist victory in 1922.

During World War I the United States had maintained throughout its participation in the war a system of embargoes through the agency of the War Trade Board, both for imports and exports. The War Trade Board employed its powers after the war ended to control among other things the importation of dyestuffs. The Emergency Tariff Act of 1921 abolished the War Trade Board. But the same act provided that certain chemicals and dyestuffs, especially those derived from coal-tar products, should for a period of three months be prohibited importation unless it was determined that such articles, or satisfactory substitutes were not obtainable in the United States in sufficient quantities and on reasonable terms as to quality, price, delivery, etc. The time of the application of the Act was later extended on August 24, 1921, for a period of three months, and on November 16, 1921, until the Tariff Act of 1922 abolished embargoes for dyestuffs and related products otherwise provided by law.

Economic Nationalism and the Fordney-McCumber Tariff Act of 1922. While Congress was acting on the Emergency Tariff Act, the House Ways and Means Committee had been revising the Underwood-Simmons Tariff Act. Its "permanent" tariff bill was passed by the House on July 21, 1921, but the Senate Finance Committee then spent a year in revising the House bill. The rewritten bill had over two thousand changes and was not submitted to the Senate until April, 1922. The Democrats and Republicans then engaged in an extended debate, and the agricultural bloc from the Midwest forced concessions from the industrial Northeast. Finally the Senate passed the bill on August 19 by an almost strictly party vote of 48 to 25. The bill became law on September 19, 1922.

The new act marked the return to the high protective system that the Underwood Tariff had broken for some nine years. It was also a strong obstacle to any hope of an effective restoration of a world trading system. The main increases in the tariff were imposed upon various chemical and metallurgical articles such as coal-tar products, manganese and tungsten ores, and magnesite. The duties on coal-tar products were supposedly to protect American chemicals from German imports. The duties on dyestuffs amounted in practice to an embargo. Considerably increased rates were levied on agricultural products such as wheat, sugar, wool, butter, milk, lemons, and flaxseed and on cutlery, clocks, toys, and chinaware. The rates on textiles—woolen, silk, and cotton fabrics—were restored to the 1909 level, but the duty on lace was raised to an unusually high point. While coal and iron were left on the free list, the cruder forms of iron and steel products received duties of a moderate character, even though of slight importance. In order to please the farmers, agricultural implements, binder twine, and potash were included in the free list along with hides, leather, boots, and shoes.

The increases in customs rates reflected the pressures from different economic and sectional interests. The general economic effect of the duties on agricultural products from the point of view of both the producer and the consumer was not great except in the case of sugar and wool. But the political benefits of these duties were undoubtedly great for the Republican party. Some writers justify the protection given to the chemical and other war industries in view of the later outbreak of World War II. Other authorities, however, argue that the widespread belief in the necessity for protection contributed to the building up of international tensions and helped to bring on the very war that most people wished to avoid.

An important addition to the tariff was the flexible provision that permitted the President of the United States to revise rates upward or downward by as much as 50 percent whenever it was found that existing duties failed to equalize the difference in production costs of the U.S. and major competing countries. The Tariff Commission, established in 1916 under a Democratic regime, was given the responsibility for determining the costs of production, both in the United States and in foreign countries. Although the commission had the duty to advise the President on raising or lowering rates, independent of congressional legislation, the President was under no legal obligation to follow its advice. Nor was any really serious use made of this authority by the Harding, Coolidge, and Hoover Administrations. During the years 1922–1930 only thirty-seven changes were made in the tariff, and of these thirty-two were increases and five were decreases. The lowered rates involved paintbrush handles, bobwhite quails, mill feeds, phenol, and cresylic acid. Fifteen additional requests were considered, but not granted. Even in the case of sugar, the President ignored the recommendation that the rate be reduced. During the period of 1930 to 1939, there were 101 requests for changes. Of these, twenty-five increases were granted, thirty-one decreases ordered, and forty-five refused.

CHAPTER 4

The Depression, the New Deal, and World War II

Hoover and the Hawley-Smoot Tariff of 1930. During the Presidential-election campaign of 1928, Herbert Hoover acknowledged the economic-welfare claims of American farmers and promised to put through a farm-relief program and "limited" upward revision of the tariff. Although Alfred E. Smith and the Democratic party advocated aid for the farmers and a tariff that would preserve legitimate business interests and a high wage standard for American labor, Hoover and the Republicans won a landslide victory of 21 million to 15 million votes over Smith and the Democratic party. Shortly after his inauguration in March, 1929, Hoover called Congress into special session to enact farm-relief legislation and to raise the tariff.

Some sectors of agriculture felt they had not shared in the prosperity of the mid-1920's and demanded legislative assistance. Farm leaders proposed a closer control over the home market for oils, fats, dairy products, hides, skins, and other agricultural products. They also suggested the reduction of some industrial tariffs to equalize industrial and agricultural prices. Meanwhile, certain industries were worried about increased competition from foreign imports and demanded more protection.

An Agricultural Marketing Act was made law on June 15, 1929. But the tariff took much longer for Congress to enact. In January, 1929, hearings had begun on a limited tariff revision to benefit the farmer and to correct a few other rates and some inequalities. Soon it became clear that the revision would be much more general than had been at first intended. On May 7 a tariff bill was introduced into the House by Willis C. Hawley of Oregon. This disregarded Hoover's specific limitations on tariff revision and provided for extremely extensive changes in tariff duties, most of them upward. In addition to widespread increases in farm duties, however futile or insignificant, there were increases on almost every other commodity that might possibly suffer from foreign competition. On May 24, the House, under tight Republican machine control, passed the bill by a vote of 264 to 147. While twelve Republicans voted against the bill, twenty Democrats from industrial areas were for it.

In the Senate the Democrats were supported by the insurgent Republicans from the Middle West and Far West, in opposition to the revised tariff bill presented by Reed Smoot of Utah for the Senate Finance Committee. This combination of Democrats and insurgent Republicans almost succeeded in passing a resolution sponsored by Senator Borah of Idaho to limit the revisions strictly to agricultural products. The resulting conflict, although Hoover pleaded for speedy action on the tariff as a stabilizer of business, continued until March 24, 1930. By that time Senator Smoot, with the assistance of Joseph R. Grundy of Pennsylvania, president of the Pennsylvania Manufacturers' Association, managed to overcome opposition to the original tariff bill by trading eastern support of agricultural duties for western support of industrial duties. The Senate passed the Hawley-Smoot Tariff Bill by a vote of 53 to 31. Despite the log-rolling in the Senate, at the final vote, twenty-six Democrats and five insurgent Republicans stood fast in their opposition to this tariff.

Grundy, who had succeeded William S. Vare as Senator in December, 1929, was important as one of the organizers of the American Tariff League, the spearhead of the business groups behind the protective tariff. He was a power in Pennsylvania and national Republican politics. Despite his and Senator Smoot's successes, the insurgents were able to force the adoption of a provision for export debentures (a bounty paid out of customs to American farmers) and a provision placing the administration of the flexibility power on tariff rates under the control of Congress rather than of the President. As the House version of the tariff bill excluded these two items, the Congressmen on the House-Senate conference committee, aided by pressure from President Hoover, forced the Senate to yield on these two major amendments of the Senate insurgents. Finally, the conference bill passed the Senate, June 13, 1930, by a vote of 44 to 42, with eleven Republicans, headed by Senators Norris and Borah, against it. The next day the House gave its approval by a majority of 222 to 153. In both the Senate and the House the majorities favoring the bill came mainly from the industrial Northeast, which expected the most benefits, but not from the agricultural South and West, for whom principally the revision was originally intended.

Hoover was flooded by protests from thirty-three foreign governments, the American Bankers' Association, importers, industries with foreign markets, and over one thousand economists throughout the United States. (*See Reading No. 10.*) But he felt he had to sign the tariff bill on June 17, 1930, in order not to embarrass his party in an election year. Hoover erred in not stating early during Congress' debate on the tariff that he would veto anything that did not conform to his recommendations. W. C. Hawley, co-author of the bill, defended his Tariff Act as a protector of American industries and labor against unfair competition, improper trade practices, and exclusion from an advantageous participation in foreign markets. On the other hand, many economists agreed that the 1930 tariff would increase the cost of living, hurt the vast majority of farmers, hamper American export trade, and induce foreign countries to levy retaliatory tariffs against American goods.

In its final form, the rates imposed by the Hawley-Smoot Tariff Act reached an all-time high in American tariff history. The average ad valorem rate for free and dutiable imports was 40.08 percent in contrast to the 33.22-percent average of the Fordney-McCumber Act. But the average ad valorem rate on dutiable imports exclusively was 52.8 percent for the years 1930–1933 under the Hawley-Smoot law as against 38.5 percent for the years 1922–1929 under the Fordney-McCumber law. There was a general increase in the duties on agricultural products, e.g. sugar, wheat, long-staple cotton, meat, and dairy products. Some of these increases, however, were considered by experts to be either mere pretense or of mild benefit to the farmer. Although the increase in the duty on sugar was the most important from the revenue point of view, the profit given to the domestic beet-sugar producers was at the cost of the consumers. Hides, leather, shoes, timber, cement, long-staple cotton, and brick were removed from the free list and made dutiable. Although the majority of rates on manufactured goods was left unchanged, there were important increases on such manufactured goods as cotton, wool, and silk goods, glass, chinaware, and watch movements. The duties on certain metals, e.g. aluminum, manganese, and tungsten-bearing ores, were also raised. Some cuts were made in industries where foreign competition was not serious such as automobiles and agricultural implements.

No change of importance was made in the powers of the Tariff Commission beyond allowing the President as well as Congress to make requests for investigations. The commission could not recommend increases or decreases that would change rates more than 50 percent or transfer articles from the dutiable list to the free list, or vice versa. The President, however, was now empowered to increase existing tariff rates by an additional 50 percent ad valorem upon goods coming from countries that discriminated against American commerce. The commission was reorganized, and higher salaries were provided for its members in the hope of increasing its quality and efficiency.

World Reaction Against the 1930 Tariff. Much to the surprise of the American public, the Hawley-Smoot Tariff Act produced a world-wide tariff retaliatory movement against the United States. As a consequence of World War I the United States had become the world's greatest creditor nation and had maintained its large export trade through extensive loans to and investments in industrial and nonindustrial countries. This policy had permitted European countries to maintain their unfavorable trade balances with the United States and to continue war-debt payments until the Great Depression of 1929. But when the United States ceased making foreign loans in the late 1920's and put through its upward revision of the tariff in 1930, the result was to cut down the imports from abroad, to increase even more the deficient trade balance of Europe with the United States, and to make more difficult the transfer of money payments to the United States. Hence, many countries resorted to "defensive" tariffs in order to create export balances for debt payment, to check domestic price declines, and to stabilize their national economies. (*See Chapter 1* for an analysis of *Tariffs: The Reasons Why.*)

Hoover lessened the strain in the international debtor-creditor relationship by establishing in 1931 a moratorium on all intergovernmental debts and reparations. Nevertheless, England felt it had to go off the gold standard in September, 1931, adopt emergency tariffs in 1931–1932, establish a tariff of considerable height, and support the imperial preference policy adopted in the Ottawa Agreements of August, 1932. During 1931 and 1932 extensive increases in tariff duties were made by a dozen other countries outside Great Britain and the British Commonwealth of Nations. These actions were part of the trend toward autarchy or national self-sufficiency that the Hawley-Smoot tariff helped to induce.

What gave the foreign retaliation such a crushing effect was the fact that the United States had enjoyed a favorable trade balance before the enactment of the 1930 tariff law. Thus the United States stood more to lose than to gain in the tariff war with the outside world. In 1932 the Republican and Democratic national party conventions met at the depth of the Great Depression. Deflation in the United States had been especially severe. Between 1929 and 1932 wholesale prices had fallen 32 percent while the national income was cut in half. The dollar value of United States exports had fallen from about $4.9 billion in 1925 and from $5.4 billion in 1929 to $1.6 billion in 1932—a drop of more than two thirds of the annual average of the previous six years. The League of Nations Information Service reported:

> The total volume of goods exchanged between countries has diminished by about 30 per cent in comparison with 1929. This aspect of world trade is especially serious. Previous crises never showed such a shrinkage in the volume of trade; on the contrary, a fall in prices used to give rise speedily . . . [to a] volume of trade which made it possible for the situation to improve.

From 1929 to 1933, the American share of world trade had fallen both in European and in the Latin-American markets while other countries were increasing their trade.

The 1932 Election, F.D.R., and the Tariff. In this context the tariff planks of the Republicans showed no awareness of the relationship between the foreign retaliations to the Hawley-Smoot tariff and the shrinking of American income and employment that had been dependent on sustained exports. Instead the Republicans credited the 1930 tariff with providing better farm prices, advocated the continuance of protective tariffs, and promised such revision as changing conditions required. By contrast the Democratic platform laid down a strong plank condemning the loss of foreign markets and the international ill will resulting from the Hawley-Smoot Act. In its place the Democrats advocated a "competitive tariff" for revenue and then went on to propose a program of bargaining with other nations to bring about reciprocal trade agreements.

The distinction between the Republican and Democratic positions, however, must not be overdrawn. The Democrats numbered among the guiding spirits of their high-tariff, big-business wing such men as John J. Raskob, the millionaire Democratic National Chairman, who stood for a protective tariff while urging that the Democrats "take the Government out of business and relieve trade from unnecessary and unfeasible Government restriction." During the Presidential campaign the Republicans pressed Roosevelt to name the items in the tariff that he would lower. In reply, Roosevelt hedged his already equivocal position by declaring that he would maintain protection of agriculture and of industries facing low-wage foreign competition.

After the Democrats defeated the Republicans by a popular vote of almost 23 million to 15¾ million and Roosevelt entered the White House, he was confronted with problems that weighed more heavily on him and on the nation than the tariff policies: e.g. the collapse of the banking system a short time before the inauguration, the inadequate relief programs for the quarter of the nation that suffered from unemployment of its wage earners, the threat of imminent economic collapse and social upheaval. Understandably, it was not until Armistice Day, 1933, that the President appointed an "Executive Committee on Commercial Policy" to coordinate the existing American bank policies and to draft a new tariff bill. The Executive Committee (composed of representatives of the Tariff Commission, the Agricultural Adjustment Administration, and the Departments of State, Treasury, Commerce, and Agriculture) came to unanimous agreement in favor of a reciprocal-trade-agreement program, drafted a bill, and presented it to Roosevelt at the end of February, 1934.

F.D.R., Hull, and Reciprocal Trade. On March 2 the President's tariff message was sent to Congress. It asked Congress to delegate to him the authority for the next three years to negotiate with other nations reciprocal trade reductions up to 50 percent of the Hawley-Smoot level. (*See Reading No. 11.*) As an early New Deal measure, the Reciprocal Trade Bill was an anomaly. Roosevelt's guiding sentiment was that the nation should control its economic destiny without being dependent on the international economy. Thus the United States freed the domestic price level from having to adjust to changes in foreign price levels by going off the gold standard in the spring of 1933 through an Executive order of the President. Likewise, agriculture, industry, and commerce were brought under national control through the passage of the Agricultural Adjustment Act and the National Industrial Recovery Act on May 12 and June 16, 1933, respectively. Amidst these measures of economic nationalism, the Reciprocal Trade Bill seemed to head the American economy and ship of state into the international trade winds.

The driving force behind the reciprocal trade program was Cordell Hull, Roosevelt's Secretary of State from 1933 to 1944. Hull was dedicated to the liberalization of commercial policy and saw tariff policy at the very heart of America's economic dilemma. He thought that the expansion of foreign trade was a highway to recovery, an instrument for escaping from domestic controls, and a path to world peace.

The new bill drafted by the Executive Committee on Commercial Policy reached the House on March 2, 1934. Thereupon the Republican Congressmen almost unanimously attacked and opposed it as a revolution in tariff making. Nevertheless, the House passed the bill on March 29 by a vote of 274 to 111. A vigorous debate then took place in the Senate. Senator Borah pronounced the bill unconstitutional, and Senator Vandenberg was so carried away by emotion as to declare: "This proposal is fascist in its philosophy, fascist in its objective"; it was "economic dictatorship come to America." But these arguments had little effect; on June 4 the Senate vote was 57 in favor to 33 against, with almost all the Democrats lined up for the bill and practically all the Republicans against it.

On June 12, 1934, the Reciprocal Trade Agreement Program became law, and the power to negotiate was to run for three years. (*See Reading No. 12.*) In 1937 this power was renewed for another three years, and similar extensions were periodically re-enacted, though modified somewhat after World War II, until replaced by the Trade Expansion Act of 1962. In form, the 1934 statute was not a new tariff act, but an amendment to the Hawley-Smoot Tariff Act to be known as "Section 350" and to be added at the end of Title III of that Act. The new Act delegated to the President the power to make foreign-trade agreements with other nations on the basis of mutual reduction of duties. Specific congressional approval of reductions was not required. The Act limited reduction to 50 percent of the then existing rates of duty and stipulated that commodities could not be transferred between the dutiable and the free lists.

Although Congress gave the Department of State the primary responsibility for negotiating with other nations, it instructed the

Tariff Commission and other Government agencies to participate in developing lists of concessions that could be made to foreign countries and corresponding lists of concessions that should be demanded in return. An interdepartmental committee was designated to conduct public hearings on forthcoming negotiations so that all interested parties might have an opportunity to present their views to the President. Tariff concessions that were negotiated between the United States and any other country were to be set forth formally in the trade agreement. Each trade agreement was to incorporate the principle of "unconditional most-favored-nation treatment." This was necessary to avoid a great multiplicity of rates. Finally, the new reciprocal-trade agreements were to become effective by proclamation of the President.

Through the Trade Agreements Extension Act of 1945, Congress increased the power of the President by authorizing him to reduce tariffs by 50 percent of the rate in effect on January 1, 1945, instead of 1934, as the original act provided. Thus duties that had been reduced by 50 percent prior to 1945 could be reduced by another 50 percent, or by 75 percent below the rates that were in effect in 1934. (*See Reading No. 13.*) But in 1956 further duty reductions were limited to 20 percent.

In negotiating agreements under the Trade Agreements Act, the United States usually proceeded by making direct concessions only to so-called "chief suppliers," namely countries that were or probably would become the main source or a major source of supply of the commodity under discussion. This approach seemed favorable to the United States since no concessions were extended to "minor" supplying countries that would benefit the chief supplying countries (through unconditional most-favored-nation treatment) without the latter countries first having granted a concession. The United States counted on first withholding a concession until it could be made to the chief supplier in return for an equivalent grant, then using its bargaining power to the maximum to secure openings to foreign markets for American exports.

Between 1934 and 1947 the United States made separate trade agreements with twenty-nine foreign countries. The Tariff Commission found that when it used dutiable imports in 1939 as its basis for comparison, the United States tariffs were reduced from an average of 48 percent to 25 percent during these years. The imports on which duties were reduced came to over $700 million in 1939.

CHAPTER 5

America's New Role in The World Economy, 1945–1970

International Trade Organization. During World War II the State Department and other United States Government agencies worked on plans for the reconstruction of world trade and payments. They then discovered important defects in the Trade Agreements Program. In some cases prior to World War II, foreign governments had been hesitant to give the United States the concessions it sought because they wanted to reserve some bargaining power for negotiations with other countries. In those cases where a foreign government had made important tariff reductions while negotiating with the United States, it found it had little or nothing to give the other governments that had inflicted import restrictions upon its commodities. American officials concluded that they could make better headway through simultaneous multi-lateral negotiations. Then each government would be able to evaluate all the gains it might make and to decide what concessions it could offer. Such a procedure also enabled each country to discover what concessions it was receiving free of charge through its use of the "most-favored-nation" treatment.

One development of the 1930's and early 1940's that disturbed the United States was the extensive replacement of tariffs by import quotas and foreign exchange controls. In some cases these quota restrictions made concessions given by other governments worthless. Sometimes the restrictive effects of the quotas were more stringent than those of the tariffs they superseded. Hence, the American government gave up on negotiating a new round of tariff treaties and instead embarked upon obtaining a comprehensive international agreement on commercial policy.

Moreover, the United States authorities decided that by 1945 they had made the maximum concessions permitted by statute on some 40 percent of American dutiable imports. Relatively few duties could be lowered by 1945 without possible injury to American industry, and the Truman Administration was committed to avoiding injury. Since the concessions the United States could grant without creating injury often involved duties that had already been lowered by the pre-World War II trade agreements, it was necessary for Truman to acquire the new authority needed to reduce American tariffs beyond the 50 percent authorized in 1934.

This gap in Presidential power was removed by the Trade Agreements Extension Act of 1945. This gave the President the power to cut in half the tariff rates in force on January 1, 1945. He could thereby reduce to 25 percent of the 1934 levels the tariffs that he had already cut, and he could bring the other rates down to 50 percent of the 1934 tariff levels. (*See Reading No. 14.*)

American support for a new comprehensive, multi-lateral approach first found expression in the World War II lend-lease program the United States, Great Britain, and various other members of the United Nations adopted. Article Seven of each of the master lend-lease agreements pledged the United States and each of the other concerned countries to coordinate their individual actions toward: ". . . the expansion . . . of production, employment, and the exchange and consumption of goods, . . . the elimination of all forms of discriminatory treatment in international commerce;" and the reduction of tariffs and other trade barriers.

The success of the lend-lease agreements and of the Bretton Woods Conference on the International Monetary Fund and the International Bank for Reconstruction and Development inspired the United States State Department in 1945 to advance some far-reaching "Proposals for the Expansion of World Trade and Employment." These provisions elicited a bitter debate because some officials in Great Britain were fearful that they would result in the elimination of imperial preference. Nevertheless these provisions became the basis for later discussions. In 1946 the United Nations Economic and Social Council created a commission to hold a global conference on international trade and employment. Two years later that conference produced the charter for an International Trade Organization that was to be affiliated with the United Nations.

But the International Trade Organization never was ratified by

Congress. Its charter was so long and complicated that it gave the foes of commercial cooperation the belief that the ITO would interfere with American domestic economic policy. On the other hand, the ITO charter disappointed the champions of cooperation because its provisions were too open to evasion. As a result the ITO charter got little support and soon ceased to be a live issue.

Geneva Agreement of 1947 on Tariffs and Trade. Despite the failure to ratify the ITO charter, the United States invited eighteen foreign countries to participate with it in the negotiation of a multilateral trade agreement at Geneva in 1947. Several changes and additions were made in the composition of the nation membership during the course of the negotiations at Geneva, with twenty-three separate countries finally participating in the final negotiations. The tariff negotiations at Geneva were conducted bilaterally on a product-by-product basis. Each country negotiated as to its concessions on each import commodity with its principal supplier of that commodity. But the various bilateral understandings were combined to form the General Agreement on Tariffs and Trade, generally referred to as the Geneva Agreement. The final act embodying the text of that agreement was signed in Geneva on October 30, 1947. (*See Reading No. 15.*) This agreement did not have to be submitted to the Senate for approval because the President was already empowered to reduce our tariffs, specifically under the authority conferred by the Trade Agreements Extension Act of 1945.

The first part of GATT set forth in broad terms the principles of international trade practice to which the participating nations promised to adhere. These principles, although formulated prior to the GATT, later were enlarged and became the basis of the charter for an International Trade Organization. After 1947 the provisions of GATT were made through reference to those nations that signed it, a part of each reciprocal trade agreement concluded by the United States. The second part of the GATT listed the tariff reductions on some forty-five thousand items made by its member governments. These trade concessions covered almost two thirds of the total world trade at that time.

The most vital part of GATT's commercial code is the "most-favored-nation" clause. This promises each member the benefit of every tariff reduction made by another. The code, in addition, forbids discrimination and prohibits quotas, protective internal taxes, restrictive customs and administrative devices, and other nontariff trade barriers. Exceptions are made for countries in balance-of-payments difficulties and for those imposing similar quantitative controls upon their domestic output, e.g. in agriculture. Underdeveloped nations are permitted to restrict imports in order to develop their infant industries. Countries invoking the escape clause for the balance-of-payments exception are required, however, to consult periodically with the other members of GATT and then to justify their prolonged use of these trade restrictions. A general "escape clause" in GATT allows a country to modify or withdraw a trade-agreement concession if a domestic industry is seriously injured by imports. But it permits the countries that are hurt by this action to withdraw equivalent concessions from the country that initiated the tariff increase.

From an original membership of twenty-three countries, GATT has increased to include more than seventy countries, a membership responsible for about four fifths of all world trade. From the numerous individual tariff negotiations carried on under the auspices of GATT, concessions covering over sixty thousand items have been agreed upon. These comprised more than two thirds of the total import trade of the participating countries and more than half the total number of commodities involved in world trade.

The Temporary Status of GATT. There is an old American saying: "Only the temporary endures." This is demonstrated in the history of GATT. Drawn up as a trade agreement pending the creation of the International Trade Organization, GATT lived on as a functioning organization after the Truman Administration felt forced in December, 1950, to withdraw the proposed charter for the ITO from consideration by Congress because of the opposition within Congress to that measure. The legal basis of GATT was insecure, and it had insufficient secretariat or budget. But it continued to act as an effective agency in international trade matters, even though it had no permanent administrative machinery, or even the sanction of all its members. The United States has been a member of GATT and participates in its activities on the basis of Executive agreements, but without the express approval of Congress. In 1955 an attempt was made to give GATT a firm, permanent administrative machinery through a new institution to be known as the Organization for Trade Cooperation (OTC), but Congress refused to approve Eisenhower's proposal.

Nevertheless, GATT has achieved much in the way of trade expansion for countries accounting for more than 80 percent of world trade. Through the leadership of its chief executive, Eric Wyndham White, during its first twenty-one years, GATT has made contributions in four ways: as a forum for trade negotiations, as a body of principles guiding trade policy, as an agency for settling trade disputes, and as an instrument for the development of trade policy.

Restrictions on Tariff Negotiating. The Reciprocal Trade Agreements Act of 1934, unfortunately for those wishing trade liberalization, required a periodic renewal of authority. Between 1934 and 1962 this Act had been renewed eleven times. Each renewal enabled the protectionist members of Congress, both Republicans and an increasing number of Democrats from coal, oil, and textile districts, to vote for restrictions on the President's authority to negotiate tariff reductions. In December, 1942, a trade agreement with Mexico was signed that included an escape clause, providing that a concession of any article might be withdrawn—in whole or in part—whenever as a result of the concession and from "unforeseen" developments, the import of that article increased to such an amount as to cause or threaten "serious injury" to the domestic producers of like or similar articles. In 1947 President Truman was pressured by Congress to issue an Executive Order requiring a similar escape clause in all future trade agreements. (*See Reading No. 16.*) After the war-devastated regions of Europe and Japan were rebuilt, American producers met with increasingly vigorous foreign competition. As a result, in 1951 Congress required an escape clause to be written not only in all future trade agreements, but in all the trade agreements currently in force. These and related subsequent measures made a mockery of earlier free trade or trade liberalization objectives.

The Tariff Commission was charged by Congress with the responsibility of conducting an escape-clause investigation whenever requested by the President, either House of Congress, the Senate Finance Committee, the House Ways and Means Committee, or any interested party. Although the President was not required to follow the Tariff Commission's recommendations, if he failed to do so he had to submit a report to Congress giving his reasons. Moreover, an amendment in 1958 provided for the overriding of the President's decision by a two-thirds vote of Congress.

The criteria that the Tariff Commission had to use in determining a complaint of injury included consideration of a downward trend in production, employment, prices, profits, or wages in the industry concerned; or a decline in sales, an increase in imports—either actual or relative to domestic production; or a decline in the proportion of the domestic market supplied by domestic producers. In 1955 Congress greatly widened the escape clause by defining the term "domestic industry" to include each single product of multi-product firms, and by permitting the finding of injury even where increased imports were not the main cause of the injury.

Another protectionist restriction on tariff reductions was the introduction by a Republican-dominated Congress in 1948 of a provision directing the Tariff Commission, before GATT negotiations, to fix the minimum rates necessary to protect domestic producers against imports of similar articles. The President was empowered to offer concessions below these "peril points," but he was required to explain his reasons to Congress. Although the Democrats repealed this provision in 1949, they helped to reinstate it in 1951. Four years later this provision was amended to require that "peril points" be set high enough to protect any segment of an industry, i.e., even the least efficient domestic producers, rather than the industry as a whole.

The escape-clause and "peril-point" provisions were framed to be complementary. The first was intended mainly to take care of injuries to American industry caused by concessions that had already been made in trade agreements. The second was designed to foreclose concessions from being proposed in new negotiations that possibly might create injury in the future.

A third protectionist device for restricting imports was invented in 1955 when Congress authorized the President to impose quotas on products entering the country in such volume as to "threaten to impair the national security." The determination of such a threat was to be made first by the Office of Civil and Defense Mobilization, but the President had the final decision. In 1958 an amendment extended the basis for such action by providing that restrictions might be extended to nondefense industries if imports were weakening the internal economy and thereby affecting national security. As a result, the next year President Eisenhower ordered quotas on imports of crude oil and residual oil. The explanation given for these quotas was that they helped to stimulate the exploration necessary to assure an adequate domestic supply of oil in the event of a national emergency, but they also served to protect the soft-coal industry, which had been seriously affected by the changeover from coal to fuel oil.

Another restraint on trade other than that of tariffs created by the

United States was the imposition of import quotas on various agricultural commodities found to interfere with domestic production-control and price-support programs that were authorized by Section 22 of the Agricultural Adjustment Acts of 1937, 1948, and 1949. In 1939, for example, almost all imports of raw cotton were shut off. In 1951 Congress prohibited trade agreements that were in conflict with Section 22. As a result of foreign protest, the United States had to request a waiver of GATT rules. The countries that agreed to this waiver were authorized to take compensating action against American exports. Nevertheless, in recent years import restrictions based on Section 22 were imposed upon cotton, wheat, wheat flour, certain dairy products, peanuts, oats, rye, and barley.

An ingenious import-quota device is the "voluntary" limitation imposed by other countries on their exports to the United States. A notable instance involves cotton textiles. When warned that the United States would impose import quotas unless Japan took action, Japan agreed from 1956 on to limit its exports of various types of cotton textiles. This device has been extended in recent years to other countries' export and import textiles under an International Textile Agreement.

In addition to these general restrictions on imports considered injurious to American economic interests, the United States imposed special limitations on trade with the Communist bloc of nations for strategic reasons. Exports of strategic items to the Soviet Union and satellites were eliminated, beginning in 1948, under export-control laws going back to 1940. All American trade with Communist China and North Korea was forbidden after the Korean War began in 1950. Once the Mutual Defense Assistance Control Act of 1951 was passed, the United States tried to cut off strategic exports to the Communist bloc of nations from other countries by threatening to withhold American foreign aid. The Trade Agreements Act of 1951 also directed the President to suspend the obligation of any trade-agreements concession to imports from the Soviet Union and from any Soviet-controlled countries or areas. During 1951 and 1952, the President took action on imports from nineteen countries or areas. But in 1972 President Nixon initiated a new Soviet-Chinese policy.

Another interference with a free-trade policy by the United States was the "Buy American" Act of 1933, which gave preference to American bidders for national Governmental orders. By Administrative order, this act was interpreted in its early years to mean that foreign goods might be purchased by the national Government when comparable domestic goods were 25 percent or more higher in price. In December, 1954, President Eisenhower released an Executive Order that the United States might buy abroad if the foreign offer was 6 percent or more below any American bid. An exception up to 12 percent was made for domestic bidders in areas of high unemployment, even if their bids were higher than the new standards. In the late 1960's, foreign producers had been heavily discriminated against in American Government purchases, mainly for balance-of-payments reasons. American domestic producers were given preference regardless of the price differential whenever national security and domestic unemployment seemed relevant to Government officials.

European Common Market. In 1948, three years after the end of World War II, the United States initiated a monumental financial effort to reconstruct the economic power of Western Europe through the Marshall Plan. (*See Reading No. 17.*) America was determined to strengthen Europe against Soviet Russian expansion and aggression and to make West Germany part of the federation of democratic nations in the hope that this would help to prevent future wars. By mid-1951 the countries receiving aid from the Marshall Plan, called the Organization for European Economic Cooperation (OEEC), had achieved most of the recovery needed by the European countries outside the Soviet bloc and had spent some $10.3 billion, about 90 percent of which was in outright grants from the United States. In return for this fiscal aid the European countries agreed, not only to raise output and to increase efficiency of production, but also to eliminate restrictive trade barriers and to check inflation as a precondition to the most effective use of Europe's resources.

The start of European economic integration may be dated with the establishment in 1951 by France, West Germany, Italy, Belgium, the Netherlands, and Luxembourg of the European Coal and Steel Community. This created a common continental market in coal and steel by the abolition of national quotas and tariffs. In addition, a supra-national high authority was created with the power to regulate pricing policies and commercial practices. The six countries, known as the Six, or the Inner Six, took this action by themselves because Soviet foreign policy prevented the linking together of Eastern and Western Europe and because Great Britain's relations with the British Commonwealth of Nations at that time limited her participation.

The success of the ECSC led the foreign ministers of these six European countries to move for a complete customs union. In 1957 they signed the Treaty of Rome establishing a European Economic Community (EEC) or Common Market. Thereby they agreed to eliminate all trade barriers among themselves and to replace their national tariff structures with a common tariff wall. This new system of duties was built by averaging the separate national tariffs. Another treaty established the European Atomic Energy Community, or the Euratom.

European Free Trade Association. Great Britain, after refusing to join the Common Market, persuaded Denmark, Norway, Sweden, Austria, Switzerland, and Portugal to join with her in forming a European Free Trade Association (EFTA) in 1960. This was organized like the Common Market to remove trade barriers among the nation-members, but differed from the Common Market in that it did not erect a common external tariff. Two years later, Great Britain applied for membership in the Common Market because it concluded that EFTA could not compete with EEC in technology or in size of market. However, Charles de Gaulle, the President of France, in 1963 and on later occasions vetoed the British attempt at entry into the Common Market. In 1971 Britain finally voted to join the Common Market. This led to similar action by Norway, Denmark and Ireland. The rest of the EFTA then formed with the Common Market the biggest free-trading bloc in the world. This raises for the United States some important problems in trade policy.

Far Eastern Textiles. Another area where American national security interests were involved was the Far East. After World War II, especially after the 1949 victory of Communism in China, the United States displayed a special concern for building up the Japanese economy. In this objective America succeeded and also became Japan's largest customer. The rapid increase in Japanese exports of competitive manufactures to the United States, however, created strong protectionist reactions from textile, electronic, and other industries in the United States. Anticipating possible tariff restrictions, the Japanese in 1957 imposed quotas on several of their own textile exports to the United States. Some years later the rising textile exports to America from Hong Kong and other areas persuaded the United States to seek an international agreement by textile-exporting countries to restrict their exports in exchange for a more liberal access to European and other restricted markets. The agreements that were negotiated in 1961–1962 were not a permanent solution to the problem, and the United States was left with the obligation to secure equalization of export opportunities for Japan in the future.

The United States and the Alliance for Progress. During World War II many underdeveloped areas in Asia, Africa, and Latin America experienced prosperity because of the need for their primary products by the United States and other highly industrialized countries that were fighting the Axis. After World War II, however, these underdeveloped countries experienced great difficulties in their trading relationships with the highly industrialized countries when the prices of these primary products went down due to decreased demand in peacetime or contractions in the business cycle. During this postwar period these backward areas often felt forced to industrialize their economies in order to keep pace with the demands of nationalism and of anti-colonialism. After 1953 the United States became a competitor with the Communist bloc of nations in responding to the demands in trade and foreign aid by the underdeveloped countries.

As the European Common Market developed after 1958, it created problems for Latin America because the former African colonies of France and Belgium received preferential treatment under the common external tariff, and when Britain joined the Market, its former colonies would benefit similarly. Hence, Latin America's primary exports to Europe might be seriously hurt. To avoid this was one reason that the United States helped to launch in Latin America the "Alliance for Progress" development program in 1961. This ten-year $20-billion program of public and private investment in Latin America was designed to raise per-capita income there 2.5 percent annually. It was hoped that this might be achieved in part through an increase in Latin American exports to Europe and America. As part of this scheme an international coffee agreement was negotiated in 1962, but Congress unfortunately refused to approve implementation procedures in 1964. Congress in the same year also ordered that import quotas be imposed on beef imports. It thereby hurt economically some of the countries in the Alliance for Progress and helped to make it less likely to succeed.

The Soviet Bloc: Aid and Trade. After the death of Stalin in 1953, the new leadership of Soviet Russia developed an increasing interest in underdeveloped countries. Aid and trade agreements between Communist-bloc countries and some forty-one non-Commu-

nist countries in backward areas soon multiplied. Usually these
agreements, estimated to be over two hundred in number by 1962,
involved the barter of industrial goods for raw materials. This exchange was desirable to countries that had difficulty in finding markets for their chief exports. Although the entire Sino-Soviet world
had less than half the capacity of the United States and Western Europe to extend aid and to absorb imports of primary goods, such
trade became a major weapon in Communist attempts to erode the
American and Western Europe position throughout the underdeveloped countries.

Kennedy and the Trade Expansion Act of 1962. With the expiration on June 30, 1962, of the eleventh renewal of the Reciprocal
Trade Agreements Act, the United States was faced with a major decision on its future foreign-trade policy: to choose between continuing the program as it had evolved over the past twenty-eight years,
or to replace it with a new and expanded program. The second alternative was the one chosen by the Kennedy Administration. On January 25, 1962, President Kennedy boldly asked Congress for an unprecedented authority to negotiate with the European Common
Market for reciprocal-trade negotiations. He identified five basically
new developments that made a new trade policy imperative: (1) the
growth of the Common Market, (2) increasing pressure on American
balance of payments, (3) the need to accelerate domestic economic
growth, (4) the threat of the Communist aid and trade offensive, and
(5) the need for new markets by Japan and the developing countries.
(*See Reading No. 18.*)

The President was able to win strong support from powerful business and labor groups. The outcome of his astute campaign was that
the House passed the Trade Expansion Bill on June 28 by a vote of
298 to 125, and the Senate on September 19 by a 78 to 8 vote. When
Kennedy signed the bill on October 11, 1962, he praised it as the
most important international piece of economic legislation "since
the passage of the Marshall Plan." (*See Reading No. 19.*)

The Trade Expansion Act of 1962 differed from its predecessors in
two important ways: It granted to the President far greater authority
to lower or even to eliminate American import duties, and it replaced the negative policy of preventing dislocation by the positive
one of promoting and facilitating adjustment to the domestic dislocation caused by foreign competition. The President was authorized,

through trade agreements with foreign countries, to reduce any duty by 50 percent of the rate in effect on July 1, 1962. Whereas in the past the United States had negotiated on an "item-by-item, rate-by-rate," basis, in the future the President could decide to cut tariffs on an industry or "across-the-board" basis for all products in exchange for similar reductions by the other countries. In order to deal with the tariff problems created by the European Common Market, the President was empowered to reduce tariffs on industrial products by more than 50 percent, or to eliminate them completely in those cases where the United States and the Common Market together accounted for 80 percent or more of the world export value. In the case of agricultural products, even when the 80-percent trade coverage could not be met, the President was authorized in an agreement with the Common Market to reduce by more than 50 percent or to eliminate the duty on an agricultural commodity, if he decided that such action would help to maintain or to expand American exports of the same kind of commodity.

In an attempt to enlarge the export markets of the underdeveloped countries, the President was empowered to reduce or eliminate the duties or other import restrictions on tropical agricultural and forestry commodities not produced in significant quantities in the United States. This authority was made conditional upon the Common Market's taking comparable action on a nondiscriminatory basis so as to assure the maximum possible access to the markets of the EEC countries of commodities from the less developed countries. Finally, the President was authorized to eliminate categorically all so-called "nuisance" duties, defined as ones amounting to 5 percent or less as of July 1, 1962.

One important innovation in the 1962 law provided new ways to deal with injury to domestic industry from foreign competition created through tariff reductions. The President was authorized to assist businessmen through advice on efficiency or shifts in products, tax allowances for operating losses, and loans to help employers in diversifying or modernizing their plants. Workers were to be aided through extended unemployment compensation, re-training for new types of jobs, and re-location allowances to assist the worker's family in moving from an area where employment was lacking to an area where employment was available. These provisions in the 1962 law encouraged gains from the more efficient allocation of resources that foreign trade stimulated, and it avoided the losses in national income that limiting foreign trade and subsidizing inefficient industries brought to the nation.

As a result of these constructive devices, no peril-point provision against imports was required in the Trade Expansion Act. Nevertheless, the President was required to inform the Tariff Commission on what commodities he planned to negotiate, and to obtain from them their advice on the probable economic effect of any tariff cut domestically and internationally. But the new law allowed the President to decide for himself by balancing gains against losses from contemplated tariff cuts. Where he deemed the injury to a domestic industry required such action, he was authorized to raise tariffs or to negotiate an international quota system.

Among the restrictive sections of the Act was the retention of the much-debated National Security Amendment with its proviso for restricting imports if they threatened American national security. Under this clause the President was directed to suspend "as soon as practicable" any trade benefits granted after 1930 under most-favored-nation treatment to any country or area that was Communist dominated or controlled; Poland and Yugoslavia were the targets. But Kennedy abstained from taking action on this provision and persuaded Congress in 1963 to repeal it.

If the Tariff Commission finds serious injury threatens a domestic industry, and the President fails to increase or to impose the appropriate tariff duty or other import restrictions, both houses of Congress by a majority vote could compel him to take such action. Moreover, if a foreign country that benefited from American trade concessions imposes nontariff restrictions or discriminatory practices against American commerce, the President is directed to suspend or withdraw American trade concessions to that country. Finally the Trade Expansion Act in no way removes or modifies the power of the President to restrict the import of agricultural products that are subject to domestic price supports.

On the whole, the Trade Expansion Act of 1962 laid the firm basis for "a bold new program" in the realm of foreign commercial policy. The innovations were to prove more important than the restrictions in the succeeding years.

Johnson and the Kennedy Round. One month after John Kennedy signed the 1962 Trade Expansion Act, he was assassinated in Dallas, Texas, and Lyndon B. Johnson became President. Although some thought him more conservative than Kennedy, Johnson carried out more of Kennedy's policies, including that on foreign trade, than many of Johnson's critics have admitted. In any case, Johnson was ultimately responsible for the start in May, 1964, of a new round of tariff bargaining. This was the sixth in the series of major bargaining rounds that GATT, as a forum for trade negotiations, had promoted: at Geneva in 1947, at Annecy in 1949, at Torquay in 1950–1951, at Geneva in 1956, 1960–1961 (the "Dillon Round"), and 1964–1967 (the "Kennedy Round"). In 1967, after three years of continued efforts, the United States and fifty-two other countries, all members of GATT, concluded the Kennedy Round of tariff-cutting negotiations. Their success was a major step forward in international trade liberalization and was achieved against strong protectionist pressures in the United States by the steel, chemical, textile, and oil industries. The agreement reached on June 30, 1967, reduced tariff duties an average of about 35 percent on some sixty thousand items representing an estimated $40 billion in world trade (based on 1964 figures, the base year for the negotiations). (*See Reading No. 20.*)

Another provision included a U. S. agreement to obtain congressional repeal of a special tariff-valuation procedure, named the American Selling Price (ASP), which resulted in higher tariffs on certain chemical imports. In the industrial sector, the United States and other participant countries agreed on cuts averaging 35 percent. Some of these percentage cuts did less in reducing protection than they seemed to, since in the textile and metal industries the tariffs on raw materials were often reduced much more than the tariffs on fabricated products. The reductions in agriculture, however, were less important. Other countries in GATT agreed to the American request for a new international grains arrangement setting up a system of minimum-and-maximum world export grain prices and on a world food-aid program. Negotiations on textiles resulted in an extension of the cotton-textile Import Agreement that President Kennedy had developed in 1962 in order to secure passage of the Trade Expansion Act. (In 1968 the Senate approved a new Grains Treaty, but legislation to repeal the ASP was not enacted in that year or the next few years.)

To help less developed nations expand their trade, it was suggested during the Kennedy Round that industrial countries immediately implement full tariff cuts on products of particular interest to those countries. While the results of the negotiations fell somewhat short of the expectations of the developing countries, the United States granted concessions on more than $900 million of their products without attempting to obtain full reciprocity. On $432 million of this trade the U. S. duties were eliminated.

Whatever the defects or gaps in the tariff reductions achieved during the Kennedy Round may be, the overall results were impressive. When the last annual tariff-reduction installments of the Kennedy Round are carried out by the United States around 1973, the average height of tariffs in the major industrial countries, it is estimated, will come down to about 8 or 9 percent. Barring any contrary action by Congress, the United States by then should have reduced its average tariff height to this level from the 60 percent that prevailed before the Trade Agreements Program began in 1934.

President Johnson regarded the Kennedy Round Agreements as a magnificent achievement that would open new markets abroad for American industrialists and farmers. On May 28, 1968, he asked Congress to adopt a trade-expansion measure that would have extended until June 30, 1970, the President's authority to cut tariffs and to eliminate the American Selling Price (ASP) system with its special protection to the chemical industry. (*See Reading No. 21.*) But no action was taken by Congress except some hearings in June and July by the House Ways and Means Committee. This congressional inaction was due largely to pressure on Congress by high-tariff protectionist lobbyists representing such industrial groups as the textile, oil, steel, and chemical industries.

Nixon and Foreign-Trade Policy. After winning the bitterly fought Presidential election of 1964 against Barry Goldwater, Johnson made a remarkable record in getting through Congress important legislation on civil rights, equal economic opportunity, education, medicare, and urban housing. But by the end of 1968 the unpopularity of the Vietnam War contributed to Richard Nixon's and the Republican party's extremely narrow victory over Hubert Humphrey and the Democrats. One important election result was the division of power between the parties: The Republicans won the Presidency; the Democrats, control of Congress. The programs of the two major parties differed greatly on many domestic and foreign issues, but on the subject of foreign trade they were closer than many old-line Republicans would have anticipated.

On November 18, 1969, a year after his election, President Nixon sent to Congress a special message on foreign trade. He submitted a bill, entitled the Tariff Act of 1969, that would restore the Presidential power to make limited tariff reductions. While proposing the elimination of the American selling price (ASP) system in order to increase certain imports, the bill would broaden the existing authority to act against countries granting export subsidies that would result in unfair competition against U. S. imports in third markets. At the same time, however, it would improve significantly the means whereby business and workers injured by competing imports could receive Government assistance. (*See Reading No. 22.*)

But President Nixon's movement toward freer world trade, after a year of strenuous debate and lobbying, was stymied in part by the House of Representatives accepting some protectionist amendments to the Administration bill, notably those imposing quotas on imports of textiles and footwear. The new bill, re-titled the "Trade Act of 1970," was finally passed by the House on November 19, 1970, by a vote of 215 to 165, but never got through the Senate. That fall the House trade bill had been added by the Senate Finance Committee to a pending social-security bill as a means of pushing it through Congress before the adjournment of the 91st Congress. But on December 28 the trade provisions were lost when the Senate voted to reject the omnibus social-security package.

The Crisis in the U. S. Balance of Payments. The United States had run a balance-of-payments deficit almost every year since 1950. For more than a decade the deficit did not present a problem. In fact, it was needed to restore the war-torn world economy and helped to rebuild the monetary reserves of the rest of the world. The big decline in the U. S. balance of payments position began in the mid-1960's as the Vietnam War escalated and the United States failed to finance the increased government expenditures in a non-inflationary way. The situation worsened in 1970 and the first half of 1971.

Despite tied foreign aid and controlled financing of U. S. private foreign investment, the deficit in the U. S. balance of payments (defined to cover imports and exports, tourism, military expenditures, investment income, and long-term capital flows), increased sharply in 1969 and 1970 to an annual level of $3 billion. In the first half of 1971 a further sharp deterioration raised the deficit to an annual rate of $9 billion. One important factor in this situation was a drastic drop in our merchandise trade balance. The 1964 trade surplus of nearly $7 billion had almost vanished by 1968–1969. In 1971 the trade balance turned into a deficit, for the first time since 1888, even though the demand for imports was well below the level that full employment would have created. Moreover, the prospects for the rest of 1971 and for 1972 were for still larger deficits as the United States economy recovered and as economic expansion abroad slowed down.

The situation in the first half of 1971 was made worse through massive short-term outflows of dollars. At first American capital was attracted by the higher interest rates available in Europe, but soon capital began to flow out in increasing amounts in anticipation of an upward revaluation of European currencies, or a devaluation of the dollar. At the same time, the United States faced difficult problems of inflation and unemployment at home. Unemployment exceeded 6 percent in August, 1971. Bringing about the needed reduction, however, would put further strains on the U. S. balance of payments, since rising employment and income at home would increase the demand for imports.

On August 15, President Nixon dramatically announced a new economic program that was a complete reversal of his previous policies and a bold adoption of key Democratic ideas. To deal with inflation, he imposed a 90-day freeze on prices, rents, and wages. This was followed in November by a second-stage program of price-wage stabilization. To stimulate the economy immediately and improve output over the longer run, the President proposed a tax program to generate new jobs and greater modernization of industrial plants.

On the international economic front, Nixon stunned the U. S.'s trading partners. First, he suspended the convertibility of the dollar into gold and other reserve assets. Second, he imposed a temporary ten-percent surcharge on imports and limited the Job Development Tax Credit to U. S.-produced equipment while the surcharge remained in effect. Third, he proposed a temporary ten-percent cut in foreign aid and a more equitable sharing of the economic burden of the common defense among the NATO countries and Japan. His first measure was not as revolutionary as it looked. In March 1968, in a move to counter gold speculation, the United States had announced it would no longer sell gold in the free market.

The major immediate objective of the United States was a realignment of exchange rates. During the period from the outbreak of World War II to 1958 the outflow of dollars, averaging about $1.5

billion a year, was regarded by the rest of the world as a way of gaining badly needed financial reserves. The tide turned in 1958 when the deficit rose to $3.5 billion, and then to some $4 billion in 1959 and in 1960. In 1961 the United States realized that the world considered the American deficit in the balance of payments as a dollar glut rather than a dollar shortage. From then on the United States tried various measures to decrease the dollar outflow. But by 1971, the American balance-of-payments problem was more serious than before.

The causes of the American payments problem were varied. Part of the problem was clearly due to the huge investment the United States had made in the defense of the non-Communist world against possible aggression from Soviet Russia or Communist China. Sometimes the cause was monetary, sometimes technological. In the late 1950's the United States in comparison to Western Europe and Japan suffered from a disadvantageous cost-price disparity which arose in part from the growth of foreign technology and in part from excessive European devaluations in 1949. This was reinforced by excessive wage inflation in the United States during the early and middle 1950's. In the late 1950's and early 1960's American prices and costs became more competitive with those of Europe and Japan. After 1964, however, American involvements in the Vietnam War led to inflation of American costs and prices. By 1967 an increasingly significant difference in this regard developed between the United States, on the one hand, and Western Europe and Japan on the other. Finally, to complicate matters still more, private long-term capital exports from the United States had steadily increased after 1956.

Although a realignment of exchange rates was overdue by 1970–1971, the United States could do little about it unilaterally. Deflation was unwise. An increase in the price of gold would not affect the exchange rate unless other countries agreed to permit their currencies to appreciate against the dollar. Few countries, however, were willing to do so because of the problems this would raise for their industries engaged either in exporting or competing with American imports.

Nevertheless, some effective revaluation of some foreign currencies occurred prior to August 15, 1971. The German mark had been revalued in 1969 and permitted to float upwards since 1971. Canada permitted its dollar to float from 1970 on, and it appreciated in value. In May, 1971, the Dutch allowed their guilder to float while Switzerland and Austria revalued their currencies in a more orthodox way. But the overall change in exchange rates was clearly insufficient to restore a better balance to world payments. Furthermore, even the revaluations which had taken place were threatened because other countries, especially France and Japan, had not changed the value of their currencies. This raised serious economic problems for their major trading partners whose currencies were appreciating.

Nixon's speech of August 15 made exchange-rate adjustment an unavoidable issue. Various countries had to decide whether they preferred to accumulate dollars or increase the quantity of real goods and services at their disposal by appreciating their currencies and making the United States more competitive in world markets. This was especially true for Japan, the main target of U. S.'s monetary action.

The latter course was taken. On December 18, the Group of Ten nations, the leading economic powers among the non-Communist states, arrived at the "Smithsonian Accord" to realign their exchange rates. (*See Reading No. 23.*) The United States agreed to devalue the dollar by 7.89 percent, to remove the 10-percent surcharge on imports imposed by the President on August 15, and to make foreign-produced equipment eligible for the 7-percent investment credit enacted by Congress on December 9. In exchange, the other nations agreed to "a pattern of exchange rate relationships" based on an upward revaluation of most of their currencies against the dollar. John Connally, Secretary of the Treasury, estimated that the realignment between these currencies and the dollar was 12 percent. The agreement reached at the Smithsonian Institution provided that exchange rates would fluctuate provisionally with a margin of 2.25 percent up or down from their official parities or central rate in contrast to the 1-percent margin called for by the Articles of Agreement of the International Monetary Fund. This action was intended to make the exchange rate system more flexible.

Yet the international monetary system needed further changes. In 1944 the United States had played a leading role in establishing the International Monetary Fund. Under its rules the dollar had been pegged to gold and the United States was obligated to redeem its currency in gold at $35 an ounce if requested to do so by a foreign holder of dollars. But after large gold outflows in the early 1960's, the United States felt forced to insulate its gold stock from further losses. In March, 1968, the United States announced boldly that it would no longer sell gold to private holders of dollars. A two-tier system of prices developed. Gold prices were unsupported in the private gold market, and the United States sold only small amounts of gold at $35 an ounce to foreign central banks. In 1970, to relieve the pressure on gold, the International Monetary Fund issued Special Drawing Rights (SDRs) which were capable of providing the world with the needed increases in monetary reserves. Hence, theoretically, after 1970, the world did not have to rely on U. S. balance-of-payments deficits or the supply of gold to provide these reserves. But the system still remains to be devised that would permit the United States as well as other countries to avoid the development of persistent surpluses or deficits in their balance-of-payments. The experiment, agreed to on December 18, 1971, to allow exchange rates to fluctuate by much wider margins than had been permitted, was one step in restructuring the international monetary system.*

The 1971–1972 Crisis in Foreign Trade. After a long period of unprecedented growth, world trade had come to a virtual stagnation point in 1971, with most of the apparent growth primarily due to increased prices. At the same time the U. S. trade balance experienced its worst year in the 20th century. The unprecedented deficit was the result of underlying factors, mainly, but not exclusively, an overvalued dollar. The situation was aggravated by labor disputes at home and an economic slowdown in the developed countries.

During the first part of 1971, the United States pressed forward in an effort to secure a reduction of barriers to U. S. exports. In response to the Government's urging, Japan accelerated its Kennedy Round tariff cuts, made unilateral reductions in tariffs on certain items including automobiles, radios, and TV sets, reduced import licensing requirements, and continued to liberalize import quotas on products of interest to U. S. businessmen, especially textiles. During the second half of 1971, after the adoption of the August 15 program, negotiations were intensified with America's major trading partners—Canada, Japan, and the European Community—to reduce the barriers against American products as part of the general plan of action to strengthen the U. S. balance-of-payments.

* For detailed background see Bank for International Settlements, *Forty-Second Annual Report* (Basle, 1972), pp. 4–33, 188–192.

Some temporary measures were also taken in 1971 to help the U. S. textile producers. An arrangement was negotiated between the United States and Japan providing for restraint on Japanese exports of manmade fiber and wool textile products to the United States. Similar arrangements were negotiated with Hong Kong, the Republic of China, and the Republic of Korea, major exporters of these products to the U. S. market. The restraint agreements reflected protectionist forces exerting pressure on Congress and led to a moderation in the exceedingly high growth of these imports. A moderate but steady increase in U. S. textile imports from these countries for the following three to five years was permitted.

The Revenue Act of 1971 provided a new incentive for American industrial firms to export their products abroad. The U. S. exporters were allowed to form a new type of corporation, to be known as a Domestic International Sales Corporation (DISC). Taxes on 50 percent of a DISC's income might be postponed indefinitely, provided that 95 percent of the DISC's receipts and assets related to qualified exports. This new tax legislation was also designed to blunt the incentive for U. S. firms to locate production facilities abroad rather than at home.

East-West Trade. A diplomatic and commercial rapprochement between the United States and Communist China developed in 1971–1972. In June, 1971, President Nixon lifted the embargo on imports from the People's Republic of China and freed a long list of U. S. goods for export to that country. At the same time action was taken to increase trade with Soviet Russia by lifting the requirement that 50 percent of U. S. exports of wheat, flour, and other grains to Eastern Europe and the Soviet Union had to be carried in U. S. vessels. An amendment to the Export-Import Bank Act in August, 1971, authorized the President to extend Export-Import Bank credits to further exports to Communist countries whenever he found this to be in the national interest. The first use of this authority was made to direct the Bank to participate in financing exports to Rumania.

Less Developed Countries. In October, 1969, President Nixon voiced his support for the adoption by all the developed countries of a liberalized system of generalized tariff preferences for the exports of lower income countries. This policy was intended to help the economic growth of less developed areas by encouraging their integration into an interdependent world economy. But action on this measure was delayed in 1971 by the unsatisfactory state of the U. S. balance of payments. The agreement of December 18, 1971 on exchange-rate realignment, however, enabled Nixon on December 21 to announce his intention to submit Generalized Preference legislation to Congress in 1972.

Continuing Problems. The President's Council of Economic Advisers in its 1972 annual report expressed the belief that the net balance between exports and imports of goods and services would probably be close to zero for 1972 as a whole. They anticipated, however, that it would take some months to gain impetus away from the $2 billion annual rate of deficit of 1971's fourth quarter. They also favored a free-trade policy and warned that "voluntary" agreements to limit imports, such as those negotiated by the United States for steel and textiles, held serious disadvantages and could aid the growth of cartels. In their judgment, the two prerequisites for continued progress toward freer trade were a more flexible international monetary system and a general "milieu of expanding employment opportunities." (Also needed was an expanded program in technological research and development to create the high productivity required to sustain both high American wages and effective American competition in world markets.) Given these conditions, the shifts in employment and production, although involving some serious dislocations, would be recognized as part of a desirable movement toward higher economic benefits in which all people could share.*

* The most authoritative statement and justification of U. S. trade policy for 1971–1972 is Peter G. Peterson, *The United States in the Changing World Economy*, 2 vols. (Washington, D.C., [1972]), written in 1971 by Peterson when he was Assistant to the President for International Economic Affairs and before he became Secretary of Commerce.

CHAPTER 6

Retrospect and Prospect

After studying in some detail the complicated evolution of American tariff policy over the past two hundred years, we should consider some of the lessons that might be derived from this history. Some of these are not obvious, nor have they been taken up by the champions or the critics of the protective tariffs in the chapters preceding this. Hence, we shall proceed to analyze some of these questions.

Political and Economic Nationalism. In the United States from 1789 to 1860 nationalism was undoubtedly a driving force in the formation of the United States, a key to its foreign policy, and an important objective of its economic development. The tariff, therefore, should be regarded as an instrument (1) for bringing in the revenue needed to maintain a strong nation-state, and (2) for building up industry as a means of acquiring economic power and independence of other countries and as the foundation of military power. Although the revenue aspect of tariffs was stressed up to the War of 1812, after that war down to 1828 the tariff became important as a means of guaranteeing the military strength of the United States. Once the danger of foreign attack faded, then the special sectional advantages that southern planters and nonindustrial groups elsewhere in the country could gain from low tariffs led to a reduction in the tariff down to 1860.

The Civil War broke out because of the sectional cleavages between the South, on the one hand, and the Northeast and Northwest, on the other, over slavery and expansion into the West by the southern planters. The tariff then became a means of (1) preserving the national unity of the country by creating revenue for the national Government, and (2) at the same time building up the industries of the Northeast. Without the outbreak of war, there seems to be little doubt that the northeastern industrialists and the protectionists would never have been able to dominate Congress and obtain the high protective tariffs that they did from 1861 down to 1913.

Subsequently the United States has been in five wars: the Spanish-American War, World War I, World War II, the Korean War, and the Vietnam War, but in none of these wars, strangely enough, has the tariff been raised. One reason is that one year before the Spanish-American War, Congress passed the Dingley protective tariff, and therefore did not need to raise the tariff the next year. In the case of both World War I and World War II, the countries under attack by the enemies of the United States were prevented from sending exports to the United States; hence, the industrialists of the United States had no cause to worry about the competition from foreign countries. The last two wars did not cause any restoration of the protective tariff, mainly because the United States had become the world's greatest industrial power and, therefore, had found it desirable to lower its tariff duties progressively while seeking large foreign markets for its exports.

Internal Free Trade and External Protectionism. Champions of the protective tariff have often stressed the advantages of the tariff for the development of new industries within the United States. But they have neglected to point out the advantages that any newly established industry inside the United States has through its access to the markets of the United States. Most students of the tariff forget that the United States of 1789 was relatively small compared to the United States after the Louisiana Purchase of 1803, the Florida Purchase of 1819, the annexations resulting from the Mexican War of 1846–1848, the annexations flowing from the Spanish-American War of 1898, as well as the annexation of Alaska in 1867 and of Hawaii in 1898. The consequence is that the fifty states of the Union today comprise an area comparable to that of Europe and are free of the tariff barriers that the numerous European nation-states have erected among themselves until very recently. The large markets that have existed inside the United States over the past two hundred years for the various commodities and services produced by Americans have been important factors in the rapid economic growth of the United States. These cannot be ignored or played down as against the protective tariff. It would seem likely that this free-trade area in the United States has been more powerful as a factor in American economic growth than the tariff, but no precise studies demonstrating this have been undertaken so far. At any rate, the student must bear in mind that whatever validity the arguments in favor of the protective tariff may have, they have taken for granted the beneficial effects of the internal free-trade policy that the foreign trade protectionists have been utilizing to their own advantage.

The Conditions of Economic Growth and the Tariff. There is no doubt that the tariff has been a major political question and has enabled the competing major parties in the United States to gain votes on the basis of the alleged merits or demerits of the protective tariff. Controversy still reigns among economic historians of great ability as to exactly how important the protective tariff has been in developing various industries, such as the cotton, woolen, and iron and steel industries. Frank W. Taussig, in *The Tariff History of the United States,* asserted eighty years ago that none of these three industries were vitally affected by the protective tariff and would have been able to sustain themselves if no such tariffs had been passed on their behalf. But later, in two other works, he came to the conclusion that the evidence was so contradictory about the complex effects of the tariff that there was the strong possibility that the protective tariff may have stimulated these industries somewhat more than free trade might have done. Here we must let the matter rest: The "infant industry" argument has some theoretical validity, but each application of it to a particular case has to be scrutinized with great care.* Otherwise, seekers of special favors or subsidies will be clamoring at the doors of legislators on behalf of various dubious new enterprises.

The "infant-industry" problem raises a much more important general question: What changes are necessary in the structure of an economy if it is to advance from a primarily agricultural, fishing, ranching, mining, and lumbering economy to one in which manufacturing plays the most important role, or one in which finally services play the dominant role? Colin Clark, a distinguished Australian economist, has argued in *The Conditions of Economic Progress* (1st ed., 1940) that an economy progresses when a majority of the working population is able to shift from the primary, production sector to the secondary or manufacturing sector, and eventually to the tertiary or service sector. For the student of economic history, the most important thing about the tariff is that it is one instrument, or possible instrument, for helping to transform a predominantly agricul-

---

* Cf. essays by Paul David, Robert Fogel, and Stanley Engerman cited on p. 199 in the *Select Bibliography.*

tural economy into a predominantly manufacturing or service economy. If we assume that protection for an infant industry can be justified as the incurring of a current loss by consumers or the Government for the sake of a future gain to the country at large, the question still remains whether this method is the best one for bringing about economic growth through the development of needed industries.

Methods of Protection. Those who have argued for the necessity of a protective tariff have often not stressed that there are other methods, such as subsidies and quantitative import restrictions. Many economists prefer using subsidies rather than tariffs because the former distort only the production pattern, and not the consumption pattern, of a country. Moreover, the cost is more clearly apparent to consumers when the subsidy comes out of their taxes rather than when they pay higher prices due to a protective tariff imposed on imports. But if outright subsidies to new industries are not feasible, then economists would prefer tariffs to quantitative import restrictions because these tend to give monopoly profits to the holders of licenses to import. Moreover, in general, economists prefer to use the price mechanism where possible.

The Effects of Tariffs on Recent Output and Employment. It has been argued that tariff reductions may damage some of our industries. This has to be demonstrated in each case, but there is a contrary fact, namely that continued protection may not help some of these industries very much in the long run. The study of employment in tariff-protected industries over the period 1947–1954 shows that the heavily protected, import-competing industries were not only predominantly declining, but were declining more than less tariff-protected, import-competing industries.* In other words, strong tariff protection by itself does not guarantee the expansion of a protected industry in the United States.

There has long been a fear that increased imports might lead to great unemployment. But research by two able economists reveals that the problem of labor adjustment to an increase in imports will not be very great. A $1 billion increase in dutiable imports spread across all industries and displacing an equivalent amount of domestic commodities would decrease employment in the import-competing industries by 63,000 men; in other industries, by 52,000 men;

* Beatrice N. Vaccara, *Employment and Output in Protected Manufacturing Industries* (Washington, D.C.: Brookings Institution, 1960), pp. 67–68.

and in all industries by 115,000 men.* These estimates, moreover, do not allow for any increase in export that might follow the reduction of the tariffs of other nations, nor for any increase that might occur as a result of foreigners earning more through their exports to us and hence being able to buy more of our exports. This research also indicates that a good part of the decrease in employment would be spread very widely and would not be entirely concentrated in the import-competing industries. The reason for this is that every enterprise buys materials and services from others.

Although much of the employment loss that might result from larger imports probably would be centered in a few firms and localities, the adjustment for both the business firms and the workers can be managed through such devices as provided by the Trade Expansion Act of 1962. Experience of countries in the European Common Market has shown that an adjustment to import competition can be made most easily when aggregate demand is growing rapidly enough for new opportunities to arise for those who lose their jobs. The American economy in recent decades has been experiencing great changes in tastes and technology, from women's and men's clothing to aerospace dynamics. Hence, every American Administration, whether Republican or Democrat, has the motivation for a commitment to a fast-growing American economy. Rapid growth permits adjustments to many types of disturbances, whether these be changes in fashions, technology, or increased import competition. A change in the allocation of human and natural resources is easier and more effective when there is an incentive from increased· demand rather than from the threat of declining sales and increased unemployment.

America's Stake in Foreign Trade: the Future Prospects. Foreign trade has played an important role in American economic development from a predominantly agricultural to a predominantly manufacturing-service economy and from a weak military power to a major world power in World War II and one of the two super pow-

---

* Walter S. Salant and Beatrice N. Vaccara, *Import Liberalization and Employment* (Washington, D.C.: Brookings Institution, 1961), pp. 214–215. The data refer to imports at 1953 prices and to the median data for seventy-two import-competing industries. "Man-years" is used as the basic term, instead of "men." CF. Peter B. Kenen, *International Economics,* 2nd ed. (Englewood Cliffs, N.J.: Prentice-Hall, 1967), pp. 47–48.

ers since World War II. In this evolutionary process the protective tariff was relied upon, probably to an unnecessary extent in the early national period, 1816–1832, and in the Civil War and post-Civil War period from 1861 down to 1934. The New Deal initiated a break with the high protectionist tariff tradition, in part because of the ideology of the Democratic party, in large part because of the maturity of the American capitalistic system. By 1930, the established industry had become so powerful that it obviously no longer needed the kind of protection that "infant industries" had required or had asked for. Consequently, American statesmen and even American industrial leaders could envisage the possibility of gradually, if not drastically, cutting down the tariff barriers through such devices as reciprocal-trade agreements. This undoubtedly was considered a means of expanding American exports and helping to increase American prosperity. But at the same time it was useful to the outside world because such import liberalization afforded other nations the opportunity to make sales and to earn dollar currency that could be useful to them for building up their own countries. Hence, the United States has moved into the kind of leadership role in world trade in the mid-twentieth century that England had occupied in the nineteenth century. Although there are Marxist and other critics of American expansionism throughout the world who see this trade liberalization as a subtle device of American imperialism, in the long run there seems to be little doubt that the benefits to other countries, including the underdeveloped, are substantial.

In the pursuit of trade liberalization, various problems arise. One is the factor of depressions affecting the rate of unemployment in the United States and thereby creating opposition to an increase in trade liberalism. The Keynesian remedy is a vigorous expansionist program to create jobs either by tax cuts or by deficit spending. There is a danger of inflation in such a course, but once the proper fiscal-monetary instruments have been used to restore high employment at home, various economic stabilization controls over inflation can be utilized. The attack on unemployment would remove one important barrier to the carrying out of the trade liberalization policies initiated by President Kennedy's Trade Expansion Act of 1962. In 1971, President Nixon's Council on International Economic Policy approved a recommendation by his Commission on International Trade and Investment Policy for a major new initiative to liberalize the national trade. This included the eventual elimination of all tariffs, and new arrangements to make trade in agricultural products responsive to factors of comparative advantage.

Another problem that threatens import expansion by the United States is that some Congressmen, trade union leaders, and industrialists fear multi-national corporations and large American capital investments abroad. In September, 1971, a bill entitled the Foreign Trade and Investment Act of 1972 was introduced into Congress by Senator Vance Hartke, a Democrat from Indiana, and Representative James A. Burke, a Democrat from Massachusetts. The bill proposed to curb imports into the United States and restrict operations of U. S. companies abroad through various import quotas and tax devices. A research team at the Harvard Graduate School of Business made a careful study of this problem, however, and concluded that, compared with the likely alternatives, direct foreign investment by American corporations was still decidedly healthy, both for employment at home and the balance of payments in the long run. Most American foreign investments are "defensive" in that had the producers continued to operate only in the United States, they would have lost their overseas markets to foreign competitors.

A third problem is a continuation of the dollar deficit in the United States balance of international payments. Since the causes are numerous, no single solution can solve the problem. Lessening of international tensions between the United States and other foreign governments, notably Soviet Russia and Communist China, may lead to a decrease in defense spending overseas, as well as an end to the Vietnam War and thereby to a drain on U. S. dollars. Further sharing of free world defense costs by other governments in Western Europe and the Far East will also cut down on the outflow of dollars. The new realignment of exchange rates should benefit American competitiveness in export markets. In 1972 there were still heavy pressures, at different times, on the dollar. But an increase in American interest rates began to draw dollars back from Europe to the United States and thereby to lessen some of the excess holding of dollars in Europe. Moreover, the Western European, Canadian, and Japanese monetary authorities were led to cooperate with the Americans in upholding the value of the dollar against speculative pressures so long as there was a possibility of some kind of convertibility for the dollar. One suggestion for accomplishing this was that new Super Special Drawing Rights (SDRs) should be created that would combine the existing SDRs with gold and dollars into one reserve unit. This new reserve unit would be used to settle international debts. A limit would be placed on foreign-held dollar balances, and the United States would not be able to churn out dollars to settle its debts.*

Whatever the new monetary reforms, as one set of problems is solved, other problems will undoubtedly arise. Difficult as it is to forecast the future, whichever administration is in power after the elections of November, 1972, it seems that major new trends have been initiated on both the domestic and the international front. Economic stabilization of wages, prices, and rents will be attempted for some time. A decrease in unemployment from 6 percent to some lower rate is likely. An important decrease in defense spending and a sharing of defense costs abroad are on the way, slowly and painfully. Incentives for increase in efficiency by both business and labor exist. The structure of the world economy and military and diplomatic power in the 1970's is vastly different from that in 1945. Threats to international peace still exist in the Mid-East, the Far East, and Western Europe. Nevertheless, the United States can continue to play a critically important role as a world leader in liberalizing foreign trade and in lowering the tariff. The results of such trade liberalism can be economically good both for the United States and for the rest of the world.

* For a more extended analysis of international monetary reform, see Alexandre Kafka, *The IMF: The Second Coming*, (Princeton, N.J., 1972). For some highly constructive proposals, see Fritz Machlup, "International Money: The Way Forward Now," *The Banker, CXXII* (March, 1972), 287–96.

Part II

READINGS

The Tariff Act of July 4, 1789 *

The tax needs of a central government had been a factor in the creation of a new national Government and Federal system under the Constitution framed in 1787 at Philadelphia. In 1789 Congress proceeded to raise revenue through the passage of a tariff act that was protectionist in intent but primarily a revenue measure in effect. This was the first of a long series of tariff laws that finally reached the heights of protectionism in 1930 with the Hawley-Smoot Tariff Act.

—An act for laying a duty on goods, wares, and merchandise imported into the United States.

SEC. 1. Whereas it is necessary for the support of government, for the discharge of the debts of the United States, and the encouragement and protection of manufactures, that duties be laid on goods, wares and merchandise imported:

Be it enacted by the Senate and House of Representatives of the United States of America in Congress assembled, That from and after the first day of August next ensuing, the several duties hereinafter mentioned shall be laid on the following goods, wares, and merchandises imported into the United States from any foreign port or place, that is to say:

On all distilled spirits of Jamaica proof, imported from any kingdom or country whatsoever, per gallon, ten cents.

On all other distilled spirits, per gallon, eight cents

On molasses, per gallon, two and a half cents.

On Madeira wine, per gallon, eighteen cents.

On all other wines, per gallon, ten cents.

On every gallon of beer, ale or porter in casks, five cents.

* *U. S. Statutes at Large,* Vol. 1, Ch. II; *Tariff Acts Passed by the Congress of the United States from 1789 to 1909,* House Doc. 671, 61st Congress, 2d Session (Washington: G.P.O., 1909), pp. 13–15.

On all cider, beer, ale or porter in bottles, per dozen, twenty cents.

On malt, per bushel, ten cents.

On brown sugars, per pound, one cent.

On loaf sugars, per pound, three cents.

On all other sugars, per pound, one and a half cents.

On coffee, per pound, two and a half cents.

On cocoa, per pound, one cent.

On all candles of tallow, per pound, two cents.

On all candles of wax or spermaceti, per pound, six cents.

On cheese, per pound, four cents.

On soap, per pound, two cents.

On boots, per pair, fifty cents.

On all shoes, slippers or goloshoes made of leather, per pair, seven cents.

On all shoes or slippers made of silk or stuff, per pair, ten cents.

On cables, for every one hundred and twelve pounds, seventy-five cents.

On tarred cordage, for every one hundred and twelve pounds, seventy-five cents.

On untarred ditto, and yarn, for every one hundred and twelve pounds, ninety cents.

On twine or packthread, for every one hundred and twelve pounds, two hundred cents.

On all steel unwrought, for every one hundred and twelve pounds, fifty-six cents.

On all nails and spikes, per pound, one cent.

On salt, per bushel, six cents.

On manufactured tobacco, per pound, six cents.

On snuff, per pound, ten cents.

On indigo, per pound, sixteen cents.

On wool and cotton cards, per dozen, fifty cents.

On coal, per bushel, two cents.

On pickled fish, per barrel, seventy-five cents.

On dried fish, per quintal, fifty cents.

On all teas imported from China or India, in ships built in the United States and belonging to a citizen or citizens thereof, or in ships or vessels built in foreign countries, and on the sixteenth day of May last wholly the property of a citizen or citizens of the United States, and so continuing until the time of importation, as follows:

On bohea tea, per pound, six cents.

On all souchong, or other black teas, per pound, ten cents.

On all hyson teas, per pound, twenty cents.

On all other green teas, per pound, twelve cents.

On all teas imported from Europe in ships or vessels built in the United States and belonging wholly to a citizen or citizens thereof, or in ships or vessels built in foreign countries, and on the sixteenth day of May last wholly the property of a citizen or citizens of the United States, and so continuing until the time of importation, as follows:

On all bohea tea, per pound, eight cents.

On all souchong, and other black teas, per pound, thirteen cents.

On all hyson teas, per pound, twenty-six cents.

On all other green teas, per pound, sixteen cents.

On all teas imported, in any other manner than as above mentioned, as follows:

On bohea tea, per pound, fifteen cents.

On all souchong, or other black teas, per pound, twenty-two cents.

On all hyson teas, per pound, forty-five cents.

On all other green teas, per pound, twenty-seven cents.

On all goods, wares and merchandises, other than teas, imported from China or India, in ships not built in the United States, and not wholly the property of a citizen or citizens thereof, nor in vessels built in foreign countries, and on the sixteenth day of May last wholly the property of a citizen or citizens of the United States, and so continuing until the time of importation, twelve and a half per centum ad valorem.

On all looking-glasses, window and other glass (except black quart bottles),

On all China, stone and earthen ware,

On gunpowder,

On all paints ground in oil,

On shoe and knee buckles,

On gold and silver lace, and

On gold and silver leaf, ten per centum ad valorem;

On all blank books,

On all writing, printing or wrapping paper, paper-hangings and pasteboard,

On all cabinet wares,

On all buttons,

On all saddles,

On all gloves of leather,

On all hats of beaver, fur, wool, or mixture of either,

On all millinery ready made,

On all castings of iron, and upon slit and rolled iron,

On all leather tanned or tawed, and all manufacture of leather, except such as shall be otherwise rated,

On canes, walking sticks and whips,

On clothing ready made,

On all brushes,

On gold, silver, and plated ware, and on jewelry and paste work,

On anchors, and on all wrought, tin, and pewter ware, seven and a half per centum ad valorem;

On playing cards, per pack, ten cents.

On every coach, chariot or other four wheel carriage, and on every chaise, solo, or other two wheel carriage, or parts thereof, fifteen per centum ad valorem.

On all other goods, wares and merchandise, five per centum on the value thereof at the time and place of importation, except as follows: Saltpetre, tin in pigs, tin plates, lead, old pewter, brass, iron and brass wire, copper in plates, wool, cotton, dyeing woods and dyeing drugs, raw hides, beaver, and all other furs, and deer skins.

SEC. 2. *And be it further enacted by the authority aforesaid,* That from and after the first day of December, which shall be in the year one thousand seven hundred and ninety, there shall be laid a duty on every one hundred and twelve pounds, weight of hemp imported as aforesaid, of sixty cents; and on cotton per pound, three cents.

SEC. 3. *And be it [further] enacted by the authority aforesaid,* That all the duties paid, or secured to be paid upon any of the goods, wares and merchandises as aforesaid, except on distilled spirits, other than brandy and geneva, shall be returned or discharged upon such of the said goods, wares, or merchandises, as shall within twelve months after payment made, or security given, be exported to any country without the limits of the United States, as settled by the late treaty of peace; except one per centum on the amount of the said duties, in consideration of the expense which shall have accrued by the entry and safe-keeping thereof.

SEC. 4. *And be it [further] enacted by the authority aforesaid,* That there shall be allowed and paid on every quintal of dried, and on every barrel of pickled fish, of the fisheries of the United States, and on every barrel of salted provision of the United States, exported to any country without the limits thereof, in lieu of a drawback of the duties imposed on the importation of the salt employed and expended therein, viz:

On every quintal of dried fish, five cents.

On every barrel of pickled fish, five cents.

On every barrel of salted provision, five cents.

SEC. 5. *And be it further enacted by the authority aforesaid,* That a discount of ten per cent. on all the duties imposed by this act shall be allowed on such goods, wares and merchandises as shall be imported in vessels built in the United States, and which shall be wholly the property of a citizen or citizens thereof, or in vessels built in foreign countries, and on the sixteenth day of May last, wholly the property of a citizen or citizens of the United States, and so continuing until the time of importation.

SEC. 6. *And be it further enacted by the authority aforesaid,* That this act

shall continue and be in force until the first day of June, which shall be in the year of our Lord one thousand seven hundred and ninety-six, and from thence until the end of the next succeeding session of Congress which shall be held thereafter, and no longer.

Approved, July 4, 1789.

READING NO. 2

Hamilton's Report on Manufactures, 1791 *

On December 5, 1791, Alexander Hamilton submitted to the House of Representatives a report on the desirability of fostering manufactures that might render the United States independent of foreign nations for military and other essential supplies. He drew heavily on Adam Smith in presenting arguments on the crucial role of industry in the growth of a country's wealth and income. But he broke with Smith in advocating Government assistance to new industries through protective tariffs, bounties, and other means. Hamilton's views had little effect, however, until the Republicans came into power in 1861 and built up the protective tariff from the Civil War to the 1930 Hawley-Smoot Tariff Act.

It is now proper to proceed a step further, and to enumerate the principal circumstances from which it may be inferred that manufacturing establishments not only occasion a positive augmentation of the produce and revenue of the society, but that they contribute essentially to rendering them greater than they could possibly be, without such establishments. These circumstances are:

1. The division of labor.
2. An extension of the use of machinery.
3. Additional employment to classes of the community not ordinarily engaged in the business.
4. The promoting of emigration from foreign countries.
5. The furnishing greater scope for the diversity of talents and dispositions, which discriminate men from each other.
6. The affording a more ample and various field for enterprise.

* *American State Papers, Finances* (Washington: Gales and Seaton, 1832), I, 125–127, 135–137.

7. The creating, in some instances, a new, and securing, in all, a more certain and steady demand for the surplus produce of the soil.

Each of these circumstances has a considerable influence upon the total mass of industrious effort in a community; together, they add to it a degree of energy and effect, which are not easily conceived. Some comments upon each of them, in the order in which they have been stated, may serve to explain their importance.

1. *As to the division of labor.*

It has justly been observed, that there is scarcely any thing of greater moment in the economy of a nation, than the proper division of labor. The separation of occupations, causes each to be carried to a much greater perfection, than it could possibly acquire if they were blended. This arises principally from three circumstances:

1st. The greater skill and dexterity naturally resulting from a constant and undivided application to a single object. . . .

2d. The economy of time, by avoiding the loss of it, incident to a frequent transition from one operation to another of a different nature. . . .

3d. An extension of the use of machinery. . . .

And from these causes united, the mere separation of the occupation of the cultivator from that of the artificer, has the effect of augmenting the productive powers of labor, and with them, the total mass of the produce or revenue of a country. In this single view of the subject, therefore, the utility of artificers or manufacturers, towards promoting an increase of productive industry, is apparent.

2. *As to an extension of the use of machinery, a point which, though partly anticipated, requires to be placed in one or two additional lights.*

The employment of machinery forms an item of great importance in the general mass of national industry. It is an artificial force brought in aid of the natural force of man; and, to all the purposes of labor, is an increase of hands, an accession of strength, unencumbered too by the expense of maintaining the laborer. May it not, therefore, be fairly inferred, that those occupations which give greatest scope to the use of this auxiliary, contribute most to the general stock of industrious effort, and, in consequence, to the general product of industry. . . .

3. *As to the additional employment of classes of the community not originally engaged in the particular business.*

This is not among the least valuable of the means, by which manufac-

turing institutions contribute to augment the general stock of industry and production. In places where those institutions prevail, besides the persons regularly engaged in them, they afford occasional and extra employment to industrious individuals and families, who are willing to devote the leisure resulting from the intermissions of their ordinary pursuits to collateral labors, as a resource for multiplying their acquisitions or their enjoyments. The husbandman himself experiences a new source of profit and support, from the increased industry of his wife and daughters, invited and stimulated by the demands of the neighboring manufactories. . . .

4. *As to the promoting of emigration from foreign countries.*

Men reluctantly quit one course of occupation and livelihood for another, unless invited to it by very apparent and proximate advantages. Many who would go from one country to another, if they had a prospect of continuing with more benefit the callings to which they have been educated, will often not be tempted to change their situation by the hope of doing better in some other way. Manufacturers, who, listening to the powerful invitations of a better price for their fabrics, or their labor, of greater cheapness of provisions and raw materials, of an exemption from the chief part of the taxes, burthens, and restraints, which they endure in the old world, of greater personal independence and consequence, under the operation of a more equal government, and of what is far more precious than mere religious toleration, a perfect equality of religious privileges, would probably flock from Europe to the United States, to pursue their own trades or professions, if they were once made sensible of the advantages they would enjoy, and were inspired with an assurance of encouragement and employment, will, with difficulty, be induced to transplant themselves, with a view to becoming cultivators of land.

If it be true, then, that it is the interest of the United States to open every possible avenue to emigration from abroad, it affords a weighty argument for the encouragement of manufactures; which, for the reasons just assigned, will have the strongest tendency to multiply the inducements to it.

Here is perceived an important resource, not only for extending the population, and with it the useful and productive labor of the country, but likewise for the prosecution of manufactures, without deducting from the number of hands, which might otherwise be drawn to tillage; and even for the indemnification of agriculture, for such as might happen to be diverted from it. Many, whom manufacturing views would induce to emigrate, would, afterwards, yield to the temptations which the particular situation of this country holds out to agricultural pursuits. And while agriculture would, in other respects, derive many signal and unmingled advantages from the growth of manufactures, it is a problem whether it would gain or lose, as to the article of the number of persons employed in carrying it on.

5. *As to the furnishing greater scope for the diversity of talents and dispositions, which discriminate men from each other.*

This is a much more powerful mean of augmenting the fund of national industry, than may at first sight appear. It is a just observation, that minds of the strongest and most active powers for their proper objects, fall below mediocrity, and labor without effect, if confined to uncongenial pursuits. And it is thence to be inferred, that the results of human exertion may be immensely increased by diversifying its objects. When all the different kinds of industry obtain in a community, each individual can find his proper element, and can call into activity, the whole vigor of his nature. And the community is benefitted by the services of its respective members, in the manner in which each can serve it with most effect.

If there be any thing in a remark often to be met with, namely, that there is, in the genius of the people of this country, a peculiar aptitude for mechanic improvements, it would operate as a forcible reason for giving opportunities to the exercise of that species of talent, by the propagation of manufactures.

6. *As to the affording a more ample and various field for enterprise.*

This also is of greater consequence in the general scale of national exertion, than might, perhaps, on a superficial view be supposed, and has effects not altogether dissimilar from those of the circumstance last noticed. To cherish and stimulate the activity of the human mind, by multiplying the objects of enterprise, is not among the least considerable of the expedients by which the wealth of a nation may be promoted. Even things in themselves not positively advantageous, sometimes become so, by their tendency to provoke exertion. Every new scene which is opened to the busy nature of man to rouse and exert itself, is the addition of a new energy to the general stock of effort.

The spirit of enterprise, useful and prolific as it is, must necessarily be contracted or expanded, in proportion to the simplicity or variety of the occupations and productions which are to be found in a society. It must be less in a nation of mere cultivators, than in a nation of cultivators and merchants; less in a nation of cultivators and merchants, than in a nation of cultivators, artificers, and merchants.

7. *As to the creating, in some instances, a new, and securing in all, a more certain and steady demand, for the surplus produce of the soil.*

This is among the most important of the circumstances which have been indicated. It is a principal mean by which the establishment of manufactures contributes to an augmentation of the produce or revenue of a country, and has an immediate and direct relation to the prosperity of agriculture.

It is evident, that the exertions of the husbandman will be steady or fluctuating, vigorous or feeble, in proportion to the steadiness or fluctuation, adequateness or inadequateness of the markets on which he must depend, for the vent of the surplus which may be produced by his labor; and that such surplus, in the ordinary course of things, will be greater or less in the same proportion.

For the purpose of this vent, a domestic market is greatly to be preferred to a foreign one; because it is, in the nature of things, far more to be relied upon. . . .

Considering how fast, and how much the progress of new settlements, in the United States, must increase the surplus produce of the soil, and weighing seriously the tendency of the system which prevails among most of the commercial nations of Europe; whatever dependence may be placed on the force of natural circumstances to counteract the effects of an artificial policy, there appear strong reasons to regard the foreign demand for that surplus, as too uncertain a reliance, and to desire a substitute for it in an extensive domestic market.

To secure such a market there is no other expedient than to promote manufacturing establishments. Manufacturers, who constitute the most numerous class, after the cultivators of land, are for that reason the principal consumers of the surplus of their labor. . . .

It merits particular observation, that the multiplication of manufactories not only furnishes a market for those articles which have been accustomed to be produced in abundance in a country; but it likewise creates a demand for such as were either unknown, or produced in inconsiderable quantities. The bowels, as well as the surface of the earth, are ransacked for articles which were before neglected. Animals, plants, and minerals, acquire an utility and value which were before unexplored.

The foregoing considerations seem sufficient to establish, as general propositions, that it is the interest of nations to diversify the industrious pursuits of the individuals who compose them. That the establishment of manufactures is calculated not only to increase the general stock of useful and productive labor, but even to improve the state of agriculture in particular; certainly to advance the interests of those who are engaged in it. There are other views that will be hereafter taken of the subject, which it is conceived will serve to confirm these inferences.

*   *   *

In order to a better judgment of the means proper to be resorted to by the United States, it will be of use to advert to those which have been employed with success in other countries. The principal of these are:

1. *Protecting duties—or duties on those foreign articles which are the rivals of the domestic ones intended to be encouraged.*

Duties of this nature evidently amount to a virtual bounty on the domestic fabrics; since, by enhancing the charges on foreign articles, they enable the national manufacturers to undersell all their foreign competitors. The propriety of this species of encouragement need not be dwelt upon, as it is not only a clear result from the numerous topics which have been suggested, but is sanctioned by the laws of the United States, in a variety of instances; it has the additional recommendation of being a resource of revenue. Indeed, all the duties imposed on imported articles, though with an exclusive view to revenue, have the effect, in contemplation, and, except where they fall on raw materials, wear a beneficent aspect towards the manufacturers of the country.

2. *Prohibitions of rival articles, or duties equivalent to prohibitions.*

This is another and an efficacious mean of encouraging national manufactures; but, in general, it is only fit to be employed when a manufacture has made such progress, and is in so many hands, as to ensure a due competition, and an adequate supply on reasonable terms. Of duties equivalent to prohibitions, there are examples in the laws of the United States; and there are other cases, to which the principle may be advantageously extended, but they are not numerous.

Considering a monopoly of the domestic market to its own manufacturers as the reigning policy of manufacturing nations, a similar policy, on the part of the United States, in every proper instance, is dictated, it might almost be said, by the principles of distributive justice; certainly, by the duty of endeavoring to secure to their own citizens a reciprocity of advantages.

3. *Prohibitions of the exportation of the materials of manufactures.*

The desire of securing a cheap and plentifull supply for the national workmen, and where the article is either peculiar to the country, or of peculiar quality there, the jealousy of enabling foreign workmen to rival those of the nation with its own materials, are the leading motives to this species of regulation. It ought not to be affirmed, that it is in no instance proper; but is, certainly, one which ought to be adopted with great circumspection, and only in very plain cases. It is seen at once, that its im-

mediate operation is to abridge the demand, and keep down the price of
the produce of some other branch of industry—generally speaking, of
agriculture—to the prejudice of those who carry it on; and though, if it
be really essential to the prosperity of any very important national manufacture, it may happen that those who are injured, in the first instance,
may be, eventually, indemnified by the superior steadiness of an extensive domestic market, depending on that prosperity; yet, in a matter in
which there is so much room for nice and difficult combinations, in
which such opposite considerations combat each other, prudence seems
to dictate that the expedient in question ought to be indulged with a
sparing hand.

4. *Pecuniary bounties.*

This has been found one of the most efficacious means of encouraging
manufactures, and is, in some views, the best. Though it has not yet been
practised upon by the Government of the United States, (unless the allowance on the exportation of dried and pickled fish and salted meat
could be considered as a bounty) and though it is less favored by public
opinion than some other modes, its advantages are these:

1. It is a species of encouragement more positive and direct than any
other, and, for that very reason, has a more immediate tendency to stimulate and uphold new enterprises, increasing the chances of profit, and
diminishing the risks of loss, in the first attempts.

2. It avoids the inconvenience of a temporary augmentation of price,
which is incident to some other modes; or it produces it to a less degree,
either by making no addition to the charges on the rival foreign article,
as in the case of protecting duties, or by making a smaller addition. The
first happens when the fund for the bounty is derived from a different
object, (which may or may not increase the price of some other article,
according to the nature of that object) the second, when the fund is derived from the same, or a similar object, of foreign manufacture. One per
cent. duty on the foreign article, converted into a bounty on the domestic, will have an equal effect with a duty of two per cent., exclusive of
such bounty; and the price of the foreign commodity is liable to be
raised, in the one case, in the proportion of one per cent.; in the other in
that of two per cent. Indeed the bounty, when drawn from another
source, is calculated to promote a reduction of price; because, without
laying any new charge on the foreign article, it serves to introduce a
competition with it, and to increase the total quantity of the article in the
market.

3. Bounties have not, like high protecting duties, a tendency to produce scarcity. An increase of price is not always the immediate, though,

where the progress of a domestic manufacture does not counteract a rise, it is, commonly, the ultimate effect of an additional duty. In the interval between the laying of the duty and the proportional increase of price, it may discourage importation, by interfering with the profits to be expected from the sale of the article.

4. Bounties are, sometimes, not only the best, but the only proper expedient for uniting the encouragement of a new object of agriculture with that of a new object of manufacture. . . .

It cannot escape notice, that a duty upon the importation of an article can no otherwise aid the domestic production of it, than by giving the latter greater advantages in the home market. It can have no influence upon the advantageous sale of the article produced in foreign markets— no tendency, therefore, to promote its exportation.

The true way to conciliate these two interests is to lay a duty on foreign manufactures of the material, the growth of which is desired to be encouraged, and to apply the produce of that duty, by way of bounty, either upon the production of the material itself, or upon its manufacture at home, or upon both. In this disposition of the thing, the manufacturer commences his enterprise under every advantage which is attainable, as to quantity or price of the raw material; and the farmer, if the bounty be immediately to him, is enabled by it to enter into a successful competition with the foreign material. If the bounty be to the manufacturer, on so much of the domestic material as he consumes, the operation is nearly the same; he has a motive of interest to prefer the domestic commodity, if of equal quality, even at a higher price than the foreign, so long as the difference of price is any thing short of the bounty which is allowed upon the article.

Except the simple and ordinary kinds of household manufacture, or those for which there are very commanding local advantages, pecuniary bounties are, in most cases, indispensable to the introduction of a new branch. A stimulus and a support, not less powerful and direct, is, generally speaking, essential to the overcoming of the obstacles which arise from the competitions of superior skill and maturity elsewhere. Bounties are especially essential in regard to articles upon which those foreigners, who have been accustomed to supply a country, are in the practice of granting them.

The continuance of bounties on manufactures long established, must almost always be of questionable policy: because a presumption would arise, in every such case, that there were natural and inherent impediments to success. But, in new undertakings, they are as justifiable as they are oftentimes necessary.

There is a degree of prejudice against bounties, from an appearance of giving away the public money without an immediate consideration, and from a supposition that they serve to enrich particular classes, at the expense of the community.

But neither of these sources of dislike will bear a serious examination. There is no purpose to which public money can be more beneficially applied, than to the acquisition of a new and useful branch of industry; no consideration more valuable, than a permanent addition to the general stock of productive labor.

As to the second source of objection, it equally lies against other modes of encouragement, which are admitted to be eligible. As often as a duty upon a foreign article makes an addition to its price, it causes an extra expense to the community, for the benefit of the domestic manufacturer. A bounty does no more. But it is the interest of the society, in each case, to submit to the temporary expense—which is more than compensated by an increase of industry and wealth; by an augmentation of resources and independence; and by the circumstance of eventual cheapness, which has been noticed in another place.

It would deserve attention, however, in the employment of this species of encouragement in the United States, as a reason for moderating the degree of it in the instances in which it might be deemed eligible, that the great distance of this country from Europe imposes very heavy charges on all the fabrics which are brought from thence, amounting to from fifteen to thirty per cent. on their value, according to their bulk. . . .

5. *Premiums.*

These are of a nature allied to bounties, though distinguishable from them in some important features.

Bounties are applicable to the whole quantity of an article produced, or manufactured, or exported, and involve a correspondent expense. Premiums serve to reward some particular excellence or superiority, some extraordinary exertion or skill, and are dispensed only in a small number of cases. But their effect is to stimulate general effort; contrived so as to be both honorary and lucrative, they address themselves to different passions—touching the chords, as well of emulation as of interest. They are, accordingly, a very economical mean of exciting the enterprise of a whole community.

6. *The exemption of the materials of manufactures from duty.*

The policy of that exemption, as a general rule, particularly in reference to new establishments, is obvious. It can hardly ever be advisable to add the obstructions of fiscal burthens to the difficulties which naturally embarrass a new manufacture; and where it is matured, and in condition to become an object of revenue, it is, generally speaking, better that the

fabric, than the material, should be the subject of taxation. Ideas of proportion between the quantum of the tax and the value of the article, can
be more easily adjusted in the former than in the latter case. An argument for exemptions of this kind, in the United States, is to be derived
from the practice, as far as their necessities have permitted, of those nations whom we are to meet as competitors in our own and in foreign
markets. . . .

The laws of the Union afford instances of the observance of the policy
here recommended, but it will probably be found advisable to extend it
to some other cases. Of a nature, bearing some affinity to that policy, is
the regulation which exempts from duty the tools and implements, as
well as the books, clothes, and household furniture, of foreign artists,
who come to reside in the United States—an advantage already secured
to them by the laws of the Union, and which it is, in every view, proper
to continue.

7. *Drawbacks of the duties which are imposed on the materials of manufactures.*

It has already been observed, as a general rule, that duties on those
materials ought, with certain exceptions, to be forborne. Of these exceptions, three cases occur, which may serve as examples. One, where the
material is itself an object of general or extensive consumption, and a fit
and productive source of revenue. Another, where a manufacture of a
simpler kind, the competition of which, with a like domestic article, is
desired to be restrained, partakes of the nature of a raw material, from
being capable, by a farther process, to be converted into a manufacture
of a different kind, the introduction or growth of which is desired to be
encouraged. A third, where the material itself is a production of the
country, and in sufficient abundance to furnish a cheap and plentiful
supply to the national manufacturers.

Under the first description comes the article of molasses. It is not only
a fair object of revenue, but, being a sweet, it is just that the consumers
of it should pay a duty as well as the consumers of sugar.

Cottons and linens, in their white state, fall under the second description. A duty upon such as are imported is proper, to promote the domestic manufacture of similar articles, in the same state. A drawback of that
duty is proper, to encourage the printing and staining, at home, of those
which are brought from abroad. When the first of these manufactures
has attained sufficient maturity in a country to furnish a full supply for
the second, the utility of the drawback ceases.

The article of hemp either now does, or may be expected soon to, ex-
emplify the third case in the United States.

Where duties on the materials of manufactures are not laid for the purpose of preventing a competition with some domestic production, the same reasons which recommend, as a general rule, the exemption of those materials from duties, would recommend, as a like general rule, the allowance of drawbacks in favor of the manufacturer. Accordingly, such drawbacks are familiar in countries which systematically pursue the business of manufactures; which furnishes an argument for the observance of a similar policy in the United States; and the idea has been adopted by the laws of the Union, in the instances of salt and molasses. It is believed that it will be found advantageous to extend it to some other articles.

8. *The encouragement of new inventions and discoveries at home, and of the introduction into the United States of such as may have been made in other countries; particularly, those which relate to machinery.*

This is among the most useful and unexceptionable of the aids which can be given to manufactures. The usual means of that encouragement are pecuniary rewards, and, for a time, exclusive privileges. The first must be employed, according to the occasion, and the utility of the invention or discovery. For the last, so far as respects "authors and inventors," provision has been made by law. But it is desirable, in regard to improvements, and secrets of extraordinary value, to be able to extend the same benefit to introducers, as well as authors and inventors; a policy which has been practised with advantage in other countries. Here, however, as in some other cases, there is cause to regret, that the competency of the authority of the National Government to the good which might be done, is not without a question. Many aids might be given to industry, many internal improvements of primary magnitude might be promoted, by an authority operating throughout the Union, which cannot be effected as well, if at all, by an authority confirmed within the limits of a single State.

But, if the Legislature of the Union cannot do all the good that might be wished, it is, at least, desirable that all may be done which is practicable. Means for promoting the introduction of foreign improvements, though less efficaciously than might be accomplished with more adequate authority, will form a part of the plan intended to be submitted in the close of this report.

It is customary with manufacturing nations to prohibit, under severe penalties, the exportation of implements and machines, which they have either invented or improved. There are already objects for a similar regulation in the United States; and others may be expected to occur, from time to time. The adoption of it seems to be dictated by the principle of reciprocity. Greater liberality, in such respects, might better comport with the general spirit of the country; but a selfish and exclusive policy, in other quarters, will not always permit the free indulgence of a spirit which would place us upon an unequal footing. As far as prohibitions tend to prevent foreign competitors from deriving the benefit of the improvements made at home, they tend to increase the advantages of those by whom they may have been introduced, and operate as an encouragement to exertion. . . .

Clay's Speech of 1824 on American Industry*

The Tariff Act of May 25, 1824, is celebrated for a great debate that took place in the House of Representatives on the merits and demerits of the protective tariff. On March 30 and 31, 1824, Henry Clay, the Speaker of the House, made a noted defense of what he called the American or domestic system for the protection of American industry. One major argument from that speech is presented here.

According to the opponents of the domestic policy, the proposed system will force capital and labor into new and reluctant employments, we are not prepared, in consequence of the high price of wages, for the successful establishment of manufactures, and we must fail in the experiment. We have seen that the existing occupations of our society, those of agriculture, commerce, navigation, and the learned professions, are overflowing with competitors, and that the want of employment is severely felt. Now what does this bill propose? To open a new and extensive field of business, in which all that choose may enter. There is no compulsion upon any one to engage in it. An option only is given to industry, to continue in the present unprofitable pursuits, or to embark in a new and promising one. The effect will be to lessen the competition in the old branches of business, and to multiply our resources for increasing our

* Daniel Mallory, ed., *Life and Speeches of the Hon. Henry Clay,* 2 vols. (New York: A. C. Barnes, 1857), I, 521–523.

comforts and augmenting the national wealth. The alleged fact of the high price of wages is not admitted. The truth is that no class of society suffers more, in the present stagnation of business, than the laboring class. That is a necessary effect of the depression of agriculture, the principal business of the community. The wages of able-bodied men vary from $5 to $8 per month, and such has been the want of employment, in some parts of the Union, that instances have not been unfrequent of men working merely for the means of present subsistence. If the wages for labor here and in England are compared, they will be found not to be essentially different. I agree with the honorable gentleman from Virginia, that high wages are a proof of national prosperity; we differ only in the means by which that desirable end shall be attained. But, if the fact were true, that the wages of labor are high, I deny the correctness of the argument founded upon it. The argument assumes that natural labor is the principal element in the business of manufacture. That was the ancient theory. But the valuable inventions and vast improvements in machinery, which have been made within a few past years, have produced a new era in the arts. The effect of this change, in the powers of production, may be estimated, from what I have already stated in relation to England and to the triumphs of European artificial labor over the natural labor of Asia. In considering the fitness of a nation for the establishment of manufactures, we must no longer limit our views to the state of its population and the price of wages. All circumstances must be regarded, of which that is, perhaps, the least important. Capital, ingenuity in the construction and adroitness in the use of machinery, and the possession of the raw materials, are those which deserve the greatest consideration. All these circumstances (except that of capital, of which there is no deficiency) exist in our country in an eminent degree, and more than counterbalance the disadvantage, if it really existed, of the lower wages of labor in Great Britain. The dependence upon foreign nations for the raw material of any great manufacture has been ever considered as a discouraging fact. The state of our population is peculiarly favorable to the most extensive introduction of machinery. We have no prejudices to combat, no persons to drive out of employment. The pamphlet to which we have had occasion so often to refer, in enumerating the causes which have brought in England their manufactures to such a state of perfection, and which now enable them, in the opinion of the writer, to defy all competition, does not specify, as one of them, low wages. It assigns three: first, capital; secondly, extent and costliness of machinery; and, thirdly, steady and persevering industry. Notwithstanding the concurrence of so many favorable causes in our country for the introduction of the arts, we are earnestly dissuaded from making the experiment, and our ultimate failure is confidently predicted. Why should we fail? Nations, like men, fail in nothing which they boldly attempt, when sustained by virtuous purpose and firm resolution. I am not willing to admit this depreciation of American skill and enterprise. I am not willing to strike before an effort is made. All our past history exhorts us to proceed, and inspires us with animating hopes of success. Past predictions of our incapacity have failed, and present predictions will not be realized. At the commencement of this government, we were told that the attempt would be idle to construct a marine adequate to the commerce of the country, or even to the business of its coasting trade. The founders of our government did not listen to these discouraging counsels; and—behold the fruits of their just comprehension of our resources! Our restrictive policy was denounced, and it was foretold that it would utterly disappoint all our expectations. But our restrictive policy has been eminently successful; and the share which our navigation now enjoys in the trade with France, and with the British West India islands, attests its victory. What were not the disheartening predictions of the opponents of the late war? Defeat, discomfiture, and disgrace, were to be the certain, but not the worst effect of it. Here, again, did prophecy prove false; and the energies of our country, and the valor and the patriotism of our people, carried us gloriously through the war. We are now, and ever will be, essentially an agricultural people. Without a material change in the fixed habits of the country, the friends of this measure desire to draw to it, as a powerful auxiliary to its industry, the manufacturing arts. The difference between a nation with and without the arts may be conceived by the difference between a keel-boat and a steamboat, combating the rapid torrent of the Mississippi. How slow does the former ascend, hugging the sinuosities of the shore, pushed on by her hardy and exposed crew, now throwing themselves in vigorous concert on their oars, and then seizing the pendant boughs of overhanging trees: she seems hardly to move; and her scanty cargo is scarcely worth the transportation! With what ease is she not passed by the steamboat, laden with the riches of all quarters of the world, with a crew of gay, cheerful, and protected passengers, now dashing into the midst of the current, or gliding through the eddies near the shore! Nature herself seems to survey with astonishment the passing wonder, and, in silent submission, reluctantly to own the magnificent triumphs, in her own vast dominion, of Fulton's immortal genius.

Webster's Speech of 1824 on the Tariff *

Daniel Webster was, until 1828, one of the most powerful opponents of the protective tariff. He represented the merchants and shippers of Massachusetts whose interests were favorable to free trade. He also represented the influential cotton-textile manufacturers of his state. But they did not demand higher tariffs at this time because their improved methods and general efficiency enabled them to make profits even during the 1819—1821 depression. Webster's speech of April 1 and 2, 1824, contains an important economic critique of one of Clay's major points.

The true course then, Sir, for us to pursue is, in my opinion, to consider what our situation is, what our means are, and how they can be best applied. What amount of population have we in comparison with our extent of soil, what amount of capital, and labor at what price? As to skill, knowledge, and enterprise, we may safely take it for granted that, in these particulars, we are on an equality with others. Keeping these considerations in view, allow me to examine two or three of those provisions of the bill to which I feel the strongest objections.

To begin with the article of iron. Our whole annual consumption of this article is supposed by the Chairman of the Committee to be 48,000 or 50,000 tons. Let us suppose the latter. The amount of our own manufacture he estimates, I think, at 17,000 tons. The present duty on the imported article is $15 per ton, and as this duty causes of course an equivalent augmentation of the price of the home manufacture, the whole increase of price is equal to $750,000 annually. This sum we pay on a raw material, and on an absolute necessary of life. The bill proposes to raise the duty from $15 to $22.50 per ton, which would be equal to $1,125,000 on the whole annual consumption. So that, suppose the point of prohibition which is aimed at by some gentlemen to be attained, the consumers of the article would pay this last mentioned sum every year to the producers of it, over and above the price at which they could supply themselves with the same article from other sources. There would be no mitigation of this burden, except from the prospect, whatever that might

---

* *The Works of Daniel Webster*, 6 vols. (14th ed., Boston: Little, Brown, 1866), III, 139–143.

be, that iron would fall in value by domestic competition after the importation should be prohibited. It will be easy, I think, to show that it cannot fall; and supposing for the present that it shall not, the result will be that we shall pay annually a sum of $1,125,000, constantly augmented, too, by increased consumption of the article, *to support a business that cannot support itself.*

It is of no consequence to the argument that this sum is expended at home; so it would be if we taxed the people to support any other useless and expensive establishment—to build another Capitol, for example, or incur an unnecessary expense of any sort. The question still is, are the money, time, and labor well laid out in these cases? The present price of iron at Stockholm, I am assured by importers, is $53 per ton on board, $48 in the yard before loading, and probably not far from $40 at the mines. Freight, insurance, etc., may be fairly estimated at $15, to which add our present duty of $15 more, and these two last sums, together with the cost on board at Stockholm, give $83 as the cost of Swedes iron in our market. In fact, it is said to have been sold last year at $81.50 to $82 per ton. We perceive by this statement that the cost of the iron is doubled in reaching us from the mine in which it is produced. In other words, our present duty, with the expense of transportation, gives an advantage to the American, over the foreign manufacturer, of 100%. Why then cannot the iron be manufactured at home? Our ore is said to be as good, and some of it better. It is under our feet, and the Chairman of the Committee tells us that it might be wrought by persons who otherwise will not be employed. Why then is it not wrought? Nothing could be more sure of constant sale. It is not an article of changeable fashion, but of absolute, permanent necessity, and such, therefore, as would always meet a steady demand. Sir, I think it would be well for the Chairman of the Committee to revise his premises, for I am persuaded that there is an ingredient properly belonging to the calculation which he has misstated or omitted. Swedes iron in England pays a duty, I think, of about $27 per ton; yet it is imported in considerable quantities, notwithstanding the vast capital, the excellent coal, and, more important than all perhaps, the highly improved state of inland navigation in England; although I am aware that the English use of Swedes iron may be thought to be owing in some degree to its superior quality.

Sir, the true explanation of this appears to me to lie in the different prices *of labor;* and here I apprehend is the grand mistake in the argument of the Chairman of the Committee. He says it would cost the nation, as a nation, nothing to make our ore into iron. Now, I think it would cost us precisely that which we can worst afford; that is, great *labor.* Although bar iron is very properly considered a raw material in respect to its various future uses, yet, as bar iron, the principal ingredient in its cost is labor. Of manual labor, no nation has more than a certain quantity, nor can it be increased at will. As to some operations, indeed, its place may be supplied by machinery; but there are other services which machinery cannot perform for it, and which it must perform for itself. A most important question for every nation, as well as for every individual, to propose to itself, is, how it can best apply that quantity of labor which it is able to perform? Labor is the great producer of wealth; it moves all other causes. If it call machinery to its aid, it is still employed not only in using the machinery, but in making it. Now, with respect to the quantity of labor, as we all know, different nations are differently circumstanced. Some need, more than anything, work for hands, others require hands for work; and if we ourselves are not absolutely in the latter class, we are still, most fortunately, very near it. I cannot find that we have those idle hands of which the Chairman of the Committee speaks. The price of labor is a conclusive and unanswerable refutation of that idea; it is known to be higher with us than in any other civilized state, and this is the greatest of all proofs of general happiness. Labor in this country is independent and proud. It has not to ask the patronage of capital, but capital solicits the aid of labor. This is the general truth in regard to the condition of our whole population, although in the large cities there are, doubtless, many exceptions. The mere capacity to labor in common agricultural employments gives to our young men the assurance of independence. We have been asked, Sir, by the Chairman of the Committee, in a tone of some pathos, whether we will allow to the serfs of Russia and Sweden the benefit of making iron for us? Let me inform the gentleman, Sir, that those same serfs do not earn more than seven cents a day, and that they work in these mines for that compensation because they are serfs. And let me ask the gentleman further, whether we have any labor in this country that cannot be better employed than in a business which does not yield the laborer more than seven cents a day? This, it appears to me, is the true question for our consideration. There is no reason for saying that we will work iron because we have mountains that contain the ore. We might for the same reason dig among our rocks for the scattered grains of gold and silver which might be found there. The true inquiry is, can we produce the article in a useful state at the same cost, or nearly at the same cost, or at any reasonable approximation towards the same cost, at which we can import it?

Some general estimates of the price and profits of labor in those countries from which we import our iron might be formed by comparing the reputed products of different mines and their prices with the number of hands employed. The mines of Danemora are said to yield about 4,000 tons, and to employ in the mines 1,200 workmen. Suppose this to be worth $50 per ton; any one will find by computation that the whole product would not pay in this country for one quarter part of the necessary labor. The whole export of Sweden was estimated, a few years ago, at 400,000 ship-pounds, or about 54,000 tons. Comparing this product with the number of workmen usually supposed to be employed in the mines which produce iron for exportation, the result will not greatly differ from the foregoing. These estimates are general, and might not conduct us to a precise result; but we know, from intelligent travelers and eye-witnesses, that the price of labor in the Swedish mines does not exceed seven cents a day.[1]

The true reason, Sir, why it is not our policy to compel our citizens to manufacture our own iron is, that they are far better employed. It is an unproductive business, and they are not poor enough to be obliged to follow it. If we had more of poverty, more of misery, and something of servitude, if we had an ignorant, idle, starving population, we might set up for iron makers against the world.

READING NO. 5

The Morrill Tariff Act of 1861 *

Justin S. Morrill, a Vermont Republican, was responsible for reversing the downward trend of the tariff after 1846 by initiating the first of a long se-

[1] The price of labor in Russia may be pretty well collected from Tooke's "View of the Russian Empire." "The workmen in the mines and the foundries are, indeed, all called master-people; but they distinguish themselves into masters, undermasters, apprentices, delvers, servants, carriers, washers, and separators. In proportion to their ability their wages are regulated, which proceed from 15 to upwards of 30 roubles per annum. The provisions which they receive from the magazines are deducted from this pay." The value of the rouble at that time (1799) was about 24 pence sterling, or 45 cents of our money.

"By the edict of 1799," it is added, "a laborer with a horse shall receive, daily, in summer 20 and in winter 12 copecks; a laborer without a horse, in summer 10, in winter 8 copecks."

A copeck is the hundredth part of a rouble, or about half a cent of our money. The price of labor may have risen, in some degree, since that period, but probably not much.

* *U. S. Statutes at Large*, Vol. 12, Ch. LXVIII; *Tariff Acts . . . 1789 to 1909*, pp. 163–164, 167–168.

ries of Civil War and post-Civil War highly protective tariffs that helped to put and to keep the Republicans in power by eliciting the support of iron, cotton, woolen, and other industrialists. The March 2, 1861 tariff law was part of a larger piece of legislation, entitled "An act to provide for the payment of outstanding treasury notes, to authorize a loan, to regulate and fix the duties on imports and for other purposes." The iron, woolen, and cotton tariff schedules are reprinted here as samples of the detailed attention Congress gave to the specific industrial products of their industrial supporters.

SEC. 7. *And be it further enacted,* That from and after the day and year aforesaid there shall be levied, collected, and paid, on the importation of the articles hereinafter mentioned, the following duties, that is to say:

First: On bar-iron, rolled or hammered, comprising flats not less than one inch, or more than seven inches wide, nor less than one quarter of an inch or more than two inches thick; rounds, not less than one-half an inch or more than four inches in diameter; and squares not less than one-half an inch or more than four inches square, fifteen dollars per ton: *Provided,* That all iron in slabs, blooms, loops or other forms, less finished than iron in bars and more advanced than pig-iron, except castings, shall be rated as iron in bars, and pay a duty accordingly: *And provided, further,* That none of the above iron shall pay a less rate of duty than twenty per centum ad valorem; on all iron imported in bars for railroads or inclined planes made to patterns and fitted to be laid down upon such roads or planes without further manufacture and not exceeding six inches high, twelve dollars per ton; on boiler plate iron, twenty dollars per ton; on iron wire drawn and finished, not more than one-fourth of one inch in diameter nor less than number sixteen wire gauge, seventy-five cents per one hundred pounds, and fifteen per centum ad valorem; over number sixteen and not over number twenty-five wire gauge, one dollar and fifty cents per one hundred pounds and in addition fifteen per centum ad valorem; over or finer than number twenty-five wire gauge, two dollars per one hundred pounds and in addition fifteen per centum ad valorem; on all other descriptions of rolled or hammered iron not otherwise provided for, twenty dollars per ton.

Second: On iron in pigs, six dollars per ton; on vessels of cast-iron not otherwise provided for, and on sad-irons, tailors and hatters irons, stoves and stove plates, one cent per pound; on cast-iron steam, gas and water pipe, fifty cents per one hundred pounds; on cast-iron butts and hinges, two cents per pound; on hollow-ware, glazed or tinned, two cents and a half per pound; on all other castings of iron not otherwise provided for, twenty-five per centum ad valorem.

Third: On old scrap iron, six dollars per ton: *Provided,* That nothing shall be deemed old iron that has not been in actual use and fit only to be remanufactured.

Fourth: On band and hoop iron, slit rods not otherwise provided for, twenty dollars per ton; on cut nails and spikes, one cent per pound; on iron cables or chains, or parts thereof, and anvils, one dollar and twenty-five cents per one hundred pounds; on anchors, or parts thereof, one dollar and fifty cents per one hundred pounds; on wrought board nails, spikes, rivets, and bolts, two cents per pound; on bed screws and wrought hinges, one cent and a half per pound; on chains, trace chains, halter chains, and fence chains made of wire or rods one-half of one inch in diameter or over, one cent and a half per pound; under one-half of one inch in diameter, and not under one-fourth of one inch in diameter, two cents per pound; under one-fourth of one inch in diameter, and not under number nine wire gauge, two cents and a half per pound; under number nine wire gauge, twenty-five per centum ad valorem; on black-smiths' hammers and sledges, axles or parts thereof, and malleable iron in castings not otherwise provided for, two cents per pound; on horse-shoe nails, three cents and a half per pound; on steam, gas, and water tubes and flues of wrought iron, two cents per pound; on wrought iron railroad chairs and on wrought iron nuts and washers, ready punched, twenty-five dollars per ton; on cut tacks, brads, and sprigs not exceeding sixteen ounces to the thousand, two cents per thousand; exceeding sixteen ounces to the thousand, two cents per pound.

Fifth: On smooth or polished sheet iron by whatever name designated, two cents per pound; on other sheet iron, common or black not thinner than number twenty wire gauge, twenty dollars per ton; thinner than number twenty and not thinner than number twenty-five wire gauge, twenty-five dollars per ton; thinner than number twenty-five wire gauge, thirty dollars per ton; on tin plates galvanized, galvanized iron, or iron coated with zinc, two cents per pound; on mill irons and mill cranks of wrought iron, and wrought iron for ships, locomotives, locomotive tire, or parts thereof, and steam engines, or parts thereof, weighing each twenty-five pounds or more, one cent and a half per pound; on screws commonly called wood screws, two inches or over in length, five cents per pound; less than two inches in length, eight cents per pound; on screws washed or plated, and all other screws of iron or any other metal, thirty per centum ad valorem; on all manufactures of iron not otherwise provided for, thirty per centum ad valorem.

Sixth: On all steel in ingots, bars, sheets, or wire not less than one fourth of one inch in diameter, valued at seven cents per pound or less, one and a half cents per pound; valued at above seven cents per pound and not above eleven cents per pound, two cents per pound; steel in any form not otherwise provided for, shall pay a duty of twenty per centum ad valorem; on steel wire less than one fourth of an inch in diameter, and not less than number sixteen wire gauge, two dollars per one hundred pounds, and in addition thereto fifteen per centum ad valorem; less or finer than number sixteen wire gauge, two dollars and fifty cents per one hundred pounds, and in addition thereto fifteen per centum ad valorem; on cross-cut saws, eight cents per lineal foot; on mill, pit, and drag saws, not over nine inches wide, twelve and a half cents per lineal foot; over nine inches wide, twenty cents per lineal foot; on skates costing twenty cents, or less per pair, six cents per pair; on those costing over twenty cents per pair, thirty per centum ad valorem; on all manufactures of steel or of which steel shall be a component part, not otherwise provided for, thirty per centum ad valorem: *Provided,* That all articles partially manufactured, not otherwise provided for, shall pay the same rate of duty as if wholly manufactured.

Seventh: On bituminous coal, one dollar per ton of twenty-eight bushels, eighty pounds to the bushels; on all other coal, fifty cents per ton of twenty-eight bushels, eighty pounds to the bushel; on coke and culm of coal, twenty-five per centum ad valorem. . . .

SEC. 13. *And be it further enacted,* That from and after the day and year aforesaid, there shall be levied, collected, and paid on the importation of the articles hereinafter mentioned the following duties, that is to say:

First: On Wilton, Saxony and Aubusson, Axminster patent velvet, Tournay velvet, and tapestry velvet carpets and carpeting, Brussels carpets wrought by the Jacquard machine, and all medallion or whole carpets, valued at one dollar and twenty-five cents or under per square yard, forty cents per square yard; valued at over one dollar and twenty-five cents per square yard, fifty cents per square yard: *Provided,* That no carpet or rugs of the above description shall pay a duty less than twenty-five per centum ad valorem; on Brussels and tapestry Brussels carpets and carpeting printed on the warp or otherwise, thirty cents per square yard; on all treble-ingrain and worsted-chain Venetian carpets and carpeting, twenty-five cents per square yard; on hemp or jute carpeting, four cents per square yard; on druggets, bockings, and felt carpets and carpeting printed, colored or otherwise, twenty cents per square yard; on all other kinds of carpets and carpeting of wool, flax or cotton, or parts of either, or other material not otherwise specified, a duty of thirty per centum ad valorem; *Provided,* That mats, rugs, screens, covers, hassocks, bedsides and other portions of carpets or carpeting shall pay the rate of duty herein imposed on carpets or carpeting of similar character; on all other mats, screens, hassocks, and rugs, a duty of thirty per centum ad valorem.

Second: On woollen cloths, woollen shawls, and all manufactures of wool of every description, made wholly or in part of wool, not otherwise provided for, a duty of twelve cents per pound, and in addition thereto twenty-five per centum ad valorem; on endless belts for paper, and blanketing for printing machines, twenty-five per centum ad valorem; on all flannels valued at thirty cents or less per square yard, twenty-five per centum ad valorem; valued above thirty cents per square yard, and on all flannels colored, printed, or plaided, and flannels composed in part of cotton or silk, thirty per centum ad valorem; on hats of wool, twenty per centum ad valorem; on woollen and worsted yarn, valued at fifty cents and not over one dollar per pound, twelve cents per pound, and in addition thereto fifteen per centum ad valorem, on woollen and worsted yarn, valued at over one dollar per pound, twelve cents per pound, and in addition thereto twenty-five per centum ad valorem; on woollen and worsted yarns, or yarns for carpets, valued under fifty cents per pound, and not exceeding in fineness number fourteen, twenty-five per centum ad valorem; exceeding number fourteen, thirty per centum ad valorem; on clothing ready made, and wearing apparel of every description, composed wholly or in part of wool, made up or manufactured wholly or in part by the tailor, seamstress, or manufacturer, twelve cents per pound, and in addition thereto twenty-five per centum ad valorem; on blankets of all kinds, made wholly or in part of wool, valued at not exceeding twenty-eight cents per pound, there shall be charged a duty of six cents per pound, and in addition thereto ten per centum ad valorem; on all valued above twenty-eight cents per pound, but not exceeding forty cents per pound, there shall be charged a duty of six cents per pound, and in addition thereto twenty-five per centum ad valorem; on all valued above forty cents per pound there shall be charged a duty of twelve cents per pound, and in addition thereto twenty per centum ad valorem; on woollen shawls, or shawls of which wool shall be the chief component material, a duty of sixteen cents per pound, and in addition thereto twenty per centum ad valorem.

Third: On all delaines, Cashmere delaines, muslin delaines, barege delaines, composed wholly or in part of wool, gray or uncolored, and on all other gray or uncolored goods of similar description, twenty-five per centum ad valorem; on bunting, and on all stained, colored, or printed, and on all other manufactures of wool, or of which wool shall be a component material, not otherwise provided for, thirty per centum ad valorem.

Fourth: On oil-cloth, for floors, stamped, painted, or printed, valued at fifty cents or less per square yard, twenty per centum ad valorem; valued at over fifty cents per square yard, and on all other oil cloth, thirty per centum ad valorem.

SEC. 14. *And be it further enacted,* That from and after the day and year aforesaid, there shall be levied, collected, and paid on the importations of the articles hereinafter mentioned the following duties, that is to say:

First: On all manufactures of cotton not bleached, colored, stained, painted, or printed, and not exceeding one hundred threads to the square inch, counting the warp and filling, and exceeding in weight five ounces per square yard, one cent per square yard; on finer or lighter goods of like description, not exceeding one hundred and forty threads to the square inch, counting the warp and filling, two cents per square yard; on goods of like description, exceeding one hundred and forty threads, and not exceeding two hundred threads to the square inch, counting the warp and filling, three cents per square yard; on like goods exceeding two hundred threads to the square inch, counting the warp and filling, four cents per square yard; on all goods embraced in the foregoing schedules, if bleached, there shall be levied, collected, and paid an additional duty of one-half of one cent per square yard; and if printed, painted, colored, or stained, there shall be levied, collected, and paid a duty of ten per centum in addition to the rates of duty provided in the foregoing schedules: *Provided,* That upon all plain woven cotton goods not included in the foregoing schedules, and upon cotton goods of every description, the value of which shall exceed sixteen cents per square yard, there shall be levied, collected, and paid a duty of twenty-five per centum ad valorem: *And provided, further,* That no cotton goods having more than two hundred threads to the square inch, counting the warp and filling, shall be admitted to a less rate of duty than is provided for goods which are of that number of threads.

Second: On spool and other thread of cotton, thirty per centum ad valorem.

Third: On shirts and drawers, wove or made on frames composed wholly of cotton and cotton velvet, twenty-five per centum ad valorem; and on all manufactures composed wholly of cotton, bleached, unbleached, printed, painted, or dyed, not otherwise provided for, thirty per centum ad valorem.

Fourth: On all brown or bleached linens, ducks, canvas paddings, cotbottoms, burlaps, drills, coatings, brown Hollands, blay linens, damasks, diapers, crash, huckabacks, handkerchiefs, lawns, or other manufactures of flax, jute, or hemp, [or of which flax, jute, or hemp] shall be the component material of chief value, being of the value of thirty cents and under per square yard, twenty-five per centum ad valorem; valued above thirty cents per square yard, thirty per centum ad valorem; on flax or linen threads, twine and pack-thread, and all other manufactures of flax, or of which flax shall be the component material of chief value, and not otherwise provided for, thirty per centum ad valorem.

READING NO. 6

Cleveland's Message of 1887 *

Grover Cleveland was the first Democrat to be elected to the Presidency after the Civil War. He was also one of the strongest champions of tariff reduction. On December 6, 1887, he made history by making his whole annual message to Congress an all-out attack on the protective tariff. His objectives were frustrated by the Republicans until 1894, and were then realized only to a very limited degree. But in 1913 Wilson carried Cleveland's hopes to victory.

To the Congress of the United States:

You are confronted at the threshold of your legislative duties with a condition of the national finances which imperatively demands immediate and careful consideration.

The amount of money annually exacted, through the operation of present laws, from the industries and necessities of the people largely exceeds the sum necessary to meet the expenses of the Government.

When we consider that the theory of our institutions guarantees to every citizen the full enjoyment of all the fruits of his industry and enterprise, with only such deduction as may be his share toward the careful and economical maintenance of the Government which protects him, it is plain that the exaction of more than this is indefensible extortion and a culpable betrayal of American fairness and justice. This wrong inflicted upon those who bear the burden of national taxation, like other wrongs, multiplies a brood of evil consequences. The public Treasury, which should only exist as a conduit conveying the people's tribute to its legitimate objects of expenditure, becomes a hoarding place for money needlessly withdrawn from trade and the people's use, thus crippling our national energies, suspending our country's development, preventing investment in productive enterprise, threatening financial disturbance, and inviting schemes of public plunder.

This condition of our Treasury is not altogether new, and it has more

* James D. Richardson, ed., *A Compilation of the Messages and Papers of the Presidents 1789–1905,* 11 vols. (n.p.: Bureau of National Literature and Art, 1907), VIII, 580–581, 584–590.

than once of late been submitted to the people's representatives in the Congress, who alone can apply a remedy. And yet the situation still continues, with aggravated incidents, more than ever presaging financial convulsion and widespread disaster.

*   *   *

Our scheme of taxation, by means of which this needless surplus is taken from the people and put into the public Treasury, consists of a tariff or duty levied upon importations from abroad and internal-revenue taxes levied upon the consumption of tobacco and spirituous and malt liquors. It must be conceded that none of the things subjected to internal-revenue taxation are, strictly speaking, necessaries. There appears to be no just complaint of this taxation by the consumers of these articles, and there seems to be nothing so well able to bear the burden without hardship to any portion of the people.

But our present tariff laws, the vicious, inequitable, and illogical source of unnecessary taxation, ought to be at once revised and amended. These laws, as their primary and plain effect, raise the price to consumers of all articles imported and subject to duty by precisely the sum paid for such duties. Thus the amount of the duty measures the tax paid by those who purchase for use these imported articles. Many of these things, however, are raised or manufactured in our own country, and the duties now levied upon foreign goods and products are called protection to these home manufactures, because they render it possible for those of our people who are manufacturers to make these taxed articles and sell them for a price equal to that demanded for the imported goods that have paid customs duty. So it happens that while comparatively a few use the imported articles, millions of our people, who never used and never saw any of the foreign products, purchase and use things of the same kind made in this country, and pay therefore nearly or quite the same enhanced price which the duty adds to the imported articles. Those who buy imports pay the duty charged thereon into the public Treasury, but the great majority of our citizens, who buy domestic articles of the same class, pay a sum at least approximately equal to this duty to the home manufacturer. This reference to the operation of our tariff laws is not made by way of instruction, but in order that we may be constantly reminded of the manner in which they impose a burden upon those who consume domestic products as well as those who consume imported articles, and thus create a tax upon all our people.

It is not proposed to entirely relieve the country of this taxation. It must be extensively continued as the source of the Government's income; and in a readjustment of our tariff the interests of American labor engaged in manufacture should be carefully considered, as well as the preservation of our manufacturers. It may be called protection or by any other name, but relief from the hardships and dangers of our present tariff laws should be devised with especial precaution against imperiling the existence of our manufacturing interests. But this existence should not mean a condition which, without regard to the public welfare or a national exigency, must always insure the realization of immense profits instead of moderately profitable returns. As the volume and diversity of our national activities increase, new recruits are added to those who desire a continuation of the advantages which they conceive the present system of tariff taxation directly affords them. So stubbornly have all efforts to reform the present condition been resisted by those of our fellow-citizens thus engaged that they can hardly complain of the suspicion, entertained to a certain extent, that there exists an organized combination all along the line to maintain their advantage.

We are in the midst of centennial celebrations, and with becoming pride we rejoice in American skill and ingenuity, in American energy and enterprise, and in the wonderful natural advantages and resources developed by a century's national growth. Yet when an attempt is made to justify a scheme which permits a tax to be laid upon every consumer in the land for the benefit of our manufacturers, quite beyond a reasonable demand for governmental regard, it suits the purposes of advocacy to call our manufactures infant industries still needing the highest and greatest degree of favor and fostering care that can be wrung from Federal legislation.

It is also said that the increase in the price of domestic manufactures resulting from the present tariff is necessary in order that higher wages may be paid to our workingmen employed in manufactories than are paid for what is called the pauper labor of Europe. All will acknowledge the force of an argument which involves the welfare and liberal compensation of our laboring people. Our labor is honorable in the eyes of every American citizen; and as it lies at the foundation of our development and progress, it is entitled, without affectation or hypocrisy, to the utmost regard. The standard of our laborers' life should not be measured by that of any other country less favored, and they are entitled to their full share of all our advantages.

By the last census it is made to appear that of the 17,392,099 of our population engaged in all kinds of industries 7,670,493 are employed in agriculture, 4,074,238 in professional and personal service (2,934,876 of whom are domestic servants and laborers), while 1,810,256 are employed in trade and transportation and 3,837,112 are classed as employed in manufacturing and mining.

For present purposes, however, the last number given should be considerably reduced. Without attempting to enumerate all, it will be conceded that there should be deducted from those which it includes 375,143 carpenters and joiners, 285,401 milliners, dressmakers, and seamstresses, 172,726 blacksmiths, 133,756 tailors and tailoresses, 102,473 masons, 76,241 butchers, 41,309 bakers, 22,083 plasterers, and 4,891 engaged in manufacturing agricultural implements, amounting in the aggregate to 1,214,023, leaving 2,623,089 persons employed in such manufacturing industries as are claimed to be benefited by a high tariff.

To these the appeal is made to save their employment and maintain their wages by resisting a change. There should be no disposition to answer such suggestions by the allegation that they are in a minority among those who labor, and therefore should forego an advantage in the interest of low prices for the majority. Their compensation, as it may be affected by the operation of tariff laws, should at all times be scrupulously kept in view; and yet with slight reflection they will not overlook the fact that they are consumers with the rest; that they too have their own wants and those of their families to supply from their earnings, and that the price of the necessaries of life, as well as the amount of their wages, will regulate the measure of their welfare and comfort.

But the reduction of taxation demanded should be so measured as not to necessitate or justify either the loss of employment by the workingman or the lessening of his wages; and the profits still remaining to the manufacturer after a necessary readjustment should furnish no excuse for the sacrifice of the interests of his employees, either in their opportunity to work or in the diminution of their compensation. Nor can the worker in manufactures fail to understand that while a high tariff is claimed to be necessary to allow the payment of remunerative wages, it certainly results in a very large increase in the price of nearly all sorts of manufactures, which, in almost countless forms, he needs for the use of himself and his family. He receives at the desk of his employer his wages, and perhaps before he reaches his home is obliged, in a purchase for family use of an article which embraces his own labor, to return in the payment of the increase in price which the tariff permits the hard-earned compensation of many days of toil.

The farmer and the agriculturist, who manufacture nothing, but who pay the increased price which the tariff imposes upon every agricultural implement, upon all he wears, and upon all he uses and owns, except the increase of his flocks and herds and such things as his husbandry produces from the soil, is invited to aid in maintaining the present situation; and he is told that a high duty on imported wool is necessary for the benefit of those who have sheep to shear, in order that the price of their wool may be increased. They, of course, are not reminded that the farmer who has no sheep is by this scheme obliged, in his purchases of clothing and woolen goods, to pay a tribute to his fellow-farmer as well as to the manufacturer and merchant; nor is any mention made of the fact that the sheep-owners themselves and their households must wear clothing and use other articles manufactured from the wool they sell at tariff prices, and thus as consumers must return their share of this increased price to the tradesman.

I think it may be fairly assumed that a large proportion of the sheep owned by the farmers throughout the country are found in small flocks, numbering from twenty-five to fifty. The duty on the grade of imported wool which these sheep yield is 10 cents each pound if of the value of 30 cents or less and 12 cents if of the value of more than 30 cents. If the liberal estimate of 6 pounds be allowed for each fleece, the duty thereon would be 60 or 72 cents; and this may be taken as the utmost enhancement of its price to the farmer by reason of this duty. Eighteen dollars would thus represent the increased price of the wool from twenty-five sheep and $36 that from the wool of fifty sheep; and at present values this addition would amount to about one-third of its price. If upon its sale the farmer receives this or a less tariff profit, the wool leaves his hands charged with precisely that sum, which in all its changes will adhere to it until it reaches the consumer. When manufactured into cloth and other goods and material for use, its cost is not only increased to the extent of the farmer's tariff profit, but a further sum has been added for the benefit of the manufacturer under the operation of other tariff laws. In the meantime the day arrives when the farmer finds it necessary to purchase woolen goods and material to clothe himself and family for the winter. When he faces the tradesman for that purpose, he discovers that he is obliged not only to return in the way of increased prices his tariff profit on the wool he sold, and which then perhaps lies before him in manufactured form, but that he must add a considerable sum thereto to meet a further increase in cost caused by a tariff duty on the manufacture. Thus in the end he is aroused to the fact that he has paid upon a moderate purchase, as a result of the tariff scheme, which when he sold his wool seemed so profitable, an increase in price more than sufficient to sweep away all the tariff profit he received upon the wool he produced and sold.

When the number of farmers engaged in wool-raising is compared with all the farmers in the country and the small proportion they bear to our population is considered; when it is made apparent that in the case of a large part of those who own sheep the benefit of the present tariff on wool is illusory; and, above all, when it must be conceded that the increase of the cost of living caused by such tariff becomes a burden upon those with moderate means and the poor, the employed and unemployed, the sick and well, and the young and old, and that it constitutes a tax which with relentless grasp is fastened upon the clothing of every man, woman, and child in the land, reasons are suggested why the removal or reduction of this duty should be included in a revision of our tariff laws.

In speaking of the increased cost to the consumer of our home manufactures resulting from a duty laid upon imported articles of the same description, the fact is not overlooked that competition among our domestic producers sometimes has the effect of keeping the price of their products below the highest limit allowed by such duty. But it is notorious that this competition is too often strangled by combinations quite prevalent at this time, and frequently called trusts, which have for their object the regulation of the supply and price of commodities made and sold by members of the combination. The people can hardly hope for any consideration in the operation of these selfish schemes.

If, however, in the absence of such combination, a healthy and free competition reduces the price of any particular dutiable article of home production, below the limit which it might otherwise reach under our tariff laws, and if, with such reduced price, its manufacture continues to thrive, it is entirely evident that one thing has been discovered which should be carefully scrutinized in an effort to reduce taxation.

The necessity of combination to maintain the price of any commodity to the tariff point furnishes proof that someone is willing to accept lower prices for such commodity and that such prices are remunerative; and lower prices produced by competition prove the same thing. Thus where either of these conditions exists a case would seem to be presented for an easy reduction of taxation.

*   *   *

The difficulty attending a wise and fair revision of our tariff laws is not underestimated. It will require on the part of the Congress great labor and care, and especially a broad and national contemplation of the subject and a patriotic disregard of such local and selfish claims as are unreasonable and reckless of the welfare of the entire country.

Under our present laws more than 4,000 articles are subject to duty. Many of these do not in any way compete with our own manufactures, and many are hardly worth attention as subjects of revenue. A considerable reduction can be made in the aggregate by adding them to the free list. The taxation of luxuries presents no features of hardship; but the necessaries of life used and consumed by all the people, the duty upon which adds to the cost of living in every home, should be greatly cheapened.

The radical reduction of the duties imposed upon raw material used in manufactures, or its free importation, is of course an important factor in any effort to reduce the price of these necessaries. It would not only relieve them from the increased cost caused by the tariff on such material, but the manufactured product being thus cheapened, that part of the tariff now laid upon such product, as a compensation to our manufacturers for the present price of raw material, could be accordingly modified. Such reduction or free importation would serve besides to largely reduce the revenue. It is not apparent how such a change can have any injurious effect upon our manufacturers. On the contrary, it would appear to give them a better chance in foreign markets with the manufacturers of other countries, who cheapen their wares by free material. Thus our people might have the opportunity of extending their sales beyond the limits of home consumption, saving them from the depression, interruption in business, and loss caused by a glutted domestic market and affording their employees more certain and steady labor, with its resulting quiet and contentment.

* * *

Our progress toward a wise conclusion will not be improved by dwelling upon the theories of protection and free trade. This savors too much of bandying epithets. It is a *condition* which confronts us, not a theory. Relief from this condition may involve a slight reduction of the advantages which we award our home productions, but the entire withdrawal of such advantages should not be contemplated. The question of free trade is absolutely irrelevant, and the persistent claim made in certain quarters that all the efforts to relieve the people from unjust and unnecessary taxation are schemes of so-called free traders is mischievous and far removed from any consideration for the public good.

The simple and plain duty which we owe the people is to reduce taxation to the necessary expenses of an economical operation of the Government and to restore to the business of the country the money which we hold in the Treasury through the perversion of governmental powers. These things can and should be done with safety to all our industries, without danger to the opportunity for remunerative labor which our workingmen need, and with benefit to them and all our people by cheapening their means of subsistence and increasing the measure of their comforts.

READING NO. 7

McKinley's Speech on
the Mills Tariff Bill *

William McKinley was noted as one of the leading Republican advocates of high protection in the House of Representatives during his seven terms of office as a Congressman from Ohio (1887–1891). His May 18, 1888 speech on the Mills Tariff Bill was regarded as one of the best Republican attempts at a rejoinder to the arguments of Cleveland and other Democratic spokesmen in the 1880's. McKinley went on to give his name to the McKinley Tariff Act of 1890 and to be elected President in 1896 and 1900. His last speech, given at Buffalo on September 5, 1901, appeared to suggest the wisdom of lowering tariffs. The next day he was shot by an anarchist, and he died eight days later. No important tariff revision was to occur until 1913, and then under a Democratic Administration.

This brings us face to face, therefore, with the two opposing systems, that of a revenue as distinguished from a protective tariff, and upon their respective merits they must stand or fall. Now, what are they? First, what is a revenue tariff? Upon what principle does it rest? It is a tariff or tax placed upon such articles of foreign production imported here as will produce the largest revenue with the smallest tax; or, as Robert J. Walker, late Secretary of the Treasury and author of the tariff of 1846, from whom the advocates of the measure draw their inspiration, put it:

"The only true maxim is that which experience demonstrates will bring in each case the largest revenue at the lowest rate of duty, and that no duty be imposed upon any article above the lowest rate which will yield the largest amount of revenue. The revenue (said Mr. Walker) from *ad valorem* duties last year (1845) exceeded that realized from specific duties, although the average of the *ad valorem* duties was only 23.57 per cent. and the average of the specific duties 41.30 per cent., presenting another strong proof that the lower duties increase the revenue."

To secure larger revenue from lower duties necessitates largely in-

* *Speeches and Addresses of William McKinley* (New York: Appleton, 1894), pp. 292–295, 301–303, 306–310.

creased importations, and if these compete with domestic products the latter must be diminished or find other and distant and I may say impossible markets or get out of the way altogether. A genuine revenue tariff imposes no tax upon foreign importations the like of which are produced at home, or, if produced at home, in quantities not capable of supplying the home consumption, in which case it may be truthfully said the tax is added to the foreign cost and is paid by the consumer. A revenue tariff seeks out those articles which domestic production can not supply, or only inadequately supply, and which the wants of our people demand, and imposes the duty upon them, and permits as far as possible the competing foreign product to be imported free of duty. This principle is made conspicuous in the bill under consideration; for example, wool, a competing foreign product, which our own flock-masters can fully supply for domestic wants, is put upon the free list, while sugar, with a home product of only one-eleventh of the home consumption, is left dutiable.

Any tax levied upon a foreign product which is a necessity to our people, and which we can not fully supply, will produce revenue in amount only measured by our necessities and ability to buy. In a word, foreign productions not competing with home productions are the proper subjects for taxation under a revenue tariff, and in case these do not furnish the requisite revenue a low duty is put upon the foreign product competing with the domestic one—low enough to encourage and stimulate importations, and low enough to break down eventually domestic competition. For example, the duty proposed under this bill upon cotton bagging will extinguish the industry here, and under its provisions we would import all of that product from Calcutta and Dundee. A large revenue would come from this source, because the foreign would take the place of the domestic production. This duty is a revenue one, and gives no protection whatever to the home producer. If it did it would not be a revenue tariff. As the Cobden school of political science puts it, "The moment it is made clear that a tax is a benefit to home producers then the free-trade dogma condemns it. The test is simple and easy of application. Free-trade or a revenue tariff does not allow any import duties being imposed on such articles as are likewise produced at home." Or if produced at home a revenue tariff would soon destroy their production.

What is a protective tariff? It is a tariff upon imports so adjusted as to secure the necessary revenue, and judiciously imposed upon those foreign products the like of which are produced at home or the like of which we are capable of producing at home. It imposes the duty upon the competing foreign product; it makes it bear the burden or duty, and, as far as possible, luxuries only excepted, permits the non-competing foreign product to come in free of duty. Articles of common use, comfort, and necessity which we can not produce here it sends to the people untaxed and free from customhouse exactions. Tea, coffee, spices, and drugs are such articles, and under our system are upon the free list. It says to our foreign competitor, If you want to bring your merchandise here, your farm products here, your coal and iron ore, your wool, your salt, your pottery, your glass, your cottons and woolens, and sell alongside of our producers in our markets, we will make your product bear a duty; in effect, pay for the privilege of doing it. Our kind of a tariff makes the competing foreign article carry the burden, draw the load, supply the revenue; and in performing this essential office it encourages at the same time our own industries and protects our own people in their chosen employments. That is the mission and purpose of a protective tariff. That is what we mean to maintain, and any measure which will destroy it we shall firmly resist, and if beaten on this floor, we will appeal from your decision to the people, before whom parties and policies must at last be tried. We have free trade among ourselves throughout thirty-eight States and the Territories and among sixty millions of people. Absolute freedom of exchange within our own borders and among our own citizens is the law of the Republic. Reasonable taxation and restraint upon those without is the dictate of enlightened patriotism and the doctrine of the Republican party.

Free trade in the United States is founded upon a community of equalities and reciprocities. It is like the unrestrained freedom and reciprocal relations and obligations of a family. Here we are one country, one language, one allegiance, one standard of citizenship, one flag, one Constitution, one nation, one destiny. It is otherwise with foreign nations, each a separate organism, a distinct and independent political society organized for its own, to protect its own, and work out its own destiny. We deny to those foreign nations free trade with us upon equal terms with our own producers. The foreign producer has no right or claim to equality with our own. He is not amenable to our laws. There are resting upon him none of the obligations of citizenship. He pays no taxes. He performs no civil duties; is subject to no demands for military service. He is exempt from State, county, and municipal obligations. He contributes nothing to the support, the progress, and glory of the nation. Why should he enjoy unrestrained equal privileges and profits in our markets with our producers, our labor, and our taxpayers? Let the gentleman who follows me answer. We put a burden upon his productions, we discriminate against his merchandise, because he is alien to us and our interests, and we do it to protect our own, defend our own, preserve our own who are always with us in adversity and prosperity, in sympathy and purpose, and, if necessary, in sacrifice. That is the principle which governs us. I submit it is a patriotic and righteous one. In our own country, each citizen competes with the other in free and unresentful rivalry, while with the rest of the world all are united and together in resisting outside competition as we would foreign interference.

Free foreign trade admits the foreigner to equal privileges with our own citizens. It invites the product of foreign cheap labor to this market in competition with the domestic product, representing higher and better paid labor. It results in giving our money, our manufactures, and our markets to other nations, to the injury of our labor, our tradespeople, and our farmers. Protection keeps money, markets, and manufactures at home for the benefit of our own people.

It is scarcely worth while to more than state the proposition that taxation upon a foreign competing product is more easily paid and less burdensome than taxation upon the non-competing product. In the latter it is always added to the foreign cost, and therefore paid by the consumer, while in the former, where the duty is upon the competing product, it is largely paid in the form of diminished profits to the foreign producer. It would be burdensome beyond endurance to collect our taxes from the products, professions, and labor of our own people.

*   *   *

I now come to consider the general effect of the protective system upon our people and their employments. There is no conflict of interests and should be none between the several classes of producers and the consumers in the United States. Their interests are one, interrelated and interdependent. That which benefits one benefits all; one man's work has relation with every other man's work in the same community; each is an essential part of the grand result to be attained, and that statesmanship which would seek to array the one against the other for any purpose is narrow, unworthy, and unpatriotic. The President's message is unhappily in that direction. The discussion had on this floor has taken that turn. Both have been calculated to create antagonism where none existed. The farmer, the manufacturer, the laborer, the tradesman, and the producer and the consumer all have a common interest in the maintenance of a protective tariff. All are alike and equally favored by the system which you seek to overthrow. It is a national system, broad and universal in its application; if otherwise it should be abandoned. It can not be invoked for one section or one interest to the exclusion of others. It must be general in its application within the contemplation of the principle upon which the system is founded. We have been living under it for twenty-seven continuous years, and it can be asserted with confidence that no country in the world has achieved such industrial advancement, and such marvelous progress in arts, science, and civilization as ours. Tested by its results, it has surpassed all other revenue systems.

From 1789 to 1888, a period of ninety-nine years, there have been forty-seven years when a Democratic revenue-tariff policy has prevailed, and fifty-two years under the protective policy, and it is a noteworthy fact that the most progressive and prosperous periods of our history in every department of human effort and material development were during the fifty-two years when the protective party was in control and protective tariffs were maintained; and the most disastrous years—years of want and wretchedness, ruin and retrogression, eventuating in insufficient revenues and shattered credits, individual and national—were during the free-trade or revenue tariff eras of our history. No man living who passed through any of the latter periods but would dread their return, and would flee from them as he would escape from fire and pestilence; and I believe the party which promotes their return will merit and receive popular condemnation. What is the trouble with our present condition? No country can point to greater prosperity or more enduring evidences of substantial progress among all the people. Too much money is being collected, it is said. We say stop it; not by indiscriminate and vicious legislation, but by simple business methods. Do it on simple, practical lines and we will help you. Buy up the bonds, objectionable as it may be, and pay the nation's debts, if you can not reduce taxation. You could have done this long ago. Nobody is chargeable for the failure and delay but your own Administration.

Who is objecting to our protective system? From what quarter does the complaint come? Not from the enterprising American citizen; not from the manufacturer; not from the laborer, whose wages it improves; not from the consumer, for he is fully satisfied, because under it he buys a cheaper and a better product than he did under the other system; not from the farmer, for he finds among the employés of the protected industries his best and most reliable customers; not from the merchant or the tradesman, for every hive of industry increases the number of his customers and enlarges the volume of his trade. Few, indeed, have been the petitions presented to this House asking for any reduction of duties upon imports. None, that I have seen or heard of, and I have watched with the deepest interest the number and character of these petitions that I might gather from them the drift of public sentiment—I say I have seen none asking for the passage of this bill, or for any such departure from the fiscal policy of the Government so long recognized and followed, while against this legislation there has been no limit to petitions, memorials, prayers, and protests, from producer and consumer alike. . . .

*   *   *

Why, Mr. Chairman, the establishment of a furnace or factory or mill in any neighborhood has the effect at once to enhance the value of all property and all values for miles surrounding it. They produce increased activity. The farmer has a better and a nearer market for his products. The merchant, the butcher, the grocer, have an increased trade. The carpenter is in greater demand; he is called upon to build more houses. Every branch of trade, every avenue of labor, will feel almost immediately the energizing influence of a new industry. The truck farm is in demand; the perishable products, the fruits, the vegetables, which in many cases will not bear exportation and for which a foreign market is too distant to be available, find a constant and ready demand at good paying prices.

What the agriculturist of this country wants more than anything else, after he has gathered his crop, are consumers, consumers at home, men who do not produce what they eat, who must purchase all they consume; men who are engaged in manufacturing, in mining, in cotton-spinning, in the potteries, and in the thousands of productive industries which command all their time and energy, and whose employments do not admit of their producing their own food. The American agriculturist further wants these consumers near and convenient to his field of supply. Cheap as inland transportation is, every mile saved is money made. Every manufacturing establishment in the United States, wherever situated, is of priceless value to the farmers of the country. The six manufacturing States of New England aptly illustrate the great value of a home market to the Western farmer. These States have reached the highest perfection in skill and manufactures. They do not raise from their own soil, with the exception of hay and potatoes, but a small fraction of what their inhabitants require and consume: they could not from their own fields and granaries feed the population which they had in 1830, much less their present population. The most intense revenue-reformer, the most unenlightened Democrat, will have to confess that New England is indebted in large part for her splendid development to the protective system. Now, have her prosperity and progress been secured at the sacrifice of other interests and other sections? I answer, No; but they have brought, as I believe I shall be able to show, a positive blessing to all of our 60,000,000 of people.

In 1880 the population of these six States was over 4,000,000. The food products required by their people, the very necessities of their daily life in a large measure, came from other States and remote sections of the Union. They raised in 1880 but one-quarter of 1 per cent. of the total wheat production of the United States. They raised in the same year but one-half of 1 per cent. of the total crop of Indian corn, 2½ per cent. of the oats, 12 per cent. of the hay, and 13 per cent. of the potatoes which were produced in the United States. What did they consume? What did they buy of the Western farmer? Fifty millions of dollars' worth of meat was consumed by their industrial people in a single year. The extent of their needs is strikingly shown by the fact (obtained from the accounts of Commissioner Fink) that during the year 1884 the "trunk lines" brought into New England no less than 470,000 tons of flour and 950,000 tons of grain. At 200 pounds to the barrel of flour, this is an importation of 4,700,000 barrels, or one and one-fifth, nearly, for each inhabitant. During the same year there were exported from Boston and Portland, the only points in New England from which breadstuffs are sent abroad, 2,100,000 barrels of flour, leaving for consumption within these States 2,600,000 barrels. These figures take no account of the large trade by water from New York. I am informed that a large part of the flour consumed in Connecticut, Rhode Island, and Southern Massachusetts is received in this way, but no reliable statistics are available. It is reasonable, however, to suppose, and this comes to me from what I deem good authority, that the amount thus received and consumed offsets a large portion of the foreign exports to which I have referred. Of the grain received during the same year rather less than 400,000 tons were exported, leaving for New England consumption 550,000 tons, for all of which these States were the customers of the West in addition to the amount grown upon their own soil. In addition to this, New England consumed, in 1886–'87 in her factories, nearly one-fourth of the entire cotton crop of the country. More than this, she used in her woolen mills in 1880 fully one-half of the entire wool clip of the United States, and during the year 1886 she consumed more than one-sixth of the entire anthracite-coal production of the country and 5½ per cent. of the bituminous-coal production, and every pound of both came from the Middle and Southern States.

Is not New England (I appeal to the gentlemen of the other side, I appeal to the farmers of the country) worth preserving? Is not the industrial system which makes such a community of consumers for agricultural products possible worth maintaining? Does not she give you a trade and an exchange of products worth your while to guard with the most considerate care? And does not her condition indicate the wisdom of the policy we advocate? Is not her market better for you than a foreign one? Is not New England a better customer for you, more reliable, more easily reached, more stable, than Old England? Is not Boston a better consumer for the people of the United States than London, New York than Liverpool, Pittsburgh than Manchester, Cincinnati than Birmingham?

New England buys of you for all her wants; Old England takes not a pound or a bushel from you except what she must have and can not get elsewhere. Let us contrast this home market of New England with the foreign market of Old England. In 1880 New England consumed

540,000,000 pounds of cotton, at 11.61 cents a pound, which in value then amounted to $62,695,000, 20 per cent. greater than the per capita value of all our domestic exports to the United Kingdom, and this was only New England's contribution to the Southern producers of cotton. She sends at least $70,000,000 to the West and Northwest for her food supplies. She sends to the wool-growers of the Middle, Western, and Pacific States $40,000,000 annually for their fleeces. I repeat, is not this market worth preserving, ay, cherishing, and does it not make us long to have New England thrift, New England enterprise, and New England politics more generally distributed throughout all sections of the country?

You can destroy this valuable home market by such legislation as is proposed in this bill; you can diminish this demand for food, for cotton, for wool, for flax, and hemp produced in other sections of the country by following the delusive theories of our friends on the other side of the House; you can diminish the capacity of the operatives to buy of you by diminishing their wages; you can drive them from the cotton and woolen factories to the farms; they will then drift to the West and Northwest, not to engage in manufacture, but in a great measure to become tillers of the soil, and instead of being as they are now, and as they will be under a proper tariff system, your consumers, they become your competitors. They go from the ranks of consumers to the ranks of producers; diminish the consumers and increase the producers. The foreign market for agricultural products is one of the delusions of free trade. If it ever had any real substance as against a good home market that has long since disappeared. The chairman of the Ways and Means Committee says to the Western farmer, "Let New England go. Pass her by and go to Old England." Well, that is about as practical as the Democratic party ordinarily is.

Why, it was only a little while ago that I remember to have heard the gentleman from Arkansas (Mr. Dunn), a prominent member of this House and chairman of one of its leading committees, say what I now read from the *Record*:

"The wheat producer of the Northwest is standing face to face with the wheat producer of India. A few years ago India shipped 40,000 bushels of wheat. Last year (1885) she put into the market 40,000,000 bushels. Can you protect the Northwest farmer against that labor? India can put wheat down in the markets of consumption in Europe cheaper than we can transport it from the fields of production to the markets of consumption; that is to say, India can produce and market her wheat in Europe for what it costs the farmer of the Northwest to transport his to the market of consumption, without allowing him for the cost of production. In other words, the transportation of wheat costs the American farmer as much as both transportation and production cost the India farmer."

In the face of a statement like this, from such high Democratic authority, how, I ask, is the wheat of the American farmer to reach the European market with any profit to our producers? And yet it is to this kind of competition the chairman of the Ways and Means Committee invites the American farmer. Do the farmers want such a market with such a competition? What their answer will be no man can doubt. They reject with indignation and scorn the chairman's invitation. The home market is the best, besides being the safest. It has got the most money to spend, and spends the most. It consumes the most; it is therefore the most profitable.

The masses of our people live better than any people in the world. Great Britain only buys our food products when she has not enough of her own and can reach no other supply. This market, therefore, is fitful and fluctuating, and can not be relied upon as we can rely upon our own consumers. The foreign market under a revenue tariff for agricultural products has not been encouraging in our own experience in the past. It promises less under such a system in the future.

READING NO. 8

Reed's Speech on the Mills Tariff, 1888 *

Thomas B. Reed was a Republican Congressman from Maine, who in his long career in the House (1877–1899) won fame as an unusually able exponent of protection. As the tyrannical Speaker of the House (1889–1891, 1895–1899), he was called "Czar Reed." His May 19, 1888 speech presents the economic arguments for a protective tariff that go back to Henry C. Carey, Clay, and Hamilton, yet have an incisiveness, wit, and skill all his own. In his day he earned the description, the mentor of the Republicans and the tormentor of the Democrats.

The system we believe in is called protection, and is founded upon the doctrine that a great nation like ours, having all varieties of climate and soil, will be richer, more independent, and more thrifty, and that its people will be better fitted to enjoy the comforts and luxuries of peace, and

* *Congressional Record,* 50th Congress, 1st Session, Vol. XIX, pp. 4442–4444.

better situated to endure the calamities of war, if its own people supply its own wants.

I do not purpose to defend protection. Its vast growth within the last quarter of a century defends it better even than eloquent orations. It was born with the Republic. It is the faith and practice of every civilized nation under the sun save one. It has survived the assaults of all the professors of the "dismal science" called political economy. It has stood up against all the half knowledge of learned men who never had sense enough to transmute their learning into wisdom.

On the face of the earth to-day there are but two sets of people who believe in free trade, whether pure and simple or disguised as revenue reform, and those two are the masked majority of the Committee on Ways and Means and their followers, and the United Kingdom of Great Britain and Ireland, with Ireland suppressed.

Russia, the granary of Europe, has abandoned free trade, with the striking result that whereas, in 1876, before the duties were raised, she bought eight million hundred-weight of British metals and paid therefor thirty million of dollars (eight for thirty), she got the same quantity in 1884 and paid only seventeen million for it (eight for seventeen). Three dollars and seventy-five cents per hundred-weight before tariff, and $2.12½ after. Austria, Germany, Italy, Mexico, and the Dominion of Canada, that child of Britain herself, have all joined the army of protection. It is the instinct of humanity against the assumptions of the book men. It is the wisdom of the race against the wisdom of the few.

Perhaps the best argument I can make for protection is to state what it is and the principles on which it is founded.

Man derives his greatest power from his association with other men, his union with his fellows. Whoever considers the human being as a creature alone, by himself, isolated and separated, and tries to comprehend mankind by mathematically adding these atoms together, has utterly failed to comprehend the human race and its tremendous mission.

Sixty millions even of such creatures without association are only so many beasts that perish. But sixty millions of men welded together by national brotherhood, each supporting, sustaining, and buttressing the other, are the sure conquerors of all those mighty powers of nature which alone constitute the wealth of this world. The great blunder of the Herr Professor of political economy is that he treats human beings as if every man were so many foot-pounds, such and such a fraction of a horse-power. All the soul of man he leaves out.

Think for a moment of the foundation principles involved in this question, which I now ask, Where does wealth come from? It comes from the power of man to let loose and yet guide those elemental forces the energy of which is infinite. It comes from the power of man to force the earth to give her increase, to hold in the bellying sail the passing breeze, to harness the tumbling waterfall, to dam up the great rivers, to put bits in the teeth of the lightning. Foot-pounds and fractions of a horse-power will never do this. It takes brains and the union of foot-pounds and fractions of a horse-power working harmoniously together.

To grasp the full powers of nature, to reap the richest wealth of the world, we must utilize the full power of man, not merely muscles and brains, but those intangible qualities which we call energy, vigor, ambition, confidence, and courage. Have you never remarked the wonderful difference between a sleepy country village, lying lazily alongside an unused waterfall, where more than half the energy of the people was lost for lack of the kind of work they wanted to do; where, whenever three men met together in the road, the rest looked out of the windows, idly wondering what the riot was about, and that same village after the banks were lined with workshops and the air was noisy with the whirr of the spindles, and every man was so eager to work that there never seemed hours enough in the day to tear from the powers of nature their imprisoned richness?

If you have, you have also seen the contrast between men left to themselves, so many foot-pounds and fractions of a horse-power, and men incited by hope, spurred on by ambition, and lighted on their way by the confidence of success.

For a nation to get out of itself or out of the earth all the wealth there is in both, it is not necessary for the nation to buy cheap or sell dear. That concerns individuals alone. What concerns the nation is how to utilize all the work there is in men, both of muscle and brain, of body and of soul, in the great enterprise of setting in motion the ever-gratuitous forces of nature.

How shall you get out of the people of a nation their full powers? Right here is precisely the dividing line. The let-alone school say leave individual man to his own devices. The protectionist school say let us stimulate combined and aggregated man to united endeavor. What made men work before governments? Was it an intellectual belief that work was good for the muscles? Not the least in the world. It was hunger and desire. Hunger has ceased to play the greater part, but desire will never pass away.

In the ever-growing desire of mankind for new worlds of comfort and luxury to conquer is the blazing promise of the unhasting, unresting march of civilization. In that column of march the whole nation must be ranged. Association is the instinct of humanity which grows with its growth. First the family, then the tribe, and then the nation. The race will come by and by. Faithfulness to each in their order is the true route to the next.

Here in the United States are 60,000,000 people with all the varied characters their numbers indicate. Some have faculties fit for farming, some for the management of machinery, some for invention. The problem before you is what system will get from all these creatures, so different from each other, the maximum of work and wealth and wisdom.

I have already said that the great incentive, the motive power of man, is desire. That is the magnet which draws him, but, like all other magnets, it must be put near the armature. The quenching of desire must not cost too much. The pathway to its accomplishment must not be too rugged. If you say to him who loves invention and hates farming, your path and your desire lies through the cultivation of the fields, he will say this thing costs too much. If you say to the man who loves the fields, your way must be through the workshop, you bar his progress.

There is only one way to get the best work out of men, and that is to give each the work he can do best. You can only accomplish this by diversifying industry. To diversify industry completely in a country such as ours, there is but one way given under Heaven among men. To enable the American people themselves to supply all their wants, you must give and assure to the American people the American markets. What does this phrase mean in practical life? It means that we, the nation, say to capital, "Embark yourself in the manufacture of such and such articles, and you shall have a market to the extent of the wants of the American people."

Capital then says to labor, "Go with me into this new field, all of you who like this work best, and we will share the results." Then begins a new industry. Multiply this by hundreds and you have a community where every man honestly minded will get what on the whole suits him best, and the nation will get the greatest amount of work from the greatest number.

To this system, so far sketched, no human being can find reasonable objections. But it is averred that there are some drawbacks. It is alleged that the people who are in the older industries—those which establish themselves without law—have to pay higher prices for the articles so manufactured, and that the employment in new industries is all at their expense. This does not in the least touch upon the utilization of human energy and natural energy which would otherwise run to waste. It does not touch upon the question of the divine right of those who are adapted to the older industries to reap alone the riches of the earth.

So seemingly unjust has this last appeared in one instance, that of the land-owner, that a prominent free-trader, Mr. Henry George, who will vote next election for revenue reform, has proposed to take away from land more or less of its value to the owner. That I do not agree to. I make no reclamations on that account.

I meet the question squarely and asseverate that protection does not raise prices. The opposite statement and the argument which backs it up, I purpose to state fairly, for we now come to the famous revenue-reform dilemma. You tell us, they say, that protection is for the purpose of enhancing prices to enable high wages to be paid, and yet you say that protection lowers prices. This is flat contradiction. So it is as you state it. But your statement, like all revenue-reform statements, flourishes only by assumption.

In order to make yourself clear, you have utterly omitted the element of time. You assume that we say that both our statements of higher prices for higher wages and lower prices for consumers are for the same instant of time. Not so. When you begin there are higher prices for higher wages, but when you establish your manufactories, at once the universal law of competition begins to work. The manufactories abroad, urged upon by the lower prices which the tariff forces them to offer in order to compete with us, cause every element of economy in manufacture to be set in motion. Every intellect is put to work to devise new machinery which will produce at lower cost, to seek out new methods of utilizing waste, to consolidation of effort to lessen general expenses, and the thousand and one devices every year invented to get more work out of the powers of nature.

At home the same causes are at work, and with redoubled energy, because on account of higher wages there are greater inducements to substitute labor-saving devices for costly labor. And this colossal struggle between two great empires of industry, the foreign and the domestic, results everywhere in the cheapness of commodities, in which progress of cheapness the world has marched on in one unbroken undeviating line, until to-day the citizens of the United States, the sovereigns of to-day, as we call them in moments of patriotic exaltation, the poorest citizens have for the commonest necessities of life the luxuries of the sovereigns of old days.

That lower prices will come at once, we have never said. That they will come and grow lower and lower so that in the series of years which make up a man's life all he needs will cost him less than under revenue reform we asseverate and maintain, and all history is behind our asseverations.

But would not all this take place under free trade; would not English manufactures, supplying all the world, have grown thus cheaper by themselves? Let me answer this question by two others. Do you believe in the lowering of prices by competition? Of course you do. Do you believe that the great production of $7,000,000,000 of manufactures have not entered into competition with those of England? You know that they have been the great power which has forced English prices down.

Do you want an example of to-day? In 1883 the importers were eager to prevent the increase of the tariff on pottery. I know it, because a gentleman was here earnestly urging me not to consent to the increase. Only three years afterwards he acknowledged to me that the foreign manufacturers were obliged, in the face of the great increase of product, both in quantity and quality, to cut their prices so as to pay even more than the tariff tax. Perhaps some revenue reformer may ask me, on the strength of this example, how our raising tariff helped manufacturers here if the foreign manufacturer lowered his prices.

I am glad to answer that question, for it answers many others. Before the raise, we were on pottery fighting foreigners gorged with profits and flushed with the spoils of our markets. To-day we are fighting them on even terms, or would have been, but for the package clause. Their profits would be going into our treasury, not into their pockets, and between them and us would still be going on that equal contest for cheaper and cheaper manufactures which, without lowering wages, is giving us every day lower prices and an ever-widening manufacture.

Perhaps some gentleman will say to me that this is all a dream; that the very fact of a barrier raised by our tariff prevents competition. Every manufacturer knows better. England must work or starve. She has piled up her capital, and if she can not get large profits she will take small. . . .

People say that these tariff discussions are dull and tiresome, but there are always delightful things in them. I don't know when I have bathed my weary soul in such a reverie of bliss as I did while the chairman, by the aid of Edward Atkinson, and the great doctrine of labor-cost, was explaining that the high wages of our work people were not an obstacle, but the very reason itself why the whole circumambient atmosphere should be flooded with the pauper sunshine of Europe.

The more you pay the workman the less the "labor-cost." The more you give your shoemaker the less the shoes cost. The former, he explained, is the cause of the latter. Less "labor-cost" is produced by higher wages. The higher the wages the lower the labor-cost. No limitation, of course, was set to so divine a principle. The only limit to lowness of "labor-cost" is our generosity to the laboring man. Give infinite dollars to the laboring man and things will cost nothing. Surely no frantic orator on labor day, the session before election, ever offered to the horny-handed sons of toil such a sweet boon as the great doctrine of "labor-cost."

But softly, my friends. This is not the millennium. It is not the Heavenly Jerusalem newly descended. It is only the old Jerusalem of the Jews, sacred but ancient. It is the old, old fact that the smarter the workman the better the pay, and the manufacturer makes more out of him besides. It is not an absolute fact. It is a relative one. It only means that a better workman in the same country can get better pay than a poor one, and is worth it and a percentage over. It is a valuable fact, but it is an old one, and if Mr. Atkinson, reputed an able man, ever gave such an extension to that idea as his pupil has he must be one of those men who discover a full-fledged planet with moons whenever an asteroid comes within his field of vision.

But the pleasure given by the great doctrine of "labor-cost" is soon lost in the admiration of the cool courage of what follows. Stimulated by the theory of "labor-cost," the chairman ordered an investigation into the oldest manufactories in New England. What was the result? Why, constantly increasing wages and constantly decreasing cost; the two very things his side has sneered at since tariff debates were invented, higher wages for the worker and lower prices for the consumer.

What industries did he select? Cotton sheetings and cotton prints; cotton goods, the very articles, and perhaps the only articles which have had continuous, unbroken, effective protection since 1824. He selects industries which, under all tariffs, have had sixty-four years of solid protection, shows by them higher wages for labor and lower prices for consumers, then boldly wraps the flag of labor-cost about him and proclaims to a wondering world that tariff has nothing to do with wages. I wonder what Edward Atkinson thought of his new disciple at that moment.

Oh, no; tariffs have nothing to do with wages. It is coal and steam and machinery. But what set up the machinery? What caused the cotton factory to be built? Why, the tariff. So, then, the tariff built the mill, set up the machinery, the machinery increased the wages, but the tariff did not. Is not that very much like saying your father was your progenitor, but your grandfather wasn't. How could you improve machinery you didn't have? How could you increase the efficiency of machinery that didn't exist?

READING NO. 9

Wilson's Tariff Reform Message of 1913 *

When Woodrow Wilson won the election of 1912, he set down as the first item on his legislative agenda the destruction of the system of high tariff pro-

* Congressional Record, 63rd Congress, 1st Session, Vol. 50, p. 130.

tection that the Republican party had carefully developed since 1861. On March 4, 1913, the day he was inaugurated, Wilson called a special session of Congress. A month later, on April 8, he appeared in person before both houses of Congress and delivered his special message asking for the immediate revision of the Payne-Aldrich tariff. For over a century no President had spoken directly to the national legislature. By so doing Wilson dramatized his personal interest in tariff reform and spurred Congress to achieve his goal, not of free trade, but of a moderate protection based on the principle of "effective competition."

Gentlemen of the Congress:

I am very glad indeed to have this opportunity to address the two Houses directly and to verify for myself the impression that the President of the United States is a person, not a mere department of the Government hailing Congress from some isolated island of jealous power, sending messages, not speaking naturally and with his own voice—that he is a human being trying to co-operate with other human beings in a common service. After this pleasant experience I shall feel quite normal in all our dealings with one another.

I have called the Congress together in extraordinary session because a duty was laid upon the party now in power at the recent elections which it ought to perform promptly, in order that the burden carried by the people under existing law may be lightened as soon as possible, and in order, also, that the business interests of the country may not be kept too long in suspense as to what the fiscal changes are to be to which they will be required to adjust themselves. It is clear to the whole country that the tariff duties must be altered. They must be changed to meet the radical alteration in the conditions of our economic life which the country has witnessed within the last generation. While the whole face and method of our industrial and commercial life were being changed beyond recognition the tariff schedules have remained what they were before the change began, or have moved in the direction they were given when no large circumstance of our industrial development was what it is to-day. Our task is to square them with the actual facts. The sooner that is done the sooner we shall escape from suffering from the facts and the sooner our men of business will be free to thrive by the law of nature—the nature of free business—instead of by the law of legislation and artificial arrangement.

We have seen tariff legislation wander very far afield in our day—very far indeed from the field in which our prosperity might have had a normal growth and stimulation. No one who looks the facts squarely in the face or knows anything that lies beneath the surface of action can fail to perceive the principles upon which recent tariff legislation has been based. We long ago passed beyond the modest notion of "protecting" the industries of the country and moved boldly forward to the idea that they were entitled to the direct patronage of the Government. For a long time—a time so long that the men now active in public policy hardly remember the conditions that preceded it—we have sought in our tariff schedules to give each group of manufacturers or producers what they themselves thought that they needed in order to maintain a practically exclusive market as against the rest of the world. Consciously or unconsciously, we have built up a set of privileges and exemptions from competition behind which it was easy by any, even the crudest, forms of combination to organize monopoly; until at last nothing is normal, nothing is obliged to stand the tests of efficiency and economy, in our world of big business, but everything thrives by concerted arrangement. Only new principles of action will save us from a final hard crystallization of monopoly and a complete loss of the influences that quicken enterprise and keep independent energy alive.

It is plain what those principles must be. We must abolish everything that bears even the semblance of privilege or of any kind of artificial advantage, and put our business men and producers under the stimulation of a constant necessity to be efficient, economical, and enterprising, masters of competitive supremacy, better workers and merchants than any in the world. Aside from the duties laid upon articles which we do not, and probably can not, produce, therefore, and the duties laid upon luxuries and merely for the sake of the revenues they yield, the object of the tariff duties henceforth laid must be effective competition, the whetting of American wits by contest with the wits of the rest of the world.

It would be unwise to move toward this end headlong, with reckless haste, or with strokes that cut at the very roots of what has grown up amongst us by long process and at our own invitation. It does not alter a thing to upset it and break it and deprive it of a chance to change. It destroys it. We must make changes in our fiscal laws, in our fiscal system, whose object is development, a more free and wholesome development, not revolution or upset or confusion. We must build up trade, especially foreign trade. We need the outlet and the enlarged field of energy more than we ever did before. We must build up industry as well, and must adopt freedom in the place of artificial stimulation only so far as it will build, not pull down. In dealing with the tariff the method by which this may be done will be a matter of judgment exercised item by item. To some not accustomed to the excitements and responsibilities of greater freedom our methods may in some respects and at some points seem heroic but remedies may be heroic and yet be remedies. It is our business to make sure that they are genuine remedies. Our object is clear. If our motive is above just challenge and only an occasional error of judgment is chargeable against us, we shall be fortunate.

We are called upon to render the country a great service in more matters than one. Our responsibility should be met and our methods should be thorough, as thorough as moderate and well considered, based upon the facts as they are, and not worked out as if we were beginners. We are to deal with the facts of our own day, with the facts of no other and to make laws which square with those facts. It is best, indeed it is necessary, to begin with the tariff. I will urge nothing upon you now at the opening of your session which can obscure that first object or divert our energies from that clearly defined duty. At a later time I may take the liberty of calling your attention to reforms which should press close upon the heels of the tariff changes, if not accompany them, of which the chief is the reform of our banking and currency laws; but just now I refrain. For the present, I put these matters on one side and think only of this one thing —of the changes in our fiscal system which may best serve to open once more the free channels of prosperity to a great people whom we would serve to the utmost and throughout both rank and file.

I sincerely thank you for your courtesy.

READING NO. **10**

The Protests of Economists Against the Hawley-Smoot Tariff *

Hoover's 1928 election-campaign promises to the farmers for a limited upward revision of the tariff soon became the basis for industrial tariff lobbyists' inducing Congress, under the stress of the 1929 Great Depression, to pass the highest tariff law in American history. A group of 1,028 American economists asked Congress and President Hoover to withhold their approval from the Hawley-Smoot Tariff Act. The originators and first signers of this petition included Professors Paul Douglas of Chicago, Irving Fisher of Yale, Frank Graham of Princeton, and Frank W. Taussig of Harvard. But Congress and Hoover disregarded the devastatingly correct forecast of the economists. When Hoover signed the new law, he said that nothing would so delay business recovery as continued agitation against the tariff. International retaliation on a massive scale soon disproved his assertion.

* *New York Times*, May 5, 1930.

The undersigned American economists and teachers of economics strongly urge that any measure which provides for a general upward revision of tariff rates be denied passage by Congress, or if passed, be vetoed by the President.

We are convinced that increased restrictive duties would be a mistake. They would operate, in general, to increase the prices which domestic consumers would have to pay. By raising prices they would encourage concerns with higher costs to undertake production, thus compelling the consumer to subsidize waste and inefficiency in industry.

At the same time they would force him to pay higher rates of profit to established firms which enjoyed lower production costs. A higher level of duties, such as is contemplated by the Smoot-Hawley bill, would therefore raise the cost of living and injure the great majority of our citizens.

Few people could hope to gain from such a change. Miners, construction, transportation, and public utility workers, professional people and those employed in banks, hotels, newspaper offices, in the wholesale and retail trades and scores of other occupations would clearly lose, since they produce no products which could be specially favored by tariff barriers.

The vast majority of farmers would also lose. Their cotton, pork, lard and wheat are export crops and are sold in the world market. They have no important competition in the home market. They cannot benefit, therefore, from any tariff which is imposed upon the basic commodities which they produce.

They would lose through the increased duties on manufactured goods, however, and in a double fashion. First, as consumers they would have to pay still higher prices for the products, made of textiles, chemicals, iron and steel, which they buy. Second, as producers their ability to sell their products would be further restricted by the barriers placed in the way of foreigners who wished to sell manufactured goods to us.

Our export trade, in general, would suffer. Countries cannot permanently buy from us unless they are permitted to sell to us, and the more we restrict the importation of goods from them by means of even higher tariffs, the more we reduce the possibility of our exporting to them.

This applies to such exporting industries as copper, automobiles, agricultural machinery, typewriters and the like fully as much as it does to farming. The difficulties of these industries are likely to be increased still further if we pass a higher tariff.

There are already many evidences that such action would inevitably provoke other countries to pay us back in kind by levying retaliatory duties against our goods. There are few more ironical spectacles than that of the American Government as it seeks, on the one hand, to promote exports through the activity of the Bureau of Foreign and Domestic

Commerce, while, on the other hand, by increasing tariffs it makes exportation even more difficult.

We do not believe that American manufacturers, in general, need higher tariffs. The report of the President's Committee on Recent Economic Changes has shown that industrial efficiency has increased, that costs have fallen, that profits have grown with amazing rapidity since the end of the World War. Already our factories supply our people with over 96% of the manufactured goods which they consume, and our own producers look to foreign markets to absorb the increasing output of their machines.

Further barriers to trade will serve them not well, but ill.

Many of our citizens have invested their money in foreign enterprises. The Department of Commerce has estimated that such investments, entirely aside from the war debts, amounted to between $12,555,000,000 and $14,555,000,000 on January 1, 1929. These investors, too, would suffer if restrictive duties were to be increased, since such action would make it still more difficult for their foreign debtors to pay them the interest due them.

America is now facing the problem of unemployment. The proponents of higher tariffs claim that an increase in rates will give work to the idle. This is not true. We cannot increase employment by restrictive trade. American industry, in the present crisis, might well be spared the burden of adjusting itself to higher schedules of duties.

Finally, we would urge our government to consider the bitterness which a policy of higher tariffs would inevitably inject into our international relations. The United States was ably represented at the world economic conference which was held under the auspices of the League of Nations in 1927. This conference adopted a resolution announcing that "the time has come to put an end to the increase in tariffs and to move in the opposite direction."

The higher duties proposed in our pending legislation violate the spirit of this agreement and plainly invite other nations to compete with us in raising further barriers to trade. A tariff wall does not furnish good soil for the growth of world peace.

READING NO. 11

Roosevelt's Request for Authority to Enter into Reciprocal Trade Agreements, March 2, 1934*

In the 1932 election the Democratic national platform had stated its advocacy for "reciprocal trade agreements with other nations." After his smashing victory against the Republicans, President Roosevelt was so busy with anti-Depression legislation that only in November, 1933, did he get the drafting of a new tariff bill under way. On March 2, 1934, he sent Congress a special message asking for authority to enter into executive commercial agreements with foreign nations for the revival of world trade.

To the Congress:

I am requesting the Congress to authorize the Executive to enter into executive commercial agreements with foreign Nations; and in pursuance thereof, within carefully guarded limits, to modify existing duties and import restrictions in such a way as will benefit American agriculture and industry. This action seems opportune and necessary at this time for several reasons.

First, world trade has declined with startling rapidity. Measured in terms of the volume of goods in 1933, it has been reduced to approximately 70 percent of its 1929 volume; measured in terms of dollars, it has fallen to 35 percent. The drop in the foreign trade of the United States has been even sharper. Our exports in 1933 were but 52 percent of the 1929 volume, and 32 percent of the 1929 value.

This has meant idle hands, still machines, ships tied to their docks, despairing farm households, and hungry industrial families. It has made infinitely more difficult the planning for economic readjustment in which the Government is now engaged.

You and I know that the world does not stand still; that trade movements and relations once interrupted can with the utmost difficulty be restored; that even in tranquil and prosperous times there is a constant shifting of trade channels.

How much greater, how much more violent is the shifting in these

* *House Doc. No. 273*, 73rd Congress, 2nd Session.

times of change and of stress is clear from the record of current history. Every Nation must at all times be in a position quickly to adjust its taxes and tariffs to meet sudden changes and avoid severe fluctuations in both its exports and its imports.

You and I know, too, that it is important that the country possess within its borders a necessary diversity and balance to maintain a rounded national life, that it must sustain activities vital to national defense and that such interests cannot be sacrificed for passing advantage. Equally clear is the fact that a full and permanent domestic recovery depends in part upon a revived and strengthened international trade and that American exports cannot be permanently increased without a corresponding increase in imports.

Second, other Governments are to an ever-increasing extent winning their share of international trade by negotiated reciprocal trade agreements. If American agricultural and industrial interests are to retain their deserved place in this trade, the American Government must be in a position to bargain for that place with other Governments by rapid and decisive negotiation based upon a carefully considered program, and to grant with discernment corresponding opportunities in the American market for foreign products supplementary to our own.

If the American Government is not in a position to make fair offers for fair opportunities, its trade will be superseded. If it is not in a position at a given moment rapidly to alter the terms on which it is willing to deal with other countries, it cannot adequately protect its trade against discriminations and against bargains injurious to its interests. Furthermore a promise to which prompt effect cannot be given is not an inducement which can pass current at par in commercial negotiations.

For this reason, any smaller degree of authority in the hands of the Executive would be ineffective. The executive branches of virtually all other important trading countries already possess some such power.

I would emphasize that quick results are not to be expected. The successful building up of trade without injury to American producers depends upon a cautious and gradual evolution of plans.

The disposition of other countries to grant an improved place to American products should be carefully sounded and considered; upon the attitude of each must somewhat depend our future course of action. With countries which are unwilling to abandon purely restrictive national programs, or to make concessions toward the reestablishment of international trade, no headway will be possible.

The exercise of the authority which I propose must be carefully weighed in the light of the latest information so as to give assurance that no sound and important American interest will be injuriously disturbed. The adjustment of our foreign trade relations must rest on the premise of undertaking to benefit and not to injure such interests. In a time of difficulty and unemployment such as this, the highest consideration of the position of the different branches of American production is required.

From the policy of reciprocal negotiation which is in prospect, I hope in time that definite gains will result to American agriculture and industry.

Important branches of our agriculture, such as cotton, tobacco, hog products, rice, cereal and fruit-raising, and those branches of American industry whose mass production methods have led the world, will find expanded opportunities and productive capacity in foreign markets, and will thereby be spared in part, at least, the heartbreaking readjustments that must be necessary if the shrinkage of American foreign commerce remains permanent.

A resumption of international trade cannot but improve the general situation of other countries, and thus increase their purchasing power. Let us well remember that this in turn spells increased opportunity for American sales.

Legislation such as this is an essential step in the program of national economic recovery which the Congress has elaborated during the past year. It is part of an emergency program necessitated by the economic crisis through which we are passing. It should provide that the trade agreements shall be terminable within a period not to exceed three years; a shorter period probably would not suffice for putting the program into effect. In its execution, the Executive must, of course, pay due heed to the requirements of other branches of our recovery program, such as the National Industrial Recovery Act.

I hope for early action. The many immediate situations in the field of international trade that today await our attention can thus be met effectively and with the least possible delay.

READING NO. 12

Reciprocal Trade Agreements Act of June 12, 1934 *

Three months after President Roosevelt asked Congress for power to consummate reciprocal-trade agreements, Congress passed the bill he had initi-

* U. S. *Statutes at Large,* Vol. 48, pp. 943–945.

*ated, and he signed it on the evening of June 12, 1934, with the joyful ap-
proval of Cordell Hull and the other internationalists in the New Deal. The
new law instituted a revolution in tariff making and was renewed periodically, with varying years of operation until it was replaced by the Trade Expansion Act of 1962.*

*Be it enacted by the Senate and House of Representatives of the United
States of America in Congress assembled,* That the Tariff Act of 1930 is
amended by adding at the end of title III the following:

"PART III—PROMOTION OF FOREIGN TRADE

"Sec. 350. (a) For the purpose of expanding foreign markets for the
products of the United States (as a means of assisting in the present
emergency in restoring the American standard of living, in overcoming
domestic unemployment and the present economic depression, in increasing the purchasing power of the American public, and in establishing and maintaining a better relationship among various branches of
American agriculture, industry, mining, and commerce) by regulating
the admission of foreign goods into the United States in accordance with
the characteristics and needs of various branches of American production so that foreign markets will be made available to those branches of
American production which require and are capable of developing such
outlets by affording corresponding market opportunities for foreign
products in the United States, the President, whenever he finds as a fact
that any existing duties or other import restrictions of the United States
or any foreign country are unduly burdening and restricting the foreign
trade of the United States and that the purpose above declared will be
promoted by the means hereinafter specified, is authorized from time to
time—

"(1) To enter into foreign trade agreements with foreign governments
or instrumentalities thereof; and

"(2) To proclaim such modifications of existing duties and other import restrictions, or such additional import restrictions, or such continuance, and for such minimum periods, of existing customs or excise
treatment of any article covered by foreign trade agreements, as are required or appropriate to carry out any foreign trade agreement that the
President has entered into hereunder. No proclamation shall be made increasing or decreasing by more than 50 per centum any existing rate of
duty or transferring any article between the dutiable and free lists. The
proclaimed duties and other import restrictions shall apply to articles the

growth, produce, or manufacture of all foreign countries, whether imported directly, or indirectly: *Provided,* That the President may suspend the application to articles the growth, produce, or manufacture of any country because of its discriminatory treatment of American commerce or because of other acts or policies which in his opinion tend to defeat the purposes set forth in this section; and the proclaimed duties and other import restrictions shall be in effect from and after such time as is specified in the proclamation. The President may at any time terminate any such proclamation in whole or in part.

"(b) Nothing in this section shall be construed to prevent the application, with respect to rates of duty established under this section pursuant to agreements with countries other than Cuba, of the provisions of the treaty of commercial reciprocity concluded between the United States and the Republic of Cuba on December 11, 1902, or to preclude giving effect to an exclusive agreement with Cuba concluded under this section, modifying the existing preferential customs treatment of any article the growth, produce, or manufacture of Cuba: *Provided,* That the duties payable on such an article shall in no case be increased or decreased by more than 50 per centum of the duties now payable thereon.

"(c) As used in this section, the term 'duties and other import restrictions' includes (1) rate and form of import duties and classification of articles, and (2) limitations, prohibitions, charges, and exactions other than duties, imposed on importation or imposed for the regulation of imports."

Sec. 2. (a) Subparagraph (d) of paragraph 369, the last sentence of paragraph 1402, and the provisos to paragraphs 371, 401, 1650, 1687, and 1803 (1) of the Tariff Act of 1930 are repealed. The provisions of sections 336 and 516 (b) of the Tariff Act of 1930 shall not apply to any article with respect to the importation of which into the United States a foreign trade agreement has been concluded pursuant to this Act, or to any provision of any such agreement. The third paragraph of section 311 of the Tariff Act of 1930 shall apply to any agreement concluded pursuant to this Act to the extent only that such agreement assures to the United States a rate of duty on wheat flour produced in the United States which is preferential in respect to the lowest rate of duty imposed by the country with which such agreement has been concluded on like flour produced in any other country; and upon the withdrawal of wheat flour from bonded manufacturing warehouses for exportation to the country with which such agreement has been concluded, there shall be levied, collected, and paid on the imported wheat used, a duty equal to the amount of such assured preference.

(b) Every foreign trade agreement concluded pursuant to this Act shall be subject to termination, upon due notice to the foreign government concerned, at the end of not more than three years from the date on which the agreement comes into force, and, if not then terminated, shall be subject to termination thereafter upon not more than six months' notice.

(c) The authority of the President to enter into foreign trade agreements under section 1 of this Act shall terminate on the expiration of three years from the date of the enactment of this Act.

Sec. 3. Nothing in this Act shall be construed to give any authority to cancel or reduce, in any manner, any of the indebtedness of any foreign country to the United States.

Sec. 4. Before any foreign trade agreement is concluded with any foreign government or instrumentality thereof under the provisions of this Act, reasonable public notice of the intention to negotiate an agreement with such government or instrumentality shall be given in order that any interested person may have an opportunity to present his views to the President, or to such agency as the President may designate, under such rules and regulations as the President may prescribe; and before concluding such agreement the President shall seek information and advice with respect thereto from the United States Tariff Commission, the Departments of State, Agriculture, and Commerce and from such other sources as he may deem appropriate.

Approved, June 12, 1934, 9:15 p.m.

READING NO. 13

Roosevelt's Request for Strengthening
the Trade Agreements Act,
March 26, 1945 *

In 1945 the Trade Agreements Act was being considered for renewal as American and Allied military operations against Nazi Germany and Japan were drawing to a close. Germany, Japan, and other highly industrialized countries that had been devastated by the war could not provide large-scale

* Congressional Record, 79th Congress, 1st Session, Vol. 91, Pt. 2, p. 2793.

exports for some time to come. But if the greatly expanded American econ-
omy were to avoid serious economic dislocations after the war, the United
States had to encourage an increase in American imports and exports. Presi-
dent Roosevelt realized the serious need for building an economically
healthy world in terms of world economic welfare and of future world peace.
His special message of March 26, 1945, was one of the last messages he sent
to Congress. Although he died on April 12, 1945, his successor to the Presi-
dency, Harry Truman, maintained the continuity of Roosevelt's foreign
trade policy.

To the Congress:

The coming victory of the United Nations means that they, and not their enemies, have power to establish the foundations of the future.

On April 25 their representatives will meet in San Francisco to draw up the Charter for the General Organization of the United Nations for security and peace. On this meeting and what comes after it our best hopes of a secure and peaceful world depend.

At the same time we know that we cannot succeed in building a peaceful world unless we build an economically healthy world. We are already taking decisive steps to this end. The efforts to improve currency relationships by the International Monetary Fund, to encourage international investments and make them more secure by the International Bank for Reconstruction and Development, to free the air for peaceful flight by the Chicago civil aviation arrangements, are part of that endeavor. So, too, is the proposed Food and Agriculture Organization of the United Nations.

We owe it to the vision of Secretary Hull that another of the essential measures we shall need to accomplish our objective has been tested and perfected by ten years of notably successful experience under his leadership. You are all familiar with the Trade Agreements Act which has been on the books since 1934 and which on three occasions, since that time, the Congress has renewed. The present law expires in June of this year. I recommend that it again be renewed so that the great work which Secretary Hull began may be continued.

Under him the reciprocal trade agreement program represented a sustained effort to reduce the barriers which the Nations of the world maintained against each other's trade. If the economic foundations of the peace are to be as secure as the political foundations, it is clear that this effort must be continued, vigorously and effectively.

Trade is fundamental to the prosperity of Nations, as it is of individuals. All of us earn our living by producing for some market, and all of us buy in some market most of the things we need. We do better, both as producers and consumers, when the markets upon which we depend are as large and rich and various and competitive as possible. The same is true of Nations.

We have not always understood this, in the United States or in any other country. We have tried often to protect some special interest by excluding strangers' goods from competition. In the long run everyone has suffered.

In 1934 this country started on a wiser course. We enacted into law a standing offer to reduce our tariff barriers against the goods of any country which would do the same for us. We have entered into reciprocal trade agreements with 28 countries. Each one of these agreements reduced some foreign barriers against the exports of this country, reduced our barriers against some products of the other party to the bargain, and gave protection against discrimination by guaranteeing most favored Nation treatment to us both. Each agreement increased the freedom of businessmen in both countries to buy and sell across national frontiers. The agreements have contributed to prosperity and good feeling here and in the other contracting countries.

The record of how trade agreements expand two-way trade is set forth in the 1943 report of the Committee on Ways and Means. This record shows that between 1934-35 and 1938-39 our exports to trade-agreement countries increased by 63 percent, while our shipments to non-agreement countries increased by only 32 percent; between these same periods, our imports from agreement countries increased by 22 percent as compared with only 12 percent from non-agreement countries. The disruptions and dislocations resulting from the war make later comparisons impossible. The record published in 1943 is, nevertheless, as valid today as it was then. We know, without any doubt, that trade agreements build trade and that they will do so after the war as they did before. All sections of our population—labor, farmers, businessmen have shared and will share in the benefits which increased trade brings.

Unfortunately, powerful forces operated against our efforts in the years after 1934. The most powerful were the steps of our present enemies to prepare themselves for the war they intended to let loose upon the world. They did this by subjecting every part of their business life, and especially their foreign trade, to the principle of guns instead of butter. In the face of the economic warfare which they waged, and the fear and countermeasures which their conduct caused in other countries, the success of Secretary Hull and his interdepartmental associates in scaling down trade barriers is all the more remarkable.

The coming total defeat of our enemies, and of the philosophy of conflict and aggression which they have represented, gives us a new chance and a better chance than we have ever had to bring about conditions under which the Nations of the world substitute cooperation and sound business principles for warfare in economic relations.

It is essential that we move forward aggressively and make the most of this opportunity. Business people in all countries want to know the rules under which the postwar world will operate. Industry today is working almost wholly on war orders but once the victory is won, immediate decisions will have to be made as to what lines of peacetime production look most profitable for either old or new plants. In this process of reconversion, decisions will necessarily be influenced by what businessmen foresee as Government policy. If it is clear that barriers to foreign trade are coming down all around the world, businessmen can and will direct production to the things that look most promising under those conditions. In that case a real and large and permanent expansion of international trade becomes possible and likely.

But if the signs are otherwise, if it appears that no further loosening of barriers can be expected, everyone will act very differently. In that event we shall see built up in all countries new vested interests in a system of restrictions, and we shall have lost our opportunity for the greater prosperity that expanding trade brings.

I have urged renewal of the Trade Agreements Act. In order to be fully effective the Act needs to be strengthened at one important point. You will remember that as passed in 1934 it authorized reductions in our tariff up to 50 percent of the rates then in effect. A good many of those reductions have been made, and those rates cannot be reduced further. Other reductions, smaller in amount, leave some remaining flexibility. In other cases, no reductions have been made at all, so that the full original authority remains.

You will realize that in negotiating agreements with any foreign country what we can accomplish depends on what both parties can contribute. In each of the agreements we have made, we have contributed reductions on products of special interest to the other party to the agreement, and we have obtained commensurate contributions in the form of concessions on products of special interest to us.

As to those countries, much of our original authority under the Act has been used up. We are left in this situation: Great Britain and Canada, our largest peacetime customers, still maintain certain high barriers against our exports, just as we still have high barriers against theirs. Under the Act as it now stands we do not have enough to offer these countries to serve as a basis for the further concessions we want from them. The same situation confronts us, although in a lesser degree, in the case of the other countries with whom we have already made agreements: these include France, The Netherlands, Belgium, Turkey, Sweden, Switzerland, and most of the American Republics.

I therefore recommend that the 50 percent limit be brought up to date by an amendment that relates it to the rates of 1945 instead of 1934. Then we shall have the powers necessary to deal with all our friends on the basis of the existing situation.

The bill which the Chairman of the Ways and Means Committee has introduced in the House of Representatives, H. R. 2652, would accomplish the objectives I have in mind, and has my support.

This legislation is essential to the substantial increase in our foreign trade which is necessary for full employment and improved standards of living. It means more exports and it also means more imports. For we cannot hope to maintain exports at the levels necessary to furnish the additional markets we need for agriculture and industry—income for the farmer and jobs for labor—unless we are willing to take payments in imports. We must recognize, too, that we are now a creditor country and are destined to be so for some time to come. Unless we make it possible for Americans to buy goods and services widely and readily in the markets of the world, it will be impossible for other countries to pay what is owed us. It is also important to remember that imports mean much more than goods for ultimate consumers. They mean jobs and income at every stage of the processing and distribution channels through which the imports flow to the consumer. By reducing our own tariff in conjunction with the reduction by other countries of their trade barriers, we create jobs, get more for our money, and improve the standard of living of every American consumer.

This is no longer a question on which Republicans and Democrats should divide. The logic of events and our clear and pressing national interest must override our old party controversies. They must also override our sectional and special interests. We must all come to see that what is good for the United States is good for each of us, in economic affairs just as much as in any others.

We all know that the reduction of Government-created barriers to trade will not solve all our trade problems. The field of trade has many fronts, and we must try to get forward on each of them as rapidly and as wisely as we can. I shall continue therefore to explore the possibility also of reaching a common understanding with the friendly Nations of the world on some of the other international trade problems that confront us. The appropriate committees of the Congress will be fully consulted as that work progresses. The purpose of the whole effort is to eliminate economic warfare, to make practical international cooperation effective on as many fronts as possible, and so to lay the economic basis for the secure and peaceful world we all desire.

When this Trade Agreements legislation and the other legislation I have recommended to this Congress is adopted, and when the general organization of the United Nations and their various special agencies, including one on trade, have been created and are functioning, we shall have made a good beginning at creating a workable kit of tools for the new world of international cooperation to which we all look forward. We shall be equipped to deal with the great overriding question of security, and with the crucial questions of money and exchange, international investment, trade, civil aviation, labor, and agriculture.

As I said in my message of February 12 on the Bretton Woods proposals:

> "The point in history at which we stand is full of promise and of danger. The world will either move toward unity and widely shared prosperity or it will move apart into necessarily competing economic blocs. We have a chance, we citizens of the United States, to use our influence in favor of a more united and cooperating world. Whether we do so will determine, as far as it is in our power, the kind of lives our grandchildren can live."

READING NO. **14**

Extension of Trade Agreements Act, July 5, 1945 *

After Congress received Roosevelt's March 26, 1945 message, the House Special Committee on Postwar Economic Policy and Planning recommended both a renewal of the Trade Agreements Act and a broadening of the President's authority under it. An extensive debate then took place on these proposals. Assistant Secretary of State Clayton testified before the House Ways and Means Committee on the importance of the program in expanding world trade through private enterprise as an alternative to trading by economic blocs and systems of government barter. He linked multi-lateral trading to the preservation of economic liberalism, capitalism, and world peace. Congress evidently responded to these arguments and in July, 1945, renewed the Trade Agreements Act for a three-year period to end in June, 1948.

* *U. S. Statutes at Large*, Vol. 59, p. 410.

An Act

To extend the authority of the President under section 350 of the Tariff Act of 1930, as amended, and for other purposes.

Be it enacted by the Senate and House of Representatives of the United States of America in Congress assembled, That the period during which the President is authorized to enter into foreign trade agreements under section 350 of the Tariff Act of 1930, as amended and extended, is hereby extended for a further period of three years from June 12, 1945.

Sec. 2. (a) The second sentence of subsection (a) (2) of such section, as amended (U.S.C., 1940 edition, Supp. IV, title 19, sec. 1351 (a) (2)), is amended to read as follows: "No proclamation shall be made increasing or decreasing by more than 50 per centum any rate of duty, however established, existing on January 1, 1945 (even though temporarily suspended by Act of Congress), or transferring any article between the dutiable and free lists."

(b) The proviso of subsection (b) of such section (U.S.C., 1940 edition, sec. 1351 (b)) is amended to read as follows: "*Provided,* That the duties on such an article shall in no case be increased or decreased by more than 50 per centum of the duties, however established, existing on January 1, 1945 (even though temporarily suspended by Act of Congress)."

Sec. 3. Such section 350 is further amended by adding at the end thereof a new subsection to read as follows:

"(d) (1) When any rate of duty has been increased or decreased for the duration of war or an emergency, by agreement or otherwise, any further increase or decrease shall be computed upon the basis of the post-war or post-emergency rate carried in such agreement or otherwise.

"(2) Where under a foreign trade agreement the United States has reserved the unqualified right to withdraw or modify, after the termination of war or an emergency, a rate on a specific commodity, the rate on such commodity to be considered as 'existing on January 1, 1945' for the purpose of this section shall be the rate which would have existed if the agreement had not been entered into.

"(3) No proclamation shall be made pursuant to this section for the purpose of carrying out any foreign trade agreement the proclamation with respect to which has been terminated in whole by the President prior to the date this subsection is enacted."

Sec. 4. Section 4 of the Act entitled "An Act to amend the Tariff Act of 1930", approved June 12, 1934 (U.S.C., 1940 edition, title 19, sec. 1354), relating to the governmental agencies from which the President shall seek information and advice with respect to foreign trade agreements, is amended by inserting after "Departments of State," the following: "War, Navy,."

READING NO. 15

General Agreement on Tariffs and Trade: Objectives and General Most-Favored-Nation Treatment*

In accordance with the procedures set up by the Trade Agreements Act of 1945 and the recommendations of a Preparatory Committee on tariff reductions that had met earlier in London, a general agreement on tariffs and trade was negotiated in Geneva during the period between April 10 and October 30, 1947. This conference was perhaps one of the longest and most complicated economic conferences in world history. But the results were more successful than many had anticipated. The General Agreement was put provisionally into effect on January 1, 1948, by the United States, Britain, France, and six other countries.

[Preamble]

The Governments of the Commonwealth of Australia, the Kingdom of Belgium, the United States of Brazil, Burma, Canada, Ceylon, the Republic of Chile, the Republic of China, the Republic of Cuba, the Czechoslovak Republic, the French Republic, India, Lebanon, the Grand Duchy of Luxemburg, the Kingdom of the Netherlands, New Zealand, the Kingdom of Norway, Pakistan, Southern Rhodesia, Syria, the Union of South Africa, the United Kingdom of Great Britain and Northern Ireland, and the United States of America:

Recognizing that their relations in the field of trade and economic endeavour should be conducted with a view to raising standards of living, ensuring full employment and a large and steadily growing volume of real income and effective demand, developing the full use of the resources of the world and expanding the production and exchange of goods;

---

* United Nations, *General Agreement on Tariffs and Trade,* 4 vols. (Lake Success, N. Y., 1947), Vol. I, pp. 1–3. For a compact analysis of GATT, see the *Department of State Bulletin,* November 30, 1947, Vol. 17, pp. 1042–1052.

Being desirous of contributing to these objectives by entering into reciprocal and mutually advantageous arrangements directed to the substantial reduction of tariffs and other barriers to trade and to the elimination of discriminatory treatment in international commerce;

Have through their Representatives agreed as follows:

PART I

ARTICLE I

General Most-Favoured-Nation Treatment

1. With respect to customs duties and charges of any kind imposed on
or in connection with importation or exportation or imposed on the international transfer of payments for imports or exports, and with respect
to the method of levying such duties and charges, and with respect to all
rules and formalities in connection with importation and exportation,
and with respect to all matters referred to in paragraphs 1 and 2 of Article III, any advantage, favour, privilege or immunity granted by any
contracting party to any product originating in or destined for any other
country shall be accorded immediately and unconditionally to the like
product originating in or destined for the territories of all other contracting parties.

2. The provisions of paragraph 1 of this Article shall not require the
elimination of any preferences in respect of import duties or charges
which do not exceed the levels provided for in paragraph 3 of this Article
and which fall within the following descriptions:

    (a) preferences in force exclusively between two or more of the terri-
        tories listed in Annex A, subject to the conditions set forth
        therein;

    (b) preferences in force exclusively between two or more territories
        which on July 1, 1939, were connected by common sovereignty or
        relations of protection or suzerainty and which are listed in An-
        nexes B, C and D, subject to the conditions set forth therein;

    (c) preferences in force exclusively between the United States of
        America and the Republic of Cuba;

    (d) preferences in force exclusively between neighbouring countries
        listed in Annexes E and F.

3. The margin of preference on any product in respect of which a preference is permitted under paragraph 2 of this Article but is not specifically set forth as a maximum margin of preference in the appropriate
Schedule annexed to this Agreement shall not exceed

    (a) in respect of duties or charges on any product described in such
        Schedule, the difference between the most-favoured-nation and

preferential rates provided for therein; if no preferential rate is provided for, the preferential rate shall for the purposes of this paragraph be taken to be that in force on April 10, 1947, and, if no most-favoured-nation rate is provided for, the margin shall not exceed the difference between the most-favoured-nation and preferential rates existing on April 10, 1947;

(b) in respect of duties or charges on any product not described in the appropriate Schedule, the difference between the most-favoured-nation and preferential rates existing on April 10, 1947.

In the case of the contracting parties named in Annex G, the date of April 10, 1947, referred to in subparagraphs (a) and (b) of this paragraph shall be replaced by the respective dates set forth in that Annex.

READING NO. 16

Truman's Executive Order for Escape Clauses from Concessions in Trade Agreements, February 25, 1947 *

In the congressional discussion preceding the 1945 extension of the Trade Agreements Act, considerable attention was given to adequate safeguards for American producers in the event of further tariff reductions during the postwar period. Administration spokesmen assured congressional committees that all future reciprocal trade agreements would contain comprehensive "escape clauses" similar to that in the 1942 trade agreement with Mexico. Shortly before the United States began tariff negotiations at Geneva, the President took such safeguarding action in Executive Order 9832, issued February 25, 1947. He also issued an accompanying Presidential statement that reaffirmed his faith in the "Cordell Hull Reciprocal Trade Agreements Program" and asserted that the new Executive Order did "not deviate from the traditional Cordell Hull principles."

By virtue of the authority vested in me by the Constitution and statutes, including section 332 of the Tariff Act of 1930 (46 Stat. 69S) and

* *Federal Register,* Vol. 12, pp. 1363–1365.

the Trade Agreements Act approved June 12, 1934, as amended (48 Stat. 943; 59 Stat. 410), in the interest of the foreign affairs functions of the United States and in order that the interests of the various branches of American production shall be effectively safeguarded in the administration of the trade-agreements program, it is hereby ordered as follows:

Part I

1. There shall be included in every trade agreement hereafter entered into under the authority of said act of June 12, 1934, as amended, a clause providing in effect that if, as a result of unforeseen developments and of the concession granted by the United States on any article in the trade agreement, such article is being imported in such increased quantities and under such conditions as to cause, or threaten, serious injury to domestic producers of like or similar articles, the United States shall be free to withdraw the concession, in whole or in part, or to modify it, to the extent and for such time as may be necessary to prevent such injury.

2. The United States Tariff Commission, upon the request of the President, upon its own motion, or upon application of any interested party when in the judgment of the Tariff Commission there is good and sufficient reason therefor, shall make an investigation to determine whether, as a result of unforeseen developments and of the concession granted on any article by the United States in a trade agreement containing such a clause, such article is being imported in such increased quantities and under such conditions as to cause or threaten serious injury to domestic producers of like or similar articles. Should the Tariff Commission find, as a result of its investigation, that such injury is being caused or threatened, the Tariff Commission shall recommend to the President, for his consideration in the light of the public interest, the withdrawal of the concession, in whole or in part, or the modification of the concession, to the extent and for such time as the Tariff Commission finds would be necessary to prevent such injury.

3. In the course of any investigation under the preceding paragraph, the Tariff Commission shall hold public hearings, giving reasonable public notice thereof, and shall afford reasonable opportunity for parties interested to be present, to produce evidence, and to be heard at such hearings. The procedure and rules and regulations for such investigations and hearings shall from time to time be prescribed by the Tariff Commission.

4. The Tariff Commission shall at all times keep informed concerning the operation and effect of provisions relating to duties or other import

restrictions of the United States contained in trade agreements heretofore or hereafter entered into by the President under the authority of said act of June 12, 1934, as amended. The Tariff Commission, at least once a year, shall submit to the President and to the Congress a factual report on the operation of the trade-agreements program.

PART II

5. An Interdepartmental Committee on Trade Agreements (hereinafter referred to as the Interdepartmental Committee) shall act as the agency through which the President shall, in accordance with section 4 of said act of June 12, 1934, as amended, seek information and advice before concluding a trade agreement. In order that the interests of American industry, labor, and farmers, and American military, financial, and foreign policy, shall be appropriately represented, the Interdepartmental Committee shall consist of a Commissioner of the Tariff Commission and of persons designated from their respective agencies by the Secretary of State, the Secretary of the Treasury, the Secretary of War, the Secretary of the Navy, the Secretary of Agriculture, the Secretary of Commerce, and the Secretary of Labor. The chairman of the Interdepartmental Committee shall be the representative from the Department of State. The Interdepartmental Committee may designate such subcommittees as it may deem necessary.

6. With respect to each dutiable import item which is considered by the Interdepartmental Committee for inclusion in a trade agreement, the Tariff Commission shall make an analysis of the facts relative to the production, trade, and consumption of the article involved, to the probable effect of granting a concession thereon, and to the competitive factors involved. Such analysis shall be submitted in digest form to the Interdepartmental Committee. The digests, excepting confidential material, shall be published by the Tariff Commission.

7. With respect to each export item which is considered by the Interdepartmental Committee for inclusion in a trade agreement, the Department of Commerce shall make an analysis of the facts relative to the production, trade, and consumption of the article involved, to the probable effect of obtaining a concession thereon, and to the competitive factors involved. Such analysis shall be submitted in digest form to the Interdepartmental Committee.

8. After analysis and consideration of the studies of the Tariff Commission and the Department of Commerce provided for in paragraphs 6 and 7 hereof, of the views of interested persons presented to the Committee for Reciprocity Information (established by Executive Order 6750, dated June 27, 1934, as amended by Executive Order 9647, dated

October 25, 1945), and of any other information available to the Interdepartmental Committee, the Interdepartmental Committee shall make such recommendations to the President relative to the conclusion of trade agreements, and to the provisions to be included therein, as are considered appropriate to carry out the purposes set forth in said act of June 12, 1934, as amended. If any such recommendation to the President with respect to the inclusion of a concession in any trade agreement is not unanimous, the President shall be provided with a full report by the dissenting member or members of the Interdepartmental Committee giving the reasons for their dissent and specifying the point beyond which they consider any reduction or concession involved cannot be made without injury to the domestic economy.

Part III

9. There shall also be included in every trade agreement hereafter entered into under the authority of said act of June 12, 1934, as amended, a most-favored-nation provision securing for the exports of the United States the benefits of all tariff concessions and other tariff advantages hereafter accorded by the other party or parties to the agreement to any third country. This provision shall be subject to the minimum of necessary exceptions and shall be designed to obtain the greatest possible benefits for exports from the United States. The Interdepartmental Committee shall keep informed of discriminations by any country against the trade of the United States which cannot be removed by normal diplomatic representations and, if the public interest will be served thereby, shall recommend to the President the withholding from such country of· the benefit of concessions granted under said act.

READING NO. 17

The Marshall Plan*

During World War II, as early as the Battle for Stalingrad, Averell Harriman and other keen analysts of Soviet Russia saw signs of Soviet withdrawal from postwar collaboration with the United States and the beginnings of a Soviet policy of expansion and aggression. In the winter of

* *Department of State Bulletin,* June 15, 1947, Vol. 16, pp. 1159–1160.

1946–1947 Soviet pressure against Greece and Turkey led President Truman on March 12, 1947, to offer direct aid to nations resisting direct or indirect subjugation by foreign dictatorships. The Truman Doctrine inspired Dean Acheson and General Marshall in the State Department to formulate a new set of principles for foreign aid by the United States to the European countries threatened by Soviet Russia. On June 5, 1947, Secretary of State Marshall, in a short address at the Harvard University commencement exercises, proposed that all European countries draw up a coordinated program designed to place Europe on its feet economically. Soviet Russia refused to allow its satellites to take part in the program and thereby confirmed the American prophets of the Soviet "Cold War" strategy. There can be little doubt that the Marshall Plan was an extremely bold, imaginative, and successful policy.

EUROPEAN INITIATIVE ESSENTIAL TO ECONOMIC RECOVERY

I need not tell you gentlemen that the world situation is very serious. That must be apparent to all intelligent people. I think one difficulty is that the problem is one of such enormous complexity that the very mass of facts presented to the public by press and radio make it exceedingly difficult for the man in the street to reach a clear appraisement of the situation. Furthermore, the people of this country are distant from the troubled areas of the earth and it is hard for them to comprehend the plight and consequent reactions of the long-suffering peoples, and the effect of those reactions on their governments in connection with our efforts to promote peace in the world.

In considering the requirements for the rehabilitation of Europe, the physical loss of life, the visible destruction of cities, factories, mines, and railroads was correctly estimated, but it has become obvious during recent months that this visible destruction was probably less serious than the dislocation of the entire fabric of European economy. For the past 10 years conditions have been highly abnormal. The feverish preparation for war and the more feverish maintenance of the war effort engulfed all aspects of national economies. Machinery has fallen into disrepair or is entirely obsolete. Under the arbitrary and destructive Nazi rule, virtually every possible enterprise was geared into the German war machine. Long-standing commercial ties, private institutions, banks, insurance companies, and shipping companies disappeared, through loss of capital, absorption through nationalization, or by simple destruction. In many countries, confidence in the local currency has been severely shaken. The breakdown of the business structure of Europe during the war was complete. Recovery has been seriously retarded by the fact that two years after the close of hostilities a peace settlement with Germany and Austria has not been agreed upon. But even given a more prompt solution of these difficult problems, the rehabilitation of the economic structure of Europe quite evidently will require a much longer time and greater effort than had been foreseen.

There is a phase of this matter which is both interesting and serious. The farmer has always produced the foodstuffs to exchange with the city dweller for the other necessities of life. This division of labor is the basis of modern civilization. At the present time it is threatened with breakdown. The town and city industries are not producing adequate goods to exchange with the food-producing farmer. Raw materials and fuel are in short supply. Machinery is lacking or worn out. The farmer or the peasant cannot find the goods for sale which he desires to purchase. So the sale of his farm produce for money which he cannot use seems to him an unprofitable transaction. He, therefore, has withdrawn many fields from crop cultivation and is using them for grazing. He feeds more grain to stock and finds for himself and his family an ample supply of food, however short he may be on clothing and the other ordinary gadgets of civilization. Meanwhile people in the cities are short of food and fuel. So the governments are forced to use their foreign money and credits to procure these necessities abroad. This process exhausts funds which are urgently needed for reconstruction. Thus a very serious situation is rapidly developing which bodes no good for the world. The modern system of the division of labor upon which the exchange of products is based is in danger of breaking down.

The truth of the matter is that Europe's requirements for the next three or four years of foreign food and other essential products—principally from America—are so much greater than her present ability to pay that she must have substantial additional help or face economic, social, and political deterioration of a very grave character.

The remedy lies in breaking the vicious circle and restoring the confidence of the European people in the economic future of their own countries and of Europe as a whole. The manufacturer and the farmer throughout wide areas must be able and willing to exchange their products for currencies the continuing value of which is not open to question.

Aside from the demoralizing effect on the world at large and the possibilities of disturbances arising as a result of the desperation of the people concerned, the consequences to the economy of the United States should be apparent to all. It is logical that the United States should do whatever it is able to do to assist in the return of normal economic health in the world, without which there can be no political stability and no assured peace. Our policy is directed not against any country or doctrine but against hunger, poverty, desperation, and chaos. Its purpose should be the revival of a working economy in the world so as to permit the emergence of political and social conditions in which free institutions can exist. Such assistance, I am convinced, must not be on a piecemeal basis as various crises develop. Any assistance that this Government may render in the future should provide a cure rather than a mere palliative. Any government that is willing to assist in the task of recovery will find full cooperation, I am sure, on the part of the United States Government. Any government which maneuvers to block the recovery of other countries cannot expect help from us. Furthermore, governments, political parties, or groups which seek to perpetuate human misery in order to profit therefrom politically or otherwise will encounter the opposition of the United States.

It is already evident that, before the United States Government can proceed much further in its efforts to alleviate the situation and help start the European world on its way to recovery, there must be some agreement among the countries of Europe as to the requirements of the situation and the part those countries themselves will take in order to give proper effect to whatever action might be undertaken by this Government. It would be neither fitting nor efficacious for this Government to undertake to draw up unilaterally a program designed to place Europe on its feet economically. This is the business of the Europeans. The initiative, I think, must come from Europe. The role of this country should consist of friendly aid in the drafting of a European program and of later support of such a program so far as it may be practical for us to do so. The program should be a joint one, agreed to by a number, if not all, European nations.

An essential part of any successful action on the part of the United States is an understanding on the part of the people of America of the character of the problem and the remedies to be applied. Political passion and prejudice should have no part. With foresight, and a willingness on the part of our people to face up to the vast responsibility which history has clearly placed upon our country, the difficulties I have outlined can and will be overcome.

READING NO. **18**

Kennedy's Special Message on Foreign-Trade Policy, January 25, 1962 *

The centerpiece of Kennedy's legislative efforts in 1962 was the Trade Expansion Act. It was the subject of special emphasis in his State of the Union Message, the sole focus of his first special legislative message that year, and the prime objective of an intense White House lobbying effort that had priority over almost all other bills. The broad vision and constructive innovations presented in this Special Message make it a notable document in American foreign-trade policy and history.

To the Congress of the United States:

Twenty-eight years ago our nation embarked upon a new experiment in international relationships—the Reciprocal Trade Agreements Program. Faced with the chaos in world trade that had resulted from the Great Depression, disillusioned by the failure of the promises that high protective tariffs would generate recovery, and impelled by a desperate need to restore our economy, President Roosevelt asked for authority to negotiate reciprocal tariff reductions with other nations of the world in order to spur our exports and aid our economic recovery and growth.

That landmark measure, guided through Congress by Cordell Hull, has been extended eleven times. It has served our country and the free world well over two decades. The application of this program brought growth and order to the free world trading system. Our total exports, averaging less than $2 billion a year in the three years preceding enactment of the law, have now increased to over $20 billion.

On June 30, 1962, the negotiating authority under the last extension of the Trade Agreements Act expires. It must be replaced by a wholly new instrument. A new American trade initiative is needed to meet the challenges and opportunities of a rapidly changing world economy.

In the brief period since this Act was last extended, five fundamentally new and sweeping developments have made obsolete our traditional trade policy:

---

* [Warren R. Reid, ed.], *Public Papers of the Presidents of the United States, John F. Kennedy . . . 1962* (Washington: G.P.O., 1963), pp. 68–77.

—The growth of the European Common Market—an economy which may soon nearly equal our own, protected by a single external tariff similar to our own—has progressed with such success and momentum that it has surpassed its original timetable, convinced those initially skeptical that there is now no turning back and laid the groundwork for a radical alteration of the economics of the Atlantic Alliance. Almost 90 percent of the free world's industrial production (if the United Kingdom and others successfully complete their negotiations for membership) may soon be concentrated in two great markets—the United States of America and the expanded European Economic Community. A trade policy adequate to negotiate item by item tariff reductions with a large number of small independent states will no longer be adequate to assure ready access for ourselves—and for our traditional trading partners in Canada, Japan, Latin America and elsewhere—to a market nearly as large as our own, whose negotiators can speak with one voice but whose internal differences make it impossible for them to negotiate item by item.

—The growing pressures on our balance of payments position have, in the past few years, turned a new spotlight on the importance of increasing American exports to strengthen the international position of the dollar and prevent a steady drain of our gold reserves. To maintain our defense, assistance and other commitments abroad, while expanding the free flow of goods and capital, we must achieve a reasonable equilibrium in our international accounts by offsetting these dollar outlays with dollar sales.

—The need to accelerate our own economic growth, following a lagging period of seven years characterized by three recessions, is more urgent than it has been in years—underlined by the millions of new job opportunities which will have to be found in this decade to provide employment for those already unemployed as well as an increasing flood of younger workers, farm workers seeking new opportunities, and city workers displaced by technological change.

—The communist aid and trade offensive has also become more apparent in recent years. Soviet bloc trade with 41 non-communist countries in the less-developed areas of the globe has more than tripled in recent years; and bloc trade missions are busy in nearly every continent attempting to penetrate, encircle and divide the free world.

—The need for new markets for Japan and the developing nations has also been accentuated as never before—both by the prospective impact of the EEC's external tariff and by their own need to acquire new outlets for their raw materials and light manufacturers.

To meet these new challenges and opportunities, I am today transmitting to the Congress a new and modern instrument of trade negotiation —the Trade Expansion Act of 1962. As I said in my State of the Union

Address, its enactment "could well affect the unity of the West, the course of the Cold War and the growth of our nation for a generation or more to come."

I. The Benefits of Increased Trade

Specifically, enactment of this measure will benefit substantially every state of the union, every segment of the American economy, and every basic objective of our domestic economy and foreign policy.

Our efforts to expand our economy will be importantly affected by our ability to expand our exports—and particularly upon the ability of our farmers and businessmen to sell to the Common Market. There is arising across the Atlantic a single economic community which may soon have a population half again as big as our own, working and competing together with no more barriers to commerce and investment than exist among our 50 states—in an economy which has been growing roughly twice as fast as ours—representing a purchasing power which will someday equal our own and a living standard growing faster than our own. As its consumer incomes grow, its consumer demands are also growing, particularly for the type of goods that we produce best, which are only now beginning to be widely sold or known in the markets of Europe or in the homes of its middle-income families.

Some 30 percent of our exports—more than $4 billion in industrial goods and materials and nearly $2 billion in agricultural products—already goes to the members and prospective members of the EEC. European manufacturers, however, have increased their share of this rapidly expanding market at a far greater rate than American manufacturers. Unless our industry can maintain and increase its share of this attractive market, there will be further temptation to locate additional American-financed plants in Europe in order to get behind the external tariff wall of the EEC. This would enable the American manufacturer to contend for that vast consumer potential on more competitive terms with his European counterparts; but it will also mean a failure on our part to take advantage of this growing market to increase jobs and investment in this country.

A more liberal trade policy will in general benefit our most efficient and expanding industries—industries which have demonstrated their advantage over other world producers by exporting on the average twice as much of their products as we import—industries which have done this while paying the highest wages in our country. Increasing investment and employment in these growth industries will make for a more healthy, efficient and expanding economy and a still higher American standard of living. Indeed, freer movement of trade between America and the Common Market would bolster the economy of the entire free world, stimulating each nation to do most what it does best and helping to achieve the OECD target of a 50 percent combined Atlantic Community increase in Gross National Product by 1970.

Our efforts to prevent inflation will be reinforced by expanded trade. Once given a fair and equal opportunity to compete in overseas markets, and once subject to healthy competition from overseas manufacturers for our own markets, American management and labor will have additional reason to maintain competitive costs and prices, modernize their plants and increase their productivity. The discipline of the world market place is an excellent measure of efficiency and a force to stability. To try to shield American industry from the discipline of foreign competition would isolate our domestic price level from world prices, encourage domestic inflation, reduce our exports still further and invite less desirable Governmental solutions.

Our efforts to correct our adverse balance of payments have in recent years roughly paralleled our ability to increase our export surplus. It is necessary if we are to maintain our security programs abroad—our own military forces overseas plus our contribution to the security and growth of other free countries—to make substantial dollar outlays abroad. These outlays are being held to the minimum necessary, and we are seeking increased sharing from our allies. But they will continue at substantial rates—and this requires us to enlarge the $5 billion export surplus which we presently enjoy from our favorable balance of trade. If that surplus can be enlarged, as exports under our new program rise faster than imports, we can achieve the equilibrium in our balance of payments which is essential to our economic stability and flexibility. If, on the other hand, our surplus should fail to grow, if our exports should be denied ready access to the EEC and other markets—our overseas position would be endangered. Moreover, if we can lower the external tariff wall of the Common Market through negotiation our manufacturers will be under less pressure to locate their plants behind that wall in order to sell in the European market, thus reducing the export of capital funds to Europe.

Our efforts to promote the strength and unity of the West are thus directly related to the strength and unity of Atlantic trade policies. An expanded export program is necessary to give this Nation both the balance of payments equilibrium and the economic growth we need to sustain our share of Western military security and economic advance. Equally important, a freer flow of trade across the Atlantic will enable the two giant markets on either side of the ocean to impart strength and vigor to each other, and to combine their resources and momentum to undertake the many enterprises which the security of free peoples demands. For the first time, as the world's greatest trading nation, we can welcome a single partner whose trade is even larger than our own—a partner no longer divided and dependent, but strong enough to share with us the responsibilities and initiatives of the free world.

The communist bloc, largely self-contained and isolated, represents an economic power already by some standards larger than that of Western Europe and hoping someday to overtake the United States. But the combined output and purchasing power of the United States and Western Europe—nearly a trillion dollars a year—is more than twice as great as that of the entire Sino-Soviet world. Though we have only half the population, and far less than half the territory, we can pool our resources and resourcefulness in an open trade partnership strong enough to outstrip any challenge, and strong enough to undertake all the many enterprises around the world which the maintenance and progress of freedom require. If we can take this step, Marxist predictions of "capitalist" empires warring over markets and stifling competition would be shattered for all time—Communist hopes for a trade war between these two great economic giants would be frustrated—and Communist efforts to split the West would be doomed to failure.

As members of the Atlantic Community we have concerted our military objectives through the North Atlantic Treaty Organization. We are concerting our monetary and economic policies through the Organization for Economic Cooperation and Development. It is time now to write a new chapter in the evolution of the Atlantic Community. The success of our foreign policy depends in large measure upon the success of our foreign trade, and our maintenance of Western political unity depends in equally large measure upon the degree of Western economic unity. An integrated Western Europe, joined in trading partnership with the United States, will further shift the world balance of power to the side of freedom.

Our efforts to prove the superiority of free choice will thus be advanced immeasurably. We will prove to the world that we believe in peacefully "tearing down walls" instead of arbitrarily building them. We will be opening new vistas of choice and opportunity to the producers and consumers of the free world. In answer to those who say to the world's poorer countries that economic progress and freedom are no longer compatible, we—who have long boasted about the virtues of the market place and of free competitive enterprise, about our ability to compete and sell in any market, and about our willingness to keep abreast of the times—will have our greatest opportunity since the Marshall Plan to demonstrate the vitality of free choice.

Communist bloc nations have negotiated more than 200 trade agreements in recent years. Inevitably the recipient nation finds its economy increasingly dependent upon Soviet goods, services and technicians. But many of these nations have also observed that the economics of free choice provide far greater benefits than the economics of coercion—and the wider we can make the area of economic freedom, the easier we make it for all free peoples to receive the benefits of our innovations and put them into practice.

Our efforts to aid the developing nations of the world and other friends, however, depend upon more than a demonstration of freedom's vitality and benefits. If their economies are to expand, if their new industries are to be successful, if they are to acquire the foreign exchange funds they will need to replace our aid efforts, these nations must find new outlets for their raw materials and new manufactures. We must make certain that any arrangements which we make with the European Economic Community are worked out in such a fashion as to insure nondiscriminatory application to all third countries. Even more important, however, the United States and Europe together have a joint responsibility to all of the less developed countries of the world—and in this sense we must work together to insure that their legitimate aspirations and requirements are fulfilled. The "open partnership" which this Bill proposes will enable all free nations to share together the rewards of a wider economic choice for all.

Our efforts to maintain the leadership of the free world thus rest, in the final analysis, on our success in this undertaking. Economic isolation and political leadership are wholly incompatible. In the next few years, the nations of Western Europe will be fixing basic economic and trading patterns vitally affecting the future of our economy and the hopes of our less-developed friends. Basic political and military decisions of vital interest to our security will be made. Unless we have this authority to negotiate and have it this year—if we are separated from the Common Market by high tariff barriers on either side of the Atlantic—then we cannot hope to play an effective part in those basic decisions.

If we are to retain our leadership, the initiative is up to us. The revolutionary changes which are occurring will not wait for us to make up our minds. The United States has encouraged sweeping changes in Free World economic patterns in order to strengthen the forces of freedom. But we cannot ourselves stand still. If we are to lead, we must act. We must adapt our own economy to the imperatives of a changing world, and once more assert our leadership.

The American businessman, once the authority granted by this bill is exercised, will have a unique opportunity to compete on a more equal basis in a rich and rapidly expanding market abroad which possesses potentially a purchasing power as large and as varied as our own. He knows that, once artificial restraints are removed, a vast array of American goods, produced by American know-how with American efficiency, can compete with any goods in any spot in the world. And almost all members of the business community, in every state, now participate or could participate in the production, processing, transporting, or distribution of either exports or imports.

Already we sell to Western Europe alone more machinery, transportation equipment, chemicals and coal than our total imports of these commodities from all regions of the world combined. Western Europe is our best customer today—and should be an even better one tomorrow. But as the new external tariff surrounding the Common Market replaces the internal tariff structure, a German producer—who once competed in the markets of France on the same terms with our own producers—will achieve free accesss to French markets while our own producers face a tariff. In short, in the absence of authority to bargain down that external tariff, as the economy of the Common Market expands, our exports will not expand with it. They may even decline.

The American farmer has a tremendous stake in expanded trade. One out of every seven farm workers produces for export. The average farmer depends on foreign markets to sell the crops grown on one out of every six acres he plants. Sixty percent of our rice, 49 percent of our cotton, 45 percent of our wheat and 42 percent of our soybean production are exported. Agriculture is one of our best sources of foreign exchange.

Our farmers are particularly dependent upon the markets of Western Europe. Our agricultural trade with that area is four to one in our favor. The agreements recently reached at Brussels both exhausted our existing authority to obtain further European concessions, and laid the groundwork for future negotiations on American farm exports to be conducted once new authority is granted. But new and flexible authority is required if we are to keep the door of the Common Market open to American agriculture, and open it wider still. If the output of our astounding productivity is not to pile up increasingly in our warehouses, our negotiators will need both the special EEC authority and the general 50 percent authority requested in the bill described later in this message.

The American worker will benefit from the expansion of our exports. One out of every three workers engaged in manufacturing is employed in establishments that export. Several hundred times as many workers owe their jobs directly or indirectly to exports as are in the small group—estimated to be less than one half of one percent of all workers—who might be adversely affected by a sharp increase in imports. As the number of job seekers in our labor force expands in the years ahead, increasing our job opportunities will require expanding our markets and economy, and making certain that new United States plants built to serve Common Market consumers are built here, to employ American workers, and not there.

The American consumer benefits most of all from an increase in foreign trade. Imports give him a wider choice of products at competitive prices. They introduce new ideas and new tastes, which often lead to new demands for American production.

Increased imports stimulate our own efforts to increase efficiency, and supplement anti-trust and other efforts to assure competition. Many industries of importance to the American consumer and economy are dependent upon imports for raw materials and other supplies. Thus American-made goods can also be made much less expensively for the American consumers if we lower the tariff on the materials that are necessary to their production.

American imports, in short, have generally strengthened rather than weakened our economy. Their competitive benefits have already been mentioned. But about 60 percent of the goods we import do not compete with the goods we produce—either because they are not produced in this country, or are not produced in any significant quantity. They provide us with products we need but cannot efficiently make or grow (such as bananas or coffee), supplement our own steadily depleting natural resources with items not available here in quantity (such as manganese or chrome ore, 90 percent or more of which must be imported if our steel mills are to operate), and contribute to our industrial efficiency, our economic growth and our high level of consumption. Those imports that do compete are equal to only one or one and one-half percent of our total national production; and even these imports create jobs directly for those engaged in their processing, distribution, or transportation, and indirectly for those employed in both export industries and in those industries dependent upon reasonably priced imported supplies for their own ability to compete.

Moreover, we must reduce our own tariffs if we hope to reduce tariffs abroad and thereby increase our exports and export surplus. There are many more American jobs dependent upon exports than could possibly be adversely affected by increased imports. And those export industries are our strongest, most efficient, highest paying growth industries.

It is obvious, therefore, that the warnings against increased imports based upon the lower level of wages paid in other countries are not telling the whole story. For this fear is refuted by the fact that American industry in general—and America's highest paid industries in particular—export more goods to other markets than any other nation; sell far more abroad to other countries than they sell to us; and command the vast preponderance of our own market here in the United States. There are three reasons for this:

(a) The skill and efficiency of American workers, with the help of our machinery and technology, can produce more units per man hour than any other workers in the world—thus making the competitive cost of our labor for many products far less than it is in countries with lower wage rates. For example, while a United States coal miner is paid eight times as much per hour as the Japanese miner, he produces fourteen times as much coal—our real cost per ton of coal is thus far smaller—and we sell the Japanese tens of millions of dollars worth of coal each year.

(b) Our best industries also possess other advantages—the adequacy of low cost raw materials or electrical power, for example. Neither wages nor total labor costs is an adequate standard of comparison if used alone.

(c) American products can frequently compete successfully even where foreign prices are somewhat lower—by virtue of their superior quality, style, packaging, servicing or assurance of delivery.

Given this strength, accompanied by increasing productivity and wages in the rest of the world, there is less need to be concerned over the level of wages in the low wage countries. These levels, moreover, are already on the rise, and, we would hope, will continue to narrow the current wage gap, encouraged by appropriate consultations on an international basis.

This philosophy of the free market—the wider economic choice for men and nations—is as old as freedom itself. It is not a partisan philosophy. For many years our trade legislation has enjoyed bi-partisan backing from those members of both parties who recognized how essential trade is to our basic security abroad and our economic health at home. This is even more true today. The Trade Expansion Act of 1962 is designed as the expression of a nation, not of any single faction, not of any single faction or section. It is in that spirit that I recommend it to the Congress for prompt and favorable action.

II. Provisions of the Bill

New Negotiating Authority. To achieve all of the goals and gains set forth above—to empower our negotiators with sufficient authority to induce the EEC to grant wider access to our goods and crops and fair treatment to those of Latin America, Japan and other countries—and to be ready to talk trade with the Common Market in practical terms—it is essential that our bargaining authority be increased in both flexibility and extent. I am therefore requesting two basic kinds of authority to be exercised over the next five years:

First, a general authority to reduce existing tariffs by 50 percent in reciprocal negotiations. It would be our intention to employ a variety of techniques in exercising this authority, including negotiations on broad categories or sub-categories of products.

Secondly, a special authority, to be used in negotiating with the EEC, to reduce or eliminate all tariffs on those groups of products where the United States and the EEC together account for 80 percent or more of world trade in a representative period. The fact that these groups of products fall within this special or "dominant supplier" authority is proof that they can be produced here or in Europe more efficiently than anywhere else in the world. They include most of the products which the members of the Common Market are especially interested in trading with us, and most of the products for which we want freer access to the Common Market; and to a considerable extent they are items in which our own ability to compete is demonstrated by the fact that our exports of these items are substantially greater than our imports. They account for nearly $2 billion of our total industrial exports to present and pro- spective Common Market members in 1960, and for about $1.4 billion of our imports from these countries. In short, this special authority will en- able us to negotiate for a dramatic agreement with the Common Market that will pool our economic strength for the advancement of freedom.

To be effective in achieving a breakthrough agreement with the EEC so that our farmers, manufacturers and other free world trading partners can participate, we will need to use both the dominant supplier authority and the general authority in combination. Reductions would be put into effect gradually in stages over five years or more. But the traditional technique of trading one brick at a time off our respective tariff walls will not suffice to assure American farm and factory exports the kind of ac- cess to the European market which they must have if trade between the two Atlantic markets is to expand. We must talk instead in terms of trading whole layers at a time in exchange for other layers, as the Euro- peans have been doing in reducing their internal tariffs, permitting the forces of competition to set new trade patterns. Trading in such an en- larged basis is not possible, the EEC has found, if traditional item by item economic histories are to dominate. But let me emphasize that we mean to see to it that all reductions and concessions are reciprocal—and that the access we gain is not limited by the use of quotas or other re- strictive devices.

Safeguarding interests of other trading partners. In our negotiations with the Common Market, we will preserve our traditional most favored- nation principle under which any tariff concessions negotiated will be generalized to our other trading partners. Obviously, in special authority agreements where the United States and the EEC are the dominant sup- pliers, the participation of other nations often would not be significant. On other items, where justified, compensating concessions from other in- terested countries should be obtained as part of the negotiations. But in essence we must strive for a non-discriminatory trade partnership with the EEC. If it succeeds only in splintering the free world, or increasing the disparity between rich and poor nations, it will have failed to achieve one of its major purposes. The negotiating authority under this bill will thus be used to strengthen the ties of both "Common Markets" with, and expand our own trade in, the Latin American republics, Canada, Japan and other non-European nations—as well as helping them maximize their opportunities to trade with the Common Market.

The bill also requests special authority to reduce or eliminate all duties and other restrictions on the importation of tropical agricultural and forestry products supplied by friendly less-developed countries and not produced here in any significant quantity, if our action is taken in concert with similar action by the Common Market. These tropical products are the staple exports of many less-developed countries. Their efforts for economic development and diversification must be advanced out of earnings from these products. By assuring them as large a market as possible, we are bringing closer the day when they will be able to finance their own development needs on a self-sustaining basis.

Safeguards to American Industry. If the authority requested in this act is used, imports as well as exports will increase; and this increase will, in the overwhelming number of cases, be beneficial for the reasons outlined above. Nevertheless ample safeguards against injury to American industry and agriculture will be retained. Escape clause relief will continue to be available with more up-to-date definitions. Temporary tariff relief will be granted where essential. The power to impose duties or suspend concessions to protect the national security will be retained. Articles will be reserved from negotiations whenever such action is deemed to be in the best interest of the nation and the economy. And the four basic stages of the traditional peril point procedures and safeguards will be retained and improved:

—the President will refer to the Tariff Commission the list of proposed items for negotiations;

—the Tariff Commission will conduct hearings to determine the effect of concessions on these products;

—the Commission will make a report to the President, specifically based, as such reports are based now, upon its findings of how new imports might lead to the idling of productive facilities, the inability of domestic producers to operate at a profit and the unemployment of workers as the result of anticipated reductions in duties; and

—the President will report to the Congress on his action after completion of the negotiations. The present arrangements will be substantially improved, however, since both the Tariff Commission recommendation and the President's report would be broader than a bare determination of specific peril points; and this should enable us to make much more informed use of these recommendations than has been true in the past.

Trade Adjustment Assistance. I am also recommending as an essential part of the new trade program that companies, farmers and workers who suffer damage from increased foreign import competition be assisted in their efforts to adjust to that competition. When considerations of national policy make it desirable to avoid higher tariffs, those injured by that competition should not be required to bear the full brunt of the impact. Rather, the burden of economic adjustment should be borne in part by the Federal Government.

Under existing law, the only alternatives available to the President are the imposition or refusal of tariff relief. These alternatives should continue to be available.

The legislation I am proposing, however, provides an additional alternative called Trade Adjustment Assistance. This alternative will permit the Executive Branch to make extensive use of its facilities, programs and resources to provide special assistance to farmers, firms and their employees in making the economic readjustments necessitated by the imports resulting from tariff concessions.

Any worker or group of workers unemployed or under-employed as a result of increased imports would, under this bill, be eligible for the following forms of assistance:

1. Readjustment allowances providing as much as 65 percent of the individual's average weekly wage for up to 52 weeks for all workers, and for as many as 13 additional weeks for workers over 60, with unemployment insurance benefits deducted from such allowances to the extent available;

2. Vocational education and training assistance to develop higher and different skills;

3. Financial assistance for those who cannot find work in their present community to relocate to a different place in the United States where suitable employment is available.

For a businessman or farmer adversely affected by imports, there should be available:

1. Technical information, advice and consultation to help plan and implement an attack on the problem;

2. Tax benefits to encourage modernization and diversification;

3. Loan guarantees and loans otherwise not commercially available to aid modernization and diversification.

Just as the Federal Government has assisted in personal readjustments made necessary by military service, just as the Federal Government met its obligation to assist industry in adjusting to war production and again to return to peacetime production, so there is an obligation to render assistance to those who suffer as a result of national trade policy.

Such a program will supplement and work in coordination with, not duplicate, what we are already doing or proposing to do for depressed areas, for small business, for investment incentives, and for the retraining and compensation of our unemployed workers.

This cannot be and will not be a subsidy program of government paternalism. It is instead a program to afford time for American initiative, American adaptability and American resiliency to assert themselves. It is consistent with that part of the proposed law which would stage tariff reductions over a five year period. Accordingly, trade adjustment assistance, like the other provisions of the Trade Expansion Act of 1962, is designed to strengthen the efficiency of our economy, not to protect inefficiencies.

Authority to grant temporary tariff relief will remain available to assist those industries injured by a sudden influx of goods under revised tariffs. But the accent is on "adjustment" more than "assistance." Through trade adjustment prompt and effective help can be given to those suffering genuine hardship in adjusting to import competition, moving men and resources out of uneconomic production into efficient production and competitive positions, and in the process preserving the employment relationships between firms and workers wherever possible. Unlike tariff relief, this assistance can be tailored to their individual needs without disrupting other policies. Experience with a similar kind of program in the Common Market, and in the face of more extensive tariff reductions than we propose here, testifies to the effective but relatively inexpensive nature of this approach. For most affected firms will find that the adjustment involved is no more than the adjustment they face every year or few years as the result of changes in the economy, consumer taste or domestic competition.

The purpose of this message has been to describe the challenge we face and the tools we need. The decision rests with the Congress. That decision will either mark the beginning of a new chapter in the alliance of free nations—or a threat to the growth of Western unity. The two great Atlantic markets will either grow together or they will grow apart. The meaning and range of free economic choice will either be widened for the benefit of free men everywhere—or confused and constricted by new barriers and delays.

Last year, in enacting a long-term foreign aid program, the Congress made possible a fundamental change in our relations with the developing nations. This bill will make possible a fundamental, far-reaching and unique change in our relations with the other industrialized nations—particularly with the other members of the Atlantic Community. As NATO was unprecedented in military history, this measure is unprecedented in economic history. But its passage will be long-remembered and its benefits widely distributed among those who work for freedom.

At rare moments in the life of this nation an opportunity comes along to fashion out of the confusion of current events a clear and bold action to show the world what it is we stand for. Such an opportunity is before us now. This bill, by enabling us to strike a bargain with the Common Market, will "strike a blow" for freedom.

READING NO. 19

The Trade Expansion Act of 1962 *

The effectiveness of President Kennedy's Special Message to Congress in Foreign-Trade Policy and of his support in Congress was demonstrated by the relative speed with which H.R. 9900, the bill embodying his proposals, passed the ordeal of Congressional hearings and debates between March 12 and October 4, 1962. The President signed the bill on October 11, 1962, whereupon it became Public Law 87-794, or the Trade Expansion Act of 1962. This law was the most detailed piece of trade-agreements legislation ever passed by Congress. Its scope, however, is indicated in the following statement of legislative intent.

1. LEGISLATIVE STATEMENT OF PURPOSE

It is the purpose of this Act, by lowering trade barriers through trade agreements affording mutual benefits, to stimulate the economic growth of the United States, maintain and enlarge foreign markets for the products of United States industry and agriculture, and make available to the people of the United States a greater variety of goods at lower prices; to strengthen economic and political relations with the European Economic Community and foreign countries through the development of an open and nondiscriminatory trading system in the free world; to assist in the sound economic progress of countries in the earlier stages of economic development; and to counter economic penetration by international communism. In addition, it is the purpose of this Act to provide appropriate assistance to enterprises, workers, and farmers of the United States in adjusting to new conditions which may result from increased trade with the European Economic Community and foreign countries.

* *U. S. Statutes at Large*, Vol. 76, pp. 872–903.

READING NO. **20**

The Kennedy Round, Geneva, 1964–1967 *

*The round of tariff bargaining under GATT that President Johnson initi-
ated in May, 1964, ended successfully in an agreement signed on June 30,
1967. Some of the highlights of that achievement were set down by a high
American authority in this incisive introduction to a volume devoted to a
general summary of the new agreement.*

INTRODUCTION

A multilateral trade negotiation of profound significance to international economic relations was successfully concluded at Geneva on June
30, 1967. This negotiation, known as the Kennedy Round, was the Sixth
Round of Trade Negotiations under the auspices of the General Agreement on Tariffs and Trade (GATT).

In terms of the number of participating nations, the amount of trade
involved, and the scope and depth of trade liberalization, it was by far
the greatest achievement in the series of negotiations in the 20-year history of the GATT.

The negotiation was called the Kennedy Round in recognition of the
late President's leadership in inaugurating this comprehensive assault on
obstacles to international trade. It was the culmination of United States
efforts since 1934 to promote expanding international commerce
through the negotiation of mutually advantageous agreements to reduce
trade barriers.

Among the most important results of the negotiations:

Tariff concessions were exchanged covering about *$40 billion of trade;*
concessions made by the United States account for $8.5 billion of this
total.

Tariff reductions of 50 percent were made on a broad range of nonagricultural products, and smaller, but significant, reductions on many

* *Office of the Special Representative for Trade Negotiations, General
Agreement on Tariffs and Trade, 1964–67 Trade Conference, Geneva,
Switzerland. Report on United States Negotiations* (Washington: G.P.O.,
n.d.), I, i-iii.

more. It is estimated that (in terms of trade coverage) roughly two-thirds of the duty reductions made by participants negotiating on a linear, or across-the-board, basis (the United States, the European Economic Community, the United Kingdom, Austria, Denmark, Finland, Norway, Sweden, Switzerland, and Japan) were reductions of 50 percent or more. The United States made concessions of this magnitude on $6.4 billion of its imports in 1964.

Tariff concessions on a wide range of *agricultural products* were made by major participants, although reductions were generally smaller than for industrial products.

The essentials of a *World Grains Arrangement* were agreed upon during the conference, and provision was made for further negotiations to complete the agreement. The arrangement provides assurance of an increased price range for wheat and establishes a program under which a number of countries will share in supplying food aid to developing countries. Further details are given in Part 2 of this report—Special Multilateral Negotiations.

In the area of *nontariff barriers,* the negotiations led to an antidumping code which reinforces the antidumping provisions of Article VI of the GATT with agreed practices and procedures to be followed by the major trading countries. Modifications of certain other nontariff barriers were agreed upon in bilateral negotiations. Further details are given in Part 2 of this report.

For *chemical products,* the negotiations led to a two-part agreement. The first part consists of an unconditional exchange of many U. S. and foreign tariff reductions in the main Kennedy Round. The second part is conditional upon elimination by the United States of the American selling price valuation system applied to benzenoid chemicals (as well as to canned clams and wool-knit gloves) and its replacement by normal methods of valuation. Subject to this condition, the second part provides for an additional exchange of concessions, including deeper tariff reductions on chemicals and removal of some European nontariff barriers, namely modification of certain automobile road taxes, elimination of a canned fruit import restriction in Switzerland, and reduction of a British excise preference for Commonwealth tobacco. Further details are in Part 2 of this report.

Useful if limited progress was made on the complex and sensitive problems in the *steel, aluminum, pulp and paper,* and *textile sectors,* including a three-year extension of the long-term cotton textile arrangement.

The *less-developed countries* (LDC's) were permitted to participate in the negotiations without being required to make fully reciprocal tariff concessions. They also benefited from special efforts of developed countries to make concessions on products of particular interest to them, and through the food aid provision of the grains arrangement. While the results of the negotiations fell somewhat short of the expectations of the developing countries, the United States made concessions benefiting over $900 million of trade of developing countries. On $432 million of this trade the duty will be eliminated.

READING NO. **21**

Johnson's Message on the Proposed
Trade-Expansion Act of 1968 *

The extent to which President Johnson attempted to carry on the Democratic foreign-trade policy of Roosevelt, Truman, and Kennedy is shown in his May 28, 1968 message to Congress. It reveals a concern for an expansion of world trade as a means to greater world prosperity and economic welfare. Although this message was not immediately successful, its objective and ideals were more influential with Johnson's successor than many would have ever thought possible.

To the Congress of the United States:
A nation's trade lines are its life lines. Open trade lines and active commerce lead to economic health and growth. Closed trade lines end in economic stagnation.

Franklin D. Roosevelt recognized these truths more than thirty years ago, when the nation and the world were in the grip of Depression.

On that March day in 1934 when he asked the Congress to pass the historic Reciprocal Trade Act, he pointed to America's declining world trade and what it meant to the nation: "idle hands, still machines, ships tied to their docks."

That Act set in motion three and a half decades of descending tariff barriers and rising world trade. Our producers and farmers found new markets abroad, and American exports multiplied twenty-fold.

This era of commercial progress was capped by the Kennedy Round

* *Weekly Compilation of Presidential Documents, June 3, 1968* (Washington: G.P.O., 1968), Vol. 4, pp. 862–867.

Agreements reached at Geneva last year—the greatest success in all the history of international trade negotiations.

When I reported to the Congress last November on the Kennedy Round, I said it would mean new factories, more jobs, lower prices to families, and higher incomes for American workers and for our trading partners throughout the world.

Already, through these Agreements, tariff barriers everywhere are falling, bringing savings to consumers, and opening new overseas markets for competitive producers.

But the problems and the promises of world trade are always changing. We must have the tools not only to adjust to change, but to turn change to our advantage.

To prepare for the era of world trade unfolding before us now, I submit to the Congress today the Trade Expansion Act of 1968. This measure will:

—maintain our negotiating authority to settle—advantageously— trade problems and disputes.

—carry out the special Geneva agreement on chemicals and other products.

—improve the means through which American firms and workers can adjust to new competition from increased imports.

OUR INTERNATIONAL RESPONSIBILITIES

The Trade Expansion Act of 1968 will strengthen relations with our trading partners in three ways.

First, it will extend through June 30, 1970 the President's authority to conduct negotiations for tariff reductions. This authority was contained in provisions of the Trade Expansion Act of 1962 that have expired.

Most of this authority was used in negotiating the Kennedy Round. The unused portion of that Authority will give the President the flexibility to adjust tariff rates as future developments might require.

For example, the United States might find it necessary to increase the duty on a particular article—as the result of an "escape clause" action or a statutory change in tariff classification. In such event, we would be obliged to give other nations compensatory tariff adjustments for their trade losses.

Without this authority, we would invite retaliation and endanger American markets abroad.

I recommend that the President's authority to make these tariff adjustments be extended through June 30, 1970.

Second, the Trade Expansion Act of 1968 will eliminate the American Selling Price system of customs valuation. This action is necessary to carry out the special agreement reached during the Kennedy Round.

The American Selling Price system has outlived its purpose. It should be ended.

The generally accepted method of valuing goods for tariff purposes—which we and all our trading partners employ—is to use the actual price of the item to the importer.

But many years ago, to protect a few of our fledgling industries, we imposed on competing foreign goods—in addition to a substantial tariff —the special requirement that their tariff value be determined by American prices. Today this unusual system often produces tariff protection of more than 100 percent of the import cost of the product.

Such excessive protection is both unfair and unnecessary.

This system is unfair because it:

—Gives to a few industries a special privilege available to no other American business.
—Rests on an arbitrary method of valuation which no other nation uses.
—Diverges from the provisions of the General Agreement on Tariffs and Trade.
—Imposes an unjustified burden on the U. S. consumer.

This system is unnecessary because the few industries which it covers no longer need special government protection.

It applies primarily to the chemical industry in the benzenoid field. Yet chemicals, and benzenoids in particular, are among our most efficient and rapidly expanding industries. They have done well at home. They have done well in the international market. They are in a strong position to face normal competition from imports.

A supplementary agreement was negotiated at Geneva which will lower foreign tariffs on American chemicals and reduce certain nontariff barriers—road taxes and tariff preferences—on American automobiles and tobacco. To receive these important concessions, the United States must eliminate the American Selling Price valuation system and thereby give foreign producers of chemicals and a few other products normal access to our markets. This bargain is clearly in our national interest—good for our industries, good for our workers, and good for our consumers.

I recommend that the Congress eliminate the American Selling Price system to remove inequities in our tariffs and enable us to take advantage of concessions negotiated in the Kennedy Round.

Third, the Trade Expansion Act of 1968 will provide for specific funding of our participation in the General Agreement on Tariffs and Trade.

This is the procedure we follow in meeting our financial responsibilities to all other international organizations.

The General Agreement on Tariffs and Trade has become the most important forum for the conduct of international trade relations. The Kennedy Round took place under its auspices. Yet since 1947, we have financed our annual contribution to this Agreement through general contingency funds rather than through a specific authorization.

I recommend that the Congress authorize specific appropriations for the American share of the expenses for the General Agreement on Tariffs and Trade.

When trade barriers fall, the American people and the American economy benefit. Open trade lines:

—Reduce prices of goods from abroad.
—Increase opportunities for American businesses and farms to export their products. This means expanded production and more job opportunities.
—Help improve the efficiency and competitive strength of our industries. This means a higher rate of economic growth for our nation and higher incomes for our people.

Some firms, however, have difficulty in meeting foreign competition, and need time and help to make the adjustment.

Since international trade strengthens the nation as a whole, it is only fair that the government assist those businessmen and workers who face serious problems as a result of increased imports.

The Congress recognized this need—in the Trade Expansion Act of 1962—by establishing a program of trade adjustment assistance to businessmen and workers adversely affected by imports.

Unfortunately, this program has been ineffective. The test of eligibility has proved to be too rigid, too technical, and too complicated.

As part of a comprehensive trade expansion policy, I propose that we make our adjustment assistance program fair and workable.

I recommend that Congress broaden the eligibility for this assistance. The test should be simple and clear: relief should be available whenever increased imports are a substantial cause of injury.

I intend to pattern the administration of this program on the Automotive Products Trade Act of 1965. Determinations of eligibility will be made jointly by the Secretaries of Labor, Commerce and Treasury.

The adjustment assistance provisions of Automotive Products Trade Act of 1965 have been successful. They have well served American automobile firms and their workers as we have moved to create an integrated U. S.-Canadian auto market.

These provisions will expire on June 30.

I recommend that the Congress extend the adjustment assistance provisions of the Automotive Products Trade Act through June 30, 1971.

TRADE INITIATIVES FOR THE FUTURE

The measures I have recommended today will help us carry forward the great tradition of our reciprocal trade policy.

But even as we consolidate our past gains, we must look to the future. *First and foremost, we must ensure that the progress we have made is not lost through new trade restrictions.*

One central fact is clear. A vicious cycle of trade restrictions harms most the nation which trades most. And America is that nation.

At the present time, proposals pending before the Congress would impose quotas or other trade restrictions on the imports of over twenty industries. These measures would cover about $7 billion of our imports—close to half of all imports subject to duty.

In a world of expanding trade, such restrictions would be self-defeating. Under international rules of trade, a nation restricts imports only at the risk of its own exports. Restriction begets restriction.

In reality, "protectionist" measures do not protect any of us:

—They do not protect the American working man. If world markets shrink, there will be fewer jobs.
—They do not protect the American businessman. In the long run, smaller markets will mean smaller profits.
—They do not protect the American consumer. He will pay more for the goods he buys.

The fact is that every American—directly or indirectly—has a stake in the growth and vitality of an open economic system.

Our policy of liberal trade has served this nation well. It will continue to advance our interests in the future.

But these are critical times for the nation's economy. We have launched a series of measures to reduce a serious balance of payments deficit. As part of this program, I have called for a major long-run effort to increase our trade surplus. This requires that we push ahead with actions to keep open the channels of trade.

Many of our trading partners have indicated a willingness to cooperate in this effort by accelerating some of their tariff reductions agreed to in the Kennedy Round, and by permitting the United States to defer a portion of our tariff reductions. Furthermore, a number of Western European countries are now taking more active steps to achieve a higher rate of economic growth. This promises to increase the demand for our exports and improve our trade position.

To take full advantage of the expanded trading opportunities that lie ahead, we must improve the competitive position of American goods.

Passage of the anti-inflation tax is the most critical action we could take now to strengthen our position at home and in world markets. The tax measure I have recommended will help prevent destructive price increases—which can sap the vitality and strength of our economy. Continued rapid increases in our prices would mean fewer exports and higher imports.

Second, other nations must join with us to put an end to non-tariff barriers.

Trade is a two-way street. A successful trade policy must be built upon reciprocity. Our own trade initiatives will founder unless our trading partners join with us in these efforts.

The Kennedy Round was an outstanding example of international cooperation. But major non-tariff barriers continue to impede the free flow of international commerce. These barriers now block many U. S. products from competing for world markets.

Some non-tariff barriers violate provisions of the General Agreement on Tariffs and Trade. We will step up our efforts to secure the prompt removal of these illegal restrictions.

Other non-tariff barriers may not be illegal, but they clearly hamper and hinder trade. Such barriers are found in all countries; the American Selling Price system is an example of one of our non-tariff barriers.

We have initiated a major international study to assess the effect of non-tariff barriers on world trade.

We have already begun action in the General Agreement on Tariffs and Trade and other international organizations to deal with some of these non-tariff barriers.

Efforts such as these are an important element in our trade policy. All sides must be prepared to dismantle unjustified or unreasonable barriers to trade.

Reciprocity and fair play are the essential standards for international trade. America will insist on these conditions in all our negotiations to lower non-tariff barriers.

Third, we must develop a long-range policy to guide American trade expansion through the 1970's.

I have directed the President's Special Representative for Trade Negotiations to make an intensive study of our future trade requirements and needs.

I would hope that Members of the Congress and leaders of Labor, Business and Agriculture will work with the Executive Branch in this effort. To help develop the foundations of a far-reaching policy, I will issue an Executive Order that establishes a wide basis for consultation and assistance in this important work.

AN EXPANDING ERA IN WORLD TRADE

The proposals in this message have been shaped to one purpose—to develop the promise of an expanding era in world trade.

We started on this road three and a half decades ago. In the course of that journey, the American farmer, the businessman, the worker and the consumer have benefitted.

The road ahead can lead to new levels of prosperity and achievement for the American people. The Trade Expansion Act of 1968 will speed us on the way.

I urge the Congress to give this important measure its prompt and favorable consideration.

READING NO. 22

Nixon's Message on U.S. Trade Policy, November 18, 1969 *

After President John F. Kennedy's New Frontier and President Lyndon B. Johnson's Great Society programs, President Richard Nixon's strongly laissez-faire economic program seemed to indicate he would repudiate most of his Democratic predecessors' positions. But first in foreign trade, (later in fiscal policy), Nixon kept closer in the objectives of Kennedy and Johnson than many Republicans would have anticipated. Nixon's proposed trade act encountered a strong protectionist counterattack and was not enacted as late as June 1972. His message is worth studying as an example of new thinking by high Republican foreign-trade strategists concerned about preserving America's strength in world affairs.

To the Congress of the United States:

For the past 35 years, the United States has steadfastly pursued a policy of freer world trade. As a nation, we have recognized that competition cannot stop at the ocean's edge. We have determined that American trade policies must advance the national interest—which means they must respond to the whole of our interests, and not be a device to favor the narrow interest.

* *Weekly Compilation of Presidential Documents, November 24, 1969* (Washington: G.P.O., 1969), Vol. 5, pp. 1617–1623.

This Administration has reviewed that policy and we find that its continuation is in our national interest. At the same time, however, it is clear that the trade problems of the 1970s will differ significantly from those of the past. New developments in the rapidly evolving world economy will require new responses and new initiatives.

As we look at the changing patterns of world trade, three factors stand out that require us to continue modernizing our own trade policies:

First, world economic interdependence has become a fact. Reductions in tariffs and in transportation costs have internationalized the world economy just as satellites and global television have internationalized the world communications network. The growth of multi-national corporations provides a dramatic example of this development.

Second, we must recognize that a number of foreign countries now compete fully with the United States in world markets.

We have always welcomed such competition. It promotes the economic development of the entire world to the mutual benefit of all, including our own consumers. It provides an additional stimulus to our own industry, agriculture and labor force. At the same time, however, it requires us to insist on fair competition among all countries.

Third, the traditional surplus in the U. S. balance of trade has disappeared. This is largely due to our own internal inflation and is one more reason why we must bring that inflation under control.

The disappearance of the surplus has suggested to some that we should abandon our traditional approach toward freer trade. I reject this argument not only because I believe in the principle of freer trade, but also for a very simple and pragmatic reason: any reduction in our imports produced by U. S. restrictions not accepted by our trading partners would invite foreign reaction against our own exports—all quite legally. Reduced imports would thus be offset by reduced exports, and both sides would lose. In the longer term, such a policy of trade restriction would add to domestic inflation and jeopardize our competitiveness in world markets at the very time when tougher competition throughout the world requires us to improve our competitive capabilities in every way possible.

In fact, the need to restore our trade surplus heightens the need for further movement toward freer trade. It requires us to persuade other nations to lower barriers which deny us fair access to their markets. An environment of freer trade will permit the widest possible scope for the genius of American industry and agriculture to respond to the competitive challenge of the 1970s.

Fourth, the less developed countries need improved access to the markets of the industrialized countries if their economic development is to proceed satisfactorily. Public aid will never be sufficient to meet their needs, nor should it be. I recently announced that, as one step toward improving their market access, the United States would press in world trade forums for a liberal system of tariff preferences for all developing countries. International discussions are now in progress on the matter and I will not deal with it in the trade bill I am submitting today. At the appropriate time, I will submit legislation to the Congress to seek authorization for the United States to extend preferences and to take any other steps toward improving the market access of the less developed countries which might appear desirable and which would require legislation.

THE TRADE ACT OF 1969

The trade bill which I am submitting today addresses these new problems of the 1970s. It is modest in scope, but significant in its impact. It continues the general drive toward freer world trade. It also explicitly recognizes that, while seeking to advance world interests, U. S. trade policies must also respect legitimate U. S. interests, and that to be fair to our trading partners does not require us to be unfair to our own people. Specifically:

—It restores the authority needed by the President to make limited tariff reductions.
—It takes concrete steps toward the increasingly urgent goal of lowering non-tariff barriers to trade.
—It recognizes the very real plight of particular industries, companies and workers faced with import competition, and provides for readier relief in these special cases.
—It strengthens GATT—the General Agreement on Tariffs and Trade—by regularizing the funding of United States participation.

While asking enactment of these proposals now, the trade program I will outline in this message also includes setting preparations under way for the more ambitious initiatives that will later be needed for the long-term future.

TARIFF REDUCTION

I recommend that the President be given authority to make modest reductions in U. S. tariffs.

The President has been without such authority for over two years. This authority is not designed to be used for major tariff negotiations, but rather to make possible minor adjustments that individual circumstances from time to time require—as, for example, when it becomes necessary to raise the duty on an article as the result of an "escape clause" action or when a statutory change is made in tariff classification.

Our trading partners are then entitled to reasonable compensation, just as we would be entitled to receive it from them in reverse circumstances. Lack of this authority exposes our exports to foreign retaliation. Therefore, the Bill would provide to the President, through June 30, 1973, the authority to reduce tariffs by limited amounts.

Non-Tariff Barriers

The time has come for a serious and sustained effort to reduce non-tariff barriers to trade. These non-tariff barriers have become increasingly important with the decline in tariff protection and the growing interdependence of the world economy. Their elimination is vital to our efforts to increase U. S. exports.

As a first step in this direction, I propose today that the United States eliminate the American Selling Price system of customs valuation.

Although this system applies only to a very few American products—mainly benzenoid chemicals—it is viewed by our principal trading partners as a major symbol of American protectionism. Its removal will bring reciprocal reductions in foreign tariffs on U. S. chemical exports, and a reduction in important foreign non-tariff barriers—including European road taxes, which discriminate against our larger automobiles, and the preferential treatment on tobacco extended by the United Kingdom to the countries of the Commonwealth. Beyond this, its removal will unlock the door to new negotiations on the entire range of non-tariff barriers. Because of the symbolic importance our trading partners attach to it, the American Selling Price system has itself become a major barrier to the removal of other barriers.

Essentially, the American Selling Price system is a device by which the value of imports for tariff purposes is set by the price of competitive American products instead of the actual price of the foreign product, which is the basis of tariff valuation for all other imports. The extraordinary protection it provides to these few products has outlived its original purposes. The special advantage it gives particular producers can no longer justify its heavy cost in terms of the obstacles it places in the way of opening foreign markets to American exports.

Reducing or eliminating other non-tariff barriers to world trade will require a great deal of detailed negotiating and hard bargaining.

Unlike tariffs, approaches to the reduction of non-tariff barriers are often difficult to embody in prior delegation of authority. Many—both here and abroad—have their roots in purely domestic concerns that are only indirectly related to foreign trade, and many arise from domestic laws.

Many would require specific legislative actions to accomplish their removal—but the nature of this action would not finally be clear until negotiation had shown what was possible.

This presents a special opportunity for Congress to be helpful in achieving international agreements in this vital area.

I would welcome a clear statement of Congressional intent with regard to non-tariff barriers to assist in our efforts to obtain reciprocal lowering of such barriers.

It is not my intention to use such a declaration as a "blank check." On the contrary, I pledge to maintain close consultation with the Congress during the course of any such negotiations, to keep the Congress fully informed on problems and progress, and to submit for Congressional consideration any agreements which would require new legislation. The purpose of seeking such an advance declaration is not to bypass Congress, but to strengthen our negotiating position.

In fact, it is precisely because ours is a system in which the Executive cannot commit the Legislative Branch that a general declaration of legislative intent would be important to those with whom we must negotiate.

At the same time, I urge private interests to work closely with the government in seeking the removal of these barriers. Close cooperation by the private sector is essential, because many non-tariff barriers are subtle, complex and difficult to appraise.

AID FOR AFFECTED INDUSTRIES

Freer trade brings benefits to the entire community, but it can also cause hardship for parts of the community. The price of a trade policy from which we all receive benefits must not fall unfairly on the few— whether on particular industries, on individual firms or on groups of workers. As we have long recognized, there should be prompt and effective means of helping those faced with adversity because of increased imports.

The Trade Act of 1969 provides significant improvements in the means by which U. S. industry, firms, and workers can receive assistance from their government to meet injury truly caused by imports.

This relief falls into two broad categories: 1) the escape clause, which is industry-wide; and 2) adjustment assistance, which provides specific aid to particular firms or groups of workers.

These improvements are needed because the assistance programs provided in the Trade Expansion Act of 1962 have simply not worked.

Escape Clause

The escape clause provisions of the 1962 Act have proved so stringent, so rigid, and so technical that in not a single case has the Tariff Commission been able to justify a recommendation for relief. This must be remedied. We must be able to provide, on a case-by-case basis, careful and expedited consideration of petitions for relief, and such relief must be available on a fair and reasonable basis.

I recommend a liberalization of the escape clause to provide, for industries adversely affected by import competition, a test that will be simple and clear: relief should be available whenever increased imports are the primary cause of actual or potential serious injury. The increase in imports should not—as it now is—have to be related to a prior tariff reduction.

While making these escape clause adjustments more readily obtainable, however, we must ensure that they remain what they are intended to be: temporary relief measures, not permanent features of the tariff landscape. An industry provided with temporary escape-clause relief must assume responsibility for improving its competitive position. The bill provides for regular reports on these efforts, to be taken into account in determining whether relief should be continued.

Adjustment Assistance

With regard to adjustment assistance for individual firms and groups of workers, the provisions of the Trade Expansion Act of 1962 again have not worked adequately.

The Act provides for loans, technical assistance and tax relief for firms, and readjustment allowances, relocation and training for workers. This direct aid to those individually injured should be more readily available than tariff relief for entire industries. It can be more closely targeted; it matches the relief to the damage; and it has no harmful side effects on overall trade policy.

I recommend that firms and workers be considered eligible for adjustment assistance when increased imports are found to be a substantial cause of actual or potential serious injury.

Again, the increase in imports would not have to be related to a prior tariff reduction. The "substantial cause" criterion for adjustment assistance would be less stringent than the "primary cause" criterion for tariff relief.

I also recommend two further changes in existing adjustment provisions:

—That the Tariff Commission continue to gather and supply the needed factual information, but that determinations of eligibility to apply for assistance be made by the President.
—That adjustment assistance be made available to separate units of multi-plant companies and to groups of workers in them, when the injury is substantial to the unit but not to the entire parent firm.

With these modifications, plus improved administrative procedures, our program of assistance to import-injured firms and workers can and will be made to work. Taken together, they will remedy what has too long been a serious shortcoming in our trade programs.

These changes in our escape clause and adjustment assistance programs will provide an adequate basis for government help in cases where such help is justified in the overall national interest. They will thus help us move away from protectionist proposals, which would reverse the trend toward interdependence, and toward a constructive attack on the existing trade barriers of others.

The textile import problem, of course, is a special circumstance that requires special measures. We are now trying to persuade other countries to limit their textile shipments to the United States. In doing so, however, we are trying to work out with our trading partners a reasonable solution which will allow both domestic and foreign producers to share equitably in the development of the U. S. market.

Such measures should not be misconstrued, nor should they be allowed to turn us away from the basic direction of our progress toward freer exchange.

Fair Treatment of U. S. Exports

By nature and by definition, trade is a two-way street. We must make every effort to ensure that American products are allowed to compete in world markets on equitable terms. These efforts will be more successful if we have the means to take effective action when confronted with illegal or unjust restrictions on American exports.

Section 252 of the Trade Expansion Act of 1962 authorizes the President to impose duties or other import restrictions on the products of any nation that places unjustifiable restrictions on U. S. agricultural products. *I recommend that this authority be expanded in two ways:*

—*By extending the existing authority to cover unfair actions against all U. S. products, rather than only against U. S. agricultural products.*
—*By providing new authority to take appropriate action against nations that practice what amounts to subsidized competition in third-country markets, when that subsidized competition unfairly affects U. S. exports.*

Any weapon is most effective if its presence makes its use unnecessary. With these new weapons in our negotiating arsenal, we should be better able to negotiate relief from the unfair restrictions to which American exports still are subject.

STRENGTHENING GATT

Ever since its beginning in 1947, U. S. participation in GATT—the General Agreement on Tariffs and Trade—has been financed through general contingency funds rather than through a specific appropriation.

GATT has proved its worth. It is the international organization we depend on for the enforcement of our trading rights, and toward which we look as a forum for the important new negotiations on non-tariff barriers which must now be undertaken.

I recommend specific authorization for the funding of our participation in GATT, thus both demonstrating our support and regularizing our procedures.

For the Long-Term Future

The trade bill I have submitted today is a necessary beginning. It corrects deficiencies in present policies; it enables us to begin the 1970s with a program geared to the start of that decade.

As we look further into the Seventies, it is clear that we must reexamine the entire range of our policies and objectives.

We must take into account the far-reaching changes which have occurred in investment abroad and in patterns of world trade. I have already outlined some of the problems which we will face in the 1970s. Many more will develop—and also new opportunities will emerge.

Intense international competition, new and growing markets, changes in cost levels, technological developments in both agriculture and industry, and large-scale exports of capital are having profound and continuing effects on international production and trade patterns. We can no longer afford to think of our trade policies in the old, simple terms of liberalism vs. protectionism. Rather, we must learn to treat investment, production, employment and trade as interrelated and interdependent.

We need a deeper understanding of the ways in which the major sectors of our economy are actually affected by international trade.

We have arrived at a point at which a careful review should also be made of our tariff structure itself—including such traditional aspects as its reliance upon specific duties, the relationships among tariff rates on various products, and adapting our system to conform more closely with that of the rest of the world.

To help prepare for these many future needs, I will appoint a Commission on World Trade to examine the entire range of our trade and related policies, to analyze the problems we are likely to face in the 1970s, and to prepare recommendations on what we should do about them. It will be empowered to call upon the Tariff Commission and the agencies

of the Executive Branch for advice, support and assistance, but its recommendations will be its own.

By expanding world markets, our trade policies have speeded the pace
of our own economic progress and aided the development of others. As
we look to the future, we must seek a continued expansion of world
trade, even as we also seek the dismantling of those other barriers—political, social and ideological—that have stood in the way of a freer exchange of people and ideas, as well as of goods and technology.

Our goal is an open world. Trade is one of the doors to that open
world. Its continued expansion requires that others move with us, and
that we achieve reciprocity in fact as well as in spirit.

Armed with the recommendations and analyses of the new Commission on World Trade, we will work toward broad new policies for the
1970s that will encourage that reciprocity, and that will lead us, in growing and shared prosperity, toward a world both open and just.

READING NO. 23

The Smithsonian Accord
of December 18, 1971 *

*President Richard Nixon's strong stand on August 15, 1971, against the
convertibility of the dollar into gold had international repercussions that
threatened relations with our main trading partners. After three months in
negotiations this situation was ironed out on December 17–18, 1971 at the
Smithsonian Institution in Washington, D. C. A few of the major compromises and agreements are printed below in excerpts from a press communi-
que issued on December 18, 1971.*

1. The Ministers and Central Bank Governors of the ten countries
participating in the General Arrangements to Borrow met at the Smithsonian Institution in Washington on 17th—18th December, 1971. . . .

2. The Ministers and Governors agreed on an inter-related set of
measures designed to restore stability to international monetary arrangements and to provide for expanding international trade. . . .

* *Background Material on Legislation Modifying the Par Value of the Dollar*, Committee on Banking and Currency, House of Representatives,
92d Congress, 2d Session, February 15, 1972 (Washington, D. C.:
G.P.O., 1972), pp. 29–30.

3. The Ministers and Governors reached agreement on a pattern of exchange rate relationships among their currencies. These decisions will be announced by individual governments, in the form of par values or central rates as they desire. Most of the countries plan to close their exchange markets on Monday. The Canadian Minister informed the Group that Canada intends temporarily to maintain a floating exchange rate and intends to permit fundamental market forces to establish the exchange rate without intervention except as required to maintain orderly conditions.

4. It was also agreed that, pending agreement on longer-term monetary reforms, provision will be made for $2\frac{1}{4}$ percent margins of exchange rate fluctuation above and below the new exchange rates. . . .

5. Questions of trade arrangements were recognized by the Ministers and Governors as a relevant factor in assuring a new and lasting equilibrium in the international economy. Urgent negotiations are now under way between the United States and the Commission of the European Community, Japan, and Canada to resolve pending short-term issues at the earliest possible date and with the European Community to establish an appropriate agenda for considering more basic issues in a framework of mutual cooperation in the course of 1972 and beyond. The United States agreed to propose to Congress a suitable means for devaluing the dollar in terms of gold to $38.00 per ounce as soon as the related set of short-term measures is available for Congressional scrutiny. Upon passage of required legislative authority in this framework, the United States will propose the corresponding new par value of the dollar to the International Monetary Fund.

6. In consideration of the agreed immediate realignment of exchange rates, the United States agreed that it will immediately suppress the recently imposed 10 percent import surcharge and related provisions of the Job Development Credit.

7. The Ministers and Governors agreed that discussions should be promptly undertaken, particularly in the framework of the IMF, to consider reform of the international monetary system over the longer term. It was agreed that attention should be directed to the appropriate monetary means and division of responsibilities for defending stable exchange rates and for insuring a proper degree of convertibility of the system; to the proper role of gold, of reserve currencies, and of Special Drawing Rights in the operation of the system; to the appropriate volume of liquidity; to re-examination of the permissible margins of fluctuation around established exchange rates and other means of establishing a suitable degree of flexibility; and to other measures dealing with movements of liquid capital. It is recognized that decisions in each of these areas are closely linked.

Select Bibliography

General Historical Background

Clark, Victor S., *History of Manufactures in the United States, 1607–1928,* 3 vols. (New York, 1929).

Davis, Lance E. et al., *American Economic Growth* (New York, 1972).

Dorfman, Joseph, *The Economic Mind in American Civilization,* 5 vols. (New York, 1946–1959).

Ellis, L. Ethan, *Republican Foreign Policy, 1921–1933* (New Brunswick, N.J., 1968).

Faulkner, Harold U., *The Decline of Laissez Faire 1897–1917* (New York & Toronto, 1951).

Fogel, Robert W. and Stanley L. Engerman, eds., *The Reinterpretation of American Economic History* (New York, 1971).

Kirkland, Edward C., *Industry Comes of Age . . . 1860–1897* (New York, 1961).

Link, Arthur S., *Woodrow Wilson and the Progressive Era 1910–1917* (New York, 1954).

Mitchell, Broadus, *Depression Decade . . . 1929–1941* (New York & Toronto, 1947).

Nettels, Curtis P., *The Emergence of a National Economy 1775–1815* (New York, 1962).

Nevins, Allan, *The Ordeal of the Union,* 6 vols. (New York, 1947–1960).

North, Douglass C., *The Economic Growth of the United States 1790–1860* (Englewood Cliffs, N.J., 1961).

Ratner, Sidney, *Taxation and Democracy in America* (New York, 1967).

Schlesinger, Jr., Arthur M., *A Thousand Days: John F. Kennedy in the White House* (Boston, 1965).

Schlesinger, Jr., Arthur M., *The Age of Roosevelt,* 3 vols. (New York, 1957–1960).

Shannon, Fred A., *The Farmer's Last Frontier . . . 1860–1897* (New York & Toronto, 1945).

Soule, George, *Prosperity Decade . . . 1917–1929* (New York & Toronto, 1947).

Taylor, George Rogers, *The Transportation Revolution 1815–1860* (New York & Toronto, 1951).

Ver Steeg, Clarence L., *The Formative Years: 1607–1763* (New York, 1964).

Wiebe, Robert H., *The Search for Order 1877–1920* (New York, 1967).

Wiltse, Charles M., *The New Nation: 1800–1845* (New York, 1961).

Wright, Esmond, *Fabric of Freedom: 1763–1800* (New York, 1961).

Specific Tariff Studies

Baker, Richard Cleveland, *The Tariff Under Roosevelt and Taft* (Hastings, Nebraska, 1941).

Balinky, Alexander, *Albert Gallatin: Fiscal Theories and Policies* (New Brunswick, N.J., 1958).

Berglund, Abraham and Philip G. Wright, *The Tariff on Iron and Steel* (Washington, D.C., 1929).

Blinken, Donald M., *Wool Tariffs and American Policy* (Washington, D.C., 1948).

Council of Economic Advisers, *Annual Reports* (Washington, D.C., 1947–72).

David, Paul A., "Learning by Doing and Tariff Protection," *Journal of Economic History*, XXX (1970), 521–601.

Douglas, Paul, *America in the Market Place* (New York, 1966).

Edminster, Lynn Ramsey, *The Cattle Industry and the Tariff* (New York, 1926).

Eiselen, Malcolm Rogers, *The Rise of Pennsylvania Protectionism* (Philadelphia, 1932).

Ellis, L. Ethan, *Reciprocity 1911: A Study in Canadian-American Relations* (New Haven, 1939).

Farnsworth, Helen C., *Wheat Growers and the Tariff* (Berkeley & Los Angeles, 1946).

Ferleger, Herbert Ronald, *David A. Wells and the American Revenue System 1865–1870* (New York, 1942).

Fogel, Robert W., and Stanley L. Engerman, "A Model for the Explanation of Industrial Expansion . . .", *Journal of Political Economy*, LXXVII (1969), 306–328.

Jones, Jr., Joseph M., *Tariff Retaliation: Repercussions of the Hawley-Smoot Bill* (Philadelphia, 1934).

Kaiser, Carl William, *History of the Academic Protectionist-Free Trade Controversy in America before 1860* (Philadelphia, 1939).

Mackenzie, Kenneth C., *Tariff-Making and Trade Policy in the U. S. and Canada: A Comparative Study* (New York, 1968).

Mason, Fránk R., *The American Silk Industry and the Tariff, American Economic Association Quarterly,* 2nd Series, Vol. XI, No. 4 (Cambridge, Mass., December, 1910).

Miller, Clarence Lee, *The States of the Old Northwest and the Tariff 1865–1888* (Emporia, Kansas, 1929).

Peterson, Peter G., *The United States in the Changing World Economy,* 2 vols. (Washington, D.C., 1971).

Salant, Walter S. and Beatrice N. Vaccara, *Import Liberalization in Employment* (Washington, D.C., 1961).

Stanwood, Edward, *American Tariff Controversies in the Nineteenth Century,* 2 vols. (Boston & New York, 1903).

Summers, Festus P., *William L. Wilson and Tariff Reform* (New Brunswick, N.J., 1953).

Swisher, Idella Gwatkin, *An Introduction to the Study of the Tariff* (Washington, D.C., 1931).

Taussig, Frank W., *Free Trade, the Tariff and Reciprocity* (New York, 1927).

Taussig, Frank W., *Some Aspects of the Tariff Question,* 3rd ed. (Cambridge, Mass., 1931).

Taussig, Frank W., *The Tariff History of the United States,* 8th ed. (New York, 1931).

U. S. State Department, *United States Foreign Policy, 1971: A Report of the Secretary of State* (Washington, D.C., 1972).

U. S. Tariff Commission, *Dictionary of Tariff Information* (Washington, D.C., 1924).

U. S. Tariff Commission, *Operation of the Trade Agreements Program, June 1934 to April 1948,* 5 pts. (Washington, D.C., 1949).

U. S. Tariff Commission, *Operation of the Trade Agreements,* Second Report. . . . (Washington, D.C., 1950–).

Vaccara, Beatrice N., *Employment and Output in Protected Manufacturing Industries* (Washington, D.C., 1960).

Wright, Chester W., *Wool-growing and the Tariff* (Cambridge, Mass., 1910).

Wright, Philip G., *Sugar in Relation to the Tariff* (New York, 1924).

Economics of International Trade, Reciprocity and Finance

American Economic Association, *Readings in the Theory of International Trade* (Philadelphia, 1949).

American Economic Association, *Readings in International Economics* (Homewood, Ill., 1967).

Balassa, Bela, *Trade Liberalization among Industrial Countries* (New York, 1967).

Baldwin, David A., *Economic Development and American Foreign Policy 1943–62* (Chicago and London, 1966).

Baldwin, Robert E., *Nontariff Distortions of International Trade* (Washington, D.C., 1970).

Bank for International Settlements, *Forty-Second Annual Report* (Basle, 1972).

Beckett, Grace, *The Reciprocal Trade Agreement Program* (New York, 1941).

Benoit, Emile, *Europe at Sixes and Sevens* (New York & London, 1961).

Bhagwati, Jagdish, ed., *International Trade* (Baltimore, 1969).

Carey, Robert Lincoln, *Daniel Webster as an Economist* (New York, 1929).

Caves, Richard E., *Trade and Economic Structure* (Cambridge, Mass., 1960).

Chalmers, Henry, *World Trade Policies . . . 1920–1953* (Berkeley and Los Angeles, 1953).

Cohen, Benjamin J., ed., *American Foreign Economic Policy* (New York, Evanston, London, 1968).

Conference on Research in Income and Wealth, *Education, Income, and Human Capital*, Vol. 35, Studies in Income and Wealth (New York, 1970).

Conference on Research in Income and Wealth, *Trends in the American Economy in the Nineteenth Century*, Vol. 24, Studies in Income and Wealth (Princeton, N.J., 1966).

Condliffe, J. B., *The Commerce of Nations* (New York, 1950).

Cooper, Richard N., *The Economics of Interdependence; Economic Policy in the Atlantic Community* (New York, 1968).

Cooper, Richard N., "Growth and Trade," *Journal of Economic History,* XXIV (December, 1964), 609–628.

Cooper, R. N., ed., *International Finance* (Baltimore, Md., 1969).

Corden, W. M., *Recent Developments in the Theory of International Trade* (Princeton, N.J., 1965).

Curzon, Gerard, *Multilateral Commercial Diplomacy* (New York, 1965).

Dam, Kenneth W., *The GATT—Law and International Economic Organization* (Chicago & London, 1970).

Ellsworth, P. T., *The International Economy,* 3rd ed. (New York & London, 1964).

English, H. Edward, ed., *World Trade and Trade Policy* (Toronto, 1968).

Gardner, Richard N. and Max F. Millikan, *The Global Partnership* (New York, 1968).

Haberler, Gottfried, *A Survey of International Trade Theory* (Princeton, N.J., 1961).

Harrod, Roy and D. C. Hague, eds., *International Trade Theory in a Developing World* (London, 1964).

Hollerman, Leon, *Japan's Dependence on the World Economy* (Princeton, N.J., 1967).

Hoselitz, Bert F., ed., *Economics and the Idea of Mankind* (New York & London, 1965).

Humphrey, Don D., *American Imports* (New York, 1955).

Humphrey, Don D., *The United States and the Common Market* (New York, 1962).

Johnson, Harry G., *Comparative Cost and Commercial Policy Theory for a Developing World Economy* (Stockholm, 1968).

Johnson, Harry G., ed., *Economic Nationalism in Old and New States* (Chicago, 1967).

Johnson, Harry G., *Economic Policies Toward Less Developed Countries* (New York, 1967).

Alexandre Kafka, *The IMF: The Second Coming* (Princeton, N.J., 1972)

Kenen, Peter B., *International Economics,* 2nd ed. (Englewood Cliffs, N.J., 1967), Foundations of Modern Economics Series, Otto Eckstein, ed.

Kenen, Peter B. and Roger Lawrence, eds. *The Open Economy* (New York & London, 1968).

Kindleberger, Charles P., *Foreign Trade and the National Economy* (New Haven, 1962).

Kolde, Endel J., *International Business Enterprise* (Englewood Cliffs, N.J., 1968).

Kottman, Richard N., *Reciprocity and the North Atlantic Triangle 1932–1938* (Ithaca, N.Y., 1968).

Krause, Lawrence B., *European Economic Integration and the United States* (Washington, D.C., 1968).

Krause, Walter, *International Economics* (New York, 1965).

Krause, Walter and F. John Mathis, eds., *International Economics and Business* (Boston, 1965).

Lary, Hal B., *Imports of Manufactures from Less Developed Countries* (New York, 1968).

Lary, Hal B., *Problems of the United States as World Trader and Banker* (New York, 1963).

Lary, Hal B., *The United States in the World Economy,* U. S. Bureau of Foreign Commerce, Economic Series No. 23 (Washington, D.C., 1943).

League of Nations, Economic Intelligence Service, *Europe's Trade* (Geneva, 1941).

League of Nations, Economic Intelligence Service, *The Network of World Trade* (Geneva, 1942).

Lipsey, Robert E., *Price and Quantity Trends in the Foreign Trade of the United States* (Princeton, N.J., 1963).

Machlup, Fritz, "International Money: The Way Forward Now," *The Banker*, CXXII (March, 1972), 287–296.

Machlup, Fritz, *International Trade and the National Income Multiplier* (Philadelphia, 1943).

Machlup, Fritz, *Remaking the International Monetary System* (Baltimore, 1968).

Maizels, Alfred, *Growth and Trade* (Cambridge, England, 1970).

Mandel, Ernest, *Europe vs America* (New York & London, 1970).

Meade, J. E., *The Theory of International Economic Policy*, 2 vols. (New York, 1951–1955).

Meerhaeghe, M. A. G. van, *International Economic Institutions* (New York, 1966).

Miller, Roger LeRoy and Rabum M. Williams, *The New Economics of Richard Nixon* (New York, 1972).

Mintz, Ilse, *Cyclical Fluctuations in the Exports of the United States Since 1879* (New York & London, 1967).

Mikesell, Raymond F., *United States Economic Policy and International Relations* (New York, 1952).

National Planning Association, *Local Impact of Foreign Trade* (Washington, D.C., 1960).

Patterson, Gardner, *Discrimination in International Trade . . . 1945–1965* (Princeton, N.J., 1966).

Patton, Donald J., *The United States and World Resources* (Princeton, N.J., 1968).

Piquet, Howard S., *Aid, Trade and the Tariff* (New York, 1953).

Pisar, Samuel, *Coexistence and Commerce* (New York, 1970).

Preeg, Ernest H., *Traders and Diplomats: An Analysis of the Kennedy Round . . .* (Washington, D.C., 1970).

Rowe, J. W. F., *Primary Commodities in International Trade* (Cambridge, England, 1965).

Samuelson, Paul, ed., *International Economic Relations* (London & New York, 1969).

Snider, Delbert A., *Introduction to International Economics* (Homewood, Ill., 1967).

Taussig, Frank W., *International Trade* (New York, 1927).

Taussig, Frank W., *Selected Readings in International Trade and Tariff Problems* (Boston, 1921).

Theberge, James D., *Economics of Trade and Development*)New York & London, 1968).

Travis, William Penfield, *The Theory of Trade and Protection* (Cambridge, Mass., 1964).

Triffin, Robert, *Our International Monetary System*)New York, 1968).

U. S. Bureau of the Census, *Historical Statistics of the United States Colonial Times to 1957* (Washington, D.C., 1960).

Vanek, Jaroslav, *General Equilibrium of International Discrimination: The Case of Customs Unions* (Cambridge, Mass., 1965).

Vernon, Raymond, ed., *The Technology Factor in International Trade* (New York, 1970).

Viner, Jacob, *The Customs Union Issue* (New York, 1950).

Viner, Jacob, *International Trade and Economic Development* (Glencoe, Ill., 1952).

Weiss, Leonard W., *Economics and American Industry* (New York, 1967).

Wiles, P. J. D., *Communist International Economics* (Oxford, 1968).

Williamson, Jeffrey G., *American Growth and the Balance of Payments 1820–1913* (Chapel Hill, N.C., 1964).

Woolley, Herbert B., *Measuring Transactions between World Areas* (New York, 1966).

Studies in Pressure Politics

Allen, William R., "Issues in Congressional Tariff Debates, 1890–1930," *Southern Economic Journal,* XX (1954), 346–355.

Burdette, Franklin L., *The Republican Party* (Princeton, N.J., 1968).

Chambers, William Nisbet, *The Democrats 1789–1964* (Princeton, N.J., 1964).

Coben, Stanley, "Northeastern Business and Radical Reconstruction," *Mississippi Valley Historical Review,* XVVI (1959), 67–90.

Fetter, Frank W., "Congressional Tariff Theory," *American Economic Review,* XXIII (1933), 413–427.

Herring, E. Pendleton, *Group Representation Before Congress* (New York, 1936).

Hesseltine, William B., *Third-Party Movements in the United States* (Princeton, N.J., 1962).

Key, Jr., V. O., *Politics, Parties and Pressure Groups,* 5th ed. (New York, 1964).

Leiter, Robert D., "Organized Labor and the Tariff," *Southern Economic Journal,* XXVIII (1961), 55–65.

McKee, Thomas Hudson, ed., *The National Conventions and Platforms of All Political Parties, 1789 to 1905,* 6th ed. (Baltimore, 1906).

Olson, Jr., Mancur, *The Logic of Collective Action* (New York, 1968).

Porter, Kirk H. and Donald Bruce Johnson, eds. *National Party Platforms 1840 to 1960* (Urbana, Ill., 1961).

Ratner, Sidney, *Taxation and Democracy in America* (New York, 1967).

Schattschneider, E. E., *Politics, Pressures and the Tariff* (New York, 1935).

Truman, David B., *The Governmental Process* (New York, 1951).

Appendix

Explanation of Some Key Economic Terms

Ad valorem duty: A duty levied as a percentage of the assessed value of an imported commodity.

American Selling Price: The basis in the United States for tariff assessment on certain benzenoid chemicals and a few other products. This appraisal is made on the selling price of a competitive American product instead of on the value of the imported commodity.

Balance of Payments: The relationship between the payments of all kinds made from one country to the rest of the world and its receipts from all other countries. The U. S. government has constructed several "balances" to represent different aspects of U. S. trading and finance relationships. See Council of Economic Advisers, 1972 *Annual Report*, pp. 149–55.

Balance of Trade: The relationship between the values of a country's imports and its exports. An excess of exports as against imports is called an active or favorable balance; the reverse is called a passive or unfavorable balance.

Debenture: (1) A rebate on duties paid on imported goods intended for export. (2) A Payment of money granted as a bounty to an exporter of certain domestic goods.

Devaluation: (1) As applied to a unit of money, a reduction of its metallic content as fixed by law. (2) The lowering of the value of one nation's currencies in terms of the currency of other nations.

Drawback: A refund made for customs duties and internal taxes collected on imported goods that are not intended for sale to domestic consumers and are reshipped to other nations.

Escape clause: A provision in U. S. trade legislation that permits the President to increase tariff duties if a domestic industry suffers injury.

Linear tariff cut: A reduction of all tariffs by the same percent. In the Kennedy Round the general linear cut for nonagricultural tariffs was 50 percent.

Most-favored-nation (MFN) treatment: The way in which the tariffs concessions extended by one country to imports from another are, or may be extended to imports from a third country. There are two forms of MFN treatment. Under *conditional* MFN treatment, one country agrees to reduce its duties upon specific imports from another country if that country also agrees to reduce its duties on particular imports originating in the first country. These reductions are extended to third countries only as the result of additional bargaining and in exchange for equivalent concessions. In the case of *unconditional* MFN treatment, concessions granted by one country to other countries are automatically extended to all third countries whether or not equivalent concessions are made in return.

Peril-point: A hypothetical limit beyond which reduction in a U. S. tariff duty could injure a domestic industry.

Quota: A quantitative form of trade restriction, used to control the flow of imports by being set up as an absolute limit upon either the physical volume of particular imports, or the total value of such imports, permitted to enter a country during a specified time period.

Special Drawing Rights (SDRs): An international reserve currency system created by the International Monetary Fund in October, 1969. It provides for a new type of money (known as "paper gold") to be used along with gold and dollars as monetary reserves between governments and central banks.

Index *

Adams, John Quincy, 15–16, 18
Africa, 67
Agricultural Adjustment Act (1933), 56, 64
agricultural interests, 36, 42, 44, 47, 50–51, 80, 85; sugar, 37, 39, 40, 41, 43, 45, 48, 52; Roosevelt and, 55; quotas and, 64
Agricultural Marketing Act (1929), 50
Alaska, 43, 81
Aldrich, Nelson W., 36, 42
Alliance for Progress, 67
American Bankers' Association, 52
American Iron and Steel Association, 30
American Revolution, 9
American Selling Price (ASP), 71, 72, 73
American Tariff League, 51
Arthur, Chester A., 33–34
Articles of Confederation (1781), 9–10
Asia, 67. See also specific countries
Austria, 37, 66, 76

balance of payments crisis (1970's), 73–78, 79, 86–87, 196–97
Ballinger, Richard A., 43
Barbados, 37
Belgium, 65, 67
Benton, Thomas Hart, 18
Birney, J. G., 21
"Black Tariff," see Tariff Act (1842)
Blaine, James G., 32, 35, 37
Borah, William, 51, 56
Brazil, 37
Bretton Woods Conference (1945), 59
British Guinea, 37

Bryan, William Jennings, 39, 41
Buchanan, James, 18, 22, 25, 26, 29
Burke, James A., 86
"Buy American" Act (1933), 64–65

Calhoun, John C., 13, 15, 20, 21, 22–23
California, 25, 26, 42, 44
Canada, 26–27, 43–44, 75, 77, 86
Canadian Reciprocity Treaty (1854), 26–27
Cannon, Joseph G., 43
Carey, Matthew, 15
Central America, 37–38, 54, 67. See also specific countries
Chase, Salmon P., 29
China, 11, 64, 66, 68, 75; rapprochement, 78, 86
China, Republic of (Taiwan), 78
Civil War, 6, 17, 27, 29–31, 80, 84; tariff reform after, 33–36
Clark, Colin, cited, 82
Clay, Henry, 13, 14–15, 16, 18, 19–20, 21–22, 23; Speech of 1824 on American Industry (text), 106–108
Cleveland, Grover, 35–36, 38, 39; Message of 1887 (text), 118–24
collection procedures, 22, 24–25, 45
Colombia, 38
Communist nations, 64, 66, 67, 70, 75; trade reopening (1970's) 78, 86
Compromise Tariff (1833), 19–21
Connally, John, 76
Continental Congress, 9
Coolidge, Calvin, 49
Copper Act (1869), 32
Corn Laws (British), 23

* Compiled by Roberta Blaché.

207

Cotton Textile Import Agreement (1962), 71
Cuba, 37, 41

Dallas, Alexander, 13
Dallas, George M., 23–24
Dawes, Henry L., 32
Democratic party, 16, 18, 21, 22, 23, 25; Morrill Tariff (1860) and, 28, 29; post-Civil War policies of, 31, 35–36; Tariff Act (1894) and, 38–39; election of 1908 and, 41; elections of 1910 and, 43, 44; Tariff Act (1922) and, 48, 49; election of 1928 and, 50; Hawley-Smoot and, 51, 54, 55; Reciprocal Trade restrictions and, 62, 63; election of 1968 and, 72; fiscal tendencies of, 74, 85, 86
Denmark, 66
Dingley, Nelson, Jr., 39–40
Dingley Tariff Act (1897), 39–41, 42, 43, 81
Domestic International Sales Corporation (DISC), 78
Dominican Republic, 37
Douglas, Paul, 142–144
Dred Scott Decision, 25

Eaton, John H., 18
economic nationalism, 55–56, 62–65, 80–81
Eisenhower, Dwight D., 61, 63, 65
embargoes, 12, 47, 48, 78
Emergency Tariff Act (1921), 46–47
employment, 74, 79, 87; protectionism and, 83–84, 85, 86
England, see Great Britain
Europe: American trade balances, 53–54, 73–79, 86; post-World War II recovery of, 62, 65, 162–165; Latin American trade, 67; American internal free trade and, 81. See also specific countries

European Atomic Energy Community (Euratom), 66
European Coal and Steel Community (ECSC), 65–66
European Common Market, 65–66, 67, 68, 69, 77, 84
European Free Trade Association (EFTA), 66
exchange rates, 74–77, 79, 86, 196–197
Executive Order for Escape Clauses from Concessions in Trade Agreements, February 25, 1947 (Truman), 62, 159–162
Export-Import Bank Act Amendment (1971), 78

Federal Income Tax Act (1913), 6, 46; precedents for, 30, 31, 38, 39
Fisher, Irving, 142–144
Florida, 81
Fordney-McCumber Tariff Act (1922), 47–49, 52
Fordney Emergency Tariff Bill (1921), 47
Foreign Trade and Investment Act (1927), 86
France, 5, 65, 66, 67, 76
free trade, internal, 81–82
Frémont, John C., 25

Garfield, James A., 32
Gaulle, Charles de, 66
General Agreement on Tariffs and Trade (1947), (GATT; Geneva Agreement), 60–62, 63, 64, 70–72, 77; . . . Objectives and General Most-Favored-Nation Treatment, text, 157–159; Kennedy Round, Geneva, 1964–1967, text, 180–182
Generalized Preference legislation, 78–79
Georgia, 19
Germany, 37, 47, 48, 75
gold, 38, 39, 53, 55; American

monetary crisis and, 74–77, 86–87, 196–197

Goldwater, Barry, 72

Graham, Frank, 142–144

Grains Treaty (1968), 71

Great Britain, 4, 5, 6, 12, 14, 85; tariff laws of, 9, 15, 23, 25, 53, 59, 65; Canadian-U.S. reciprocity and, 26; Latin America and, 37; Hawley-Smoot and, 53–54; Lend-Lease and, 59; Common Market and, 65, 66, 67

Great Depression (1930's), 53, 54, 55–56

Group of Ten, 76

Grundy, Joseph R., 51

Guatemala, 37

Guthrie, James, 25

Haiti, 38

Hamilton, Alexander, 12; Report on Manufactures, 1791, text, 95–106

Harding, Warren G., 47, 49

Harrison, Benjamin, 36, 38

Harrison, William H., 21

Hartke, Vance, 86

Hartley, Thomas, 10

Harvard Graduate School of Business, 86

Hawaii, 81

Hawley, Willis C., 50–51, 52

Hawley-Smoot Tariff Act (1930), 50–54; Reciprocal Trade Program (Section 350) and, 55, 56; Economists' Petition Against (text), 142–144

Hayes, John L., 32, 34

Honduras, 37

Hong Kong, 66, 78

Hoover, Herbert, 49, 50–53

Hull, Cordell, 44, 56

Humphrey, Hubert, 72

Hungary, 37

India, 11

International Bank for Reconstruction and Development, 59

International Coffee Agreement (1962), 67

International Monetary Fund, 59, 76; Special Drawing Rights, 77, 86–87

International Textile Agreement, 64

International Trade Organization, 58–60, 61

Ireland, 25

Italy, 65

Jackson, Andrew, 16, 18; Compromise Tariff, 19–20

Jamaica, 37

Japan, 4, 5, 62, 64, 66–67, 68, 74; exchange rates, 75, 76; trade cooperation (1971), 77, 78, 86

Jefferson, Thomas, 12, 23

Job Development Tax Credit, 74

Johnson, Lyndon B., 70–71, 72; Message on Proposed Trade-Expansion Act of 1968 (text), 182–188

Johnson, R. M., 18

Kansas-Nebraska Act (1854), 25

Kelley, William D., 32

Kennedy, John F., 68–70, 71, 77, 85; Special Message on Foreign Trade Policy, January 25, 1962 (text), 166–79; GATT Bargaining Round, Geneva, 1964–1967 (text), 180–82

Kentucky, 13, 14, 18

Keynes, John Maynard, 7, 85

Korean War, 64, 81

LaFollette, Robert M., 42, 45

Lake Michigan, 26

Laurier, Sir Wilfred, 44

League of Nations Information Service, 54

Lend-Lease, 59

Liberal party (Canada), 44

Liberty party, 21

Lincoln, Abraham, 29

List, Friedrich, 15
Louisiana, 14, 38, 39, 81
Lowndes, William, 13
Luxembourg, 65

McKinley, William, 36, 39;
Speech on the Mills Tariff Bill
(text), 125–133
McKinley Tariff Act (1890), 36–
38, 39, 40, 42
McLane, Louis, 19
Madison, James, 10, 11, 12, 13
Mallary Bill (1827), 15
Marshall, George C., 65; quoted,
162–165
Marshall Plan, 65–66, 68; text,
162–165
Massachusetts, 15, 18, 86
maximum-and-minimum values
principle, 43, 45
Merchant Marine, 46
metal industries, 17, 28, 30, 31,
33, 39, 41, 45, 82; shipbuilding
and, 14, 15, 16; copper, 32;
Tariff Act of 1833 and, 34;
McKinley Tariff Act and, 36,
37; Dingley Tariff and, 39;
Payne-Aldrich Tariff and, 42,
43; Fordney-McCumber Tariff
and, 48; Hawley-Smoot and,
52; GATT and, 71, 72; quotas,
79
Mexican War, 25, 81
Mexico, 25, 62
Middle Atlantic states, 14, 16, 17,
19, 20, 26. See also specific
states
Mills, Roger Q., 36
Mills Tariff Bill (1888), 36; Mc-
Kinley Speech on (text), 125–
133; Reed Speech on (text),
133–139
Minnesota, 44
Morrill, Justin S., 28–29, 31–32;
quoted, 30
Morrill Tariff Act (1861), 28–
29; text, 112–117
Morrison, William, 35

"most-favored-nation" principle,
57, 58; General Agreement on
Tariffs and Trade (1947) on,
60–61, 157–59
Mutual Defense Assistance Control Act (1951), 64

National Associations of Wool
Manufacturers and Wool-
growers, 30, 34
National Industrial Recovery Act
(1933), 56
National Manufacturers' Associ-
ation, 30
National Republican party, 15–16
National Security Amendment,
70
Navigation Acts (British), 9
Netherlands, 65, 76
Nevins, Allan, quoted, 28
New Deal, 55–56, 85
New England, 13, 14, 15, 19, 20,
26, 28, 30, 31; Tariff Act of
1828 and, 16, 17. See also spe-
cific states
New England Cotton Manufac-
turers' Association, 30
New Jersey, 28, 29, 38
New York State, 10, 18, 19, 22,
29, 38
Nicaragua, 37
Nixon, Richard M., 72–73, 74,
85; Smithsonian Accord
(1971) and, 76–77, 79, 196–
97; East-West trade and, 78;
Message on United States
Trade Policy, November 18,
1969 (text), 188–196
Non-Importation Act (1806), 12
Norris, George W., 51
North, The, 13, 14, 16, 18, 22,
26, 38, 48, 52, 80; Morrill
Tariff Acts (1860's) and, 28, 29
North Atlantic Treaty Organiza-
tion (NATO), 74
North Carolina, 19, 45
North Korea, 64

Norway, 66
nullification, 18, 19–21

Ohio, 14, 16, 32, 38
Oregon, 23, 50
Organization for European Economic Cooperation (OEEC), see Marshall Plan
Organization for Trade Cooperation (OTC), 61
Ottawa Agreements (1932), 53

Panic of 1819, 14
Panic of 1837, 21
Panic of 1857, 26, 28
Panic of 1873, 33
Panic of 1893, 38, 39
Payne, Sereno, 41–42
Payne-Aldrich Tariff Act (1909), 41–43, 44
Pennsylvania, 10, 15, 18, 22, 23–24, 26, 51; Republican party and, 28, 29, 35
Pennsylvania Manufacturers' Association, 51
"peril-points," 63, 70
Philippine Islands, 43
Pierce, Franklin, 25
Poindexter, Miles, 45
Poland, 70
Polk, James K., 23
Populist party, 36–37, 38, 39
Portugal, 66
pressure groups: Whig protectionism, 21–22; Canada and, 27; Wilson attack on, 45; Reciprocal Trade Program and, 62–63. See also lobbies, i.e., agricultural interests, metal industries, textile industries
Progressive party, 42, 44
"Proposals for the Expansion of World Trade and Employment" (U.S. Dept. of State), 59
Protests of Economists Against the Hawley-Smoot Tariff (1930), text, 142–144
Puerto Rico, 37

quotas, 58, 60–61, 63, 65, 70, 86; "voluntary," 64, 66–67, 79; monopoly and, 83

Randall, Samuel J., 35
Randolph, John, 13
Raskob, John J., 55
Reciprocal Trade Agreements Program Act (1934), 55–57, 58, 62–65, 68, 72; Roosevelt's Request for Authority to Enter (text), 145–147; Act (text), 147–150; Roosevelt's Request for Strengthening . . . March 26, 1945 (text), 150–155; Extension of Trade Agreements Act, July 5, 1945 (text), 155–156
reciprocity principle, 37–38, 40; Canadian treaties and, 26–27, 43–44; Roosevelt and, 55–57
Reconstruction period, 31–32, 80–81
Reed, Thomas, 36, 40; Speech on the Mills Tariff, 1888 (text), 133–139
Report on Manufactures (Hamilton), 12; text, 95–106
Republican party, 25, 28–29, 43–44, 46–47, 48, 72; tariff reform movement and, 31–32, 33, 35, 36, 38–41, 42, 43, 45; Hawley-Smoot (1930) and, 50, 51, 52, 54, 55; Reciprocal Trade Program (1934) and, 56, 62, 63
Revenue Act (1971), 71
Rhode Island, 10, 42
Roosevelt, Franklin D., 55–57; Request for Authority to Enter into Reciprocal Trade Agreements, March 2, 1934 (text), 145–47; Request for Strengthening the Trade Agreements Act, March 26, 1945 (text), 150–155
Roosevelt, Theodore, 44
Rumania, 78
Russia, 14. See also Soviet Union

St. Lawrence River, 26
Salvador, 37
Scott, Dred, 25
Second Bank of the United States, 16
Sherman, John, 32
Sherman Silver Purchase Act, repeal (1893), 38
Simmons, Furnifold M., 45
Smith, Alfred E., 50
Smithsonian Accord of December 18, 1971, 76–77, 79; text, 196–197
Smoot, Reed, 51
South, The, 13, 14, 16, 17, 22, 26, 38, 52, 80; nullification issue and, 18, 19–21; Morrill Tariff and, 28, 29. *See also specific states*
South America, 37, 54, 67. *See also specific countries*
South Carolina, 13, 18, 19, 20
South Korea, 78
Soviet Union, 64, 65, 67–68, 75; rapprochement, 78, 86
Spain, 37
Spanish-American War, 40, 81
Stanwood, Edward, cited, 31
Stevens, Thaddeus, 30
subsidies, 83
Sugar Trust, 40
Sweden, 14, 66
Switzerland, 66, 76

Taft, William Howard, 41, 42, 43
Tariff Act (1789), 10–11; text, 91–95
Tariff Act (1816), 12–14
Tariff Act (1818), 14
Tariff Act (1824), 14–15, 17, 19, 22
Tariff Act (1828), 15–18, 19, 22, 44
Tariff Act (1832), 18–19, 20, 22
Tariff Act (1842), 21–23
Tariff Act (1846), 23–25, 26
Tariff Act (1857), 25–26, 28
Tariff Act (1862), 30

Tariff Act (1864), 30, 31
Tariff Act (1870), 32
Tariff Act (1872), 33
Tariff Act (1883), 33–35
Tariff Act (1907), 40
Tariff Act (proposed, 1969), 73; Nixon's Message on United States Trade Policy, November 18, 1969 (text), 188–196
Taussig, Frank W., 82; on Hawley-Smoot, 142–144
Tennessee, 14, 18, 23
Texas, 23, 44, 70
textile industries, 19, 30, 33, 44, 45, 48, 62, 71, 72, 82; raw wool and, 14, 15, 16, 17, 28, 31, 32, 34, 39, 42; McKinley Tariff and, 36, 37; Dingley Tariff and, 40, 42, 43; quotas, 64, 66–67, 73, 77, 78, 79
Trade Act (1970), 73; Nixon's Message on United States Trade Policy, November 18, 1969, text, 188–196
Trade Agreements Act (1951), 64
Trade Agreements Extension Act (1945), 57, 59, 60; text, 155–56
Trade Expansion Act (1962), 56, 68–70, 71, 84, 85; Kennedy's Special Message on Foreign Trade Policy (text), 166–179; Act text, 179
Trade Expansion Act (1968), 72; Johnson's Message on Proposed . . . Act (text), 182–188
treaties, 40, 45–46; Canadian, 26–27, 43–44; Latin American, 37–38, 41; Hawley-Smoot Tariff and, 54, 56; concession negotiation procedures, 57, 58–63, 69, 70–72, 79; Lend-Lease, 59; Common Market, 65–66, 67; Generalized Preference, 78–79
Treaty of Rome (1957), 66
Trinidad, 37

Truman, Harry S., 59, 61, 62; Executive Order for Escape Clauses from Concessions in Trade Agreements, February 25, 1947 (text), 159–162
Tyler, John, 21–22

"underdeveloped" nations, 67, 78–79, 85
Underwood, Oscar W., 44
Underwood-Simmons Tariff Act (1913), 44–46, 47
United Kingdom, 5. *See also* Great Britain
United Nations Economic and Social Council, 59
United States Agricultural Adjustment Administration, 55
United States Congress, 10–13; sectional pressures in, 14–15, 16, 17–18, 20, 28; Tariff Act of 1842 in, 21–22; Tariff Act of 1846 in, 23–24; slavery issue in, 25; Tariff Act of 1857 in, 25–26, 28; Canadian Reciprocity Treaty and, 27; Civil War costs and, 29–30, 31, 32, 34; Reconstruction and, 31–33, 81; Tariff Commission (1882) and, 33–34; Cleveland Message (1887), 35–36, 118–24; special sessions of, 39–40, 41, 44, 47, 50; election of 1910, 43; Wilson message (1913), text, 139–142; Fordney Emergency Tariff Bill (1921), 47; rate revision powers, 51, 62–63, 70; Reciprocal Trade Agreements (1934) and, 55, 56–57, 62–63, 72; International Trade Organization Charter and, 59–60, 61; Alliance for Progress and, 67; Trade Expansion Act (1962) and, 68, 70; American Selling Price repeal in, 71, 72, 73; exchange rate crisis (1970's) and, 76; textile import restraints (1971) and, 78; investment abroad and, 86. *See also* United States House of Representatives; United States Senate
United States Constitution, 10, 46
United States Department of Agriculture, 55
United States Department of Commerce, 55
United States Department of State, 55, 56, 58, 59
United States Executive Committee on Commercial Policy, 55, 56
United States House of Representatives, 15, 16–17, 18, 19, 23, 26, 30; Morrill Tariff Acts in, 28–29, 32; Tariff Act of 1883 in, 34; Ways and Means Committee of, 35, 36, 38, 40, 41, 44, 47, 62, 72; Tariff Act of 1909 in, 41, 42; Republican revolt (1909) in, 43; Canadian reciprocity issue (1911) and, 44; Tariff Act of 1913 in, 44, 45; Hawley-Smoot Tariff in, 51–52; Reciprocal Trade Agreements (1934) and, 56; Trade Expansion Act of 1962 and, 68; Trade Act of 1970 in, 73
United States Office of Civil and Defense Mobilization, 63
United States Presidency: proclamation duties and, 37–38, 40; maximum-and-minimum values principle and, 43; Senate relations of, 45; rate revision powers of, 48–49, 51, 53, 57, 59, 60, 62–63, 68–69, 70, 73, 150–155, 155–156; reciprocal trade authority of, 55–57, 62, 68, 145–147, 166–179; quota imposition powers of, 63; domestic industry aid and, 69–70, 73; export credit powers of, 78. *See also individual presidents*

United States President's Commission on International Trade and Investment Policy, 85
United States President's Council of Economic Advisers, 79
United States President's Council on International Economic Policy, 85
United States Senate, 15, 16–17, 18, 23–24, 30, 42; Morrill Tariff Acts in, 28–29, 32; Reconstruction tariff revisions in, 32–33, 36; trade treaties and, 37, 40, 44, 60; Tariff Act of 1894 in, 38–39; Finance Committee of, 45, 47, 51, 62, 73; Tariff Act of 1922 in, 47–48; Hawley-Smoot in, 51–52; Reciprocal Trade Program and, 56, 60, 62; Trade Expansion Act of 1962 in, 68; Grains Treaty (1968), 71; Trade Act (1970), 73
United States Supreme Court, 25, 39
United States Tariff Commission, 43, 44, 48–49, 53, 70; Reciprocal Trade Agreements and, 55, 57, 62
United States Treasury, 12, 13, 25, 29, 33–35, 76; Compromise Tariff of 1833 and, 19, 20; Tariff Act of 1842 and, 21, 22, 23
United States War Trade Board, 47

Van Buren, Martin, 16, 18, 21
Vandenberg, Arthur, 56

Vare, William S., 51
Venezuela, 38
Verplanck Bill (1833), 19
Vietnam War, 72, 73, 75, 81, 86
Virginia, 13, 19, 21

Walker, Robert J., 23
War of 1812, 6, 12, 13, 80
Washington, George, 10
Weaver, James B., 38
Webster, Daniel, 13–14, 15, 17, 18, 20, 21; Speech of 1824 upon the Tariff (text), 109–112
Wells, David A., 32
West, The, 14, 16, 17, 19, 22, 25, 26, 31, 32, 38; Morrill Tariff and, 28, 29; Tariff Act of 1909 and, 41, 42; agricultural interests in, 47, 48, 51, 52, 80
West Germany, 5, 65
Whig party, 21–22, 23, 25
White, Eric Wyndham, 62
Wilson, William L., 38
Wilson, Woodrow, 44, 45, 47; Tariff Reform Message of 1913 (text), 139–142
Wilson-Gorman Tariff Act (1894), 38–39, 40, 41
Woolens Act (1867), 32
World War I, 46–47, 48, 53, 81
World War II, 4, 48, 56, 58, 59, 67, 74, 84; economic recovery after, 62, 65–66, 73, 81, 162–165
Wright, Silas, 18, 22

Yugoslavia, 70

D. VAN NOSTRAND ANVIL BOOKS

1 *MAKING OF MODERN FRENCH MIND*—Kohn
2 *THE AMERICAN REVOLUTION*—Morris
3 *THE LATE VICTORIANS*—Ausubel
4 *WORLD IN THE 20th CENTURY*—Rev. Ed.—Snyder
5 *50 DOCUMENTS OF THE 20th CENTURY*—Snyder
6 *THE AGE OF REASON*—Snyder
7 *MARX AND THE MARXISTS*—Hook
8 *NATIONALISM*—Kohn
9 *MODERN JAPAN*—Rev. Ed.—Tiedemann
10 *50 DOCUMENTS OF THE 19th CENTURY*—Snyder
11 *CONSERVATISM*—Viereck
12 *THE PAPACY*—Corbett
13 *AGE OF THE REFORMATION*—Bainton
14 *DOCUMENTS IN AMERICAN HISTORY*—Rev. Ed.—Morris
15 *CONTEMPORARY AFRICA*—Rev. Ed.—Wallbank
16 *THE RUSSIAN REVOLUTIONS OF 1917*—Curtiss
17 *THE GREEK MIND*—Agard
18 *BRITISH CONSTITUTIONAL HISTORY SINCE 1832*—Schuyler and Weston
19 *THE NEGRO IN THE U.S., Vol. I: A History to 1945*—Logan
20 *AMERICAN CAPITALISM*—Hacker
21 *LIBERALISM*—Schapiro
22 *THE FRENCH REVOLUTION, 1789-1799*—Gershoy
23 *HISTORY OF MODERN GERMANY*—Snyder
24 *HISTORY OF MODERN RUSSIA*—Kohn
25 *NORTH ATLANTIC CIVILIZATION*—Kraus
26 *NATO*—Salvadori
27 *DOCUMENTS IN U.S. FOREIGN POLICY*—Brockway
28 *AMERICAN FARMERS' MOVEMENTS*—Shannon
29 *HISTORIC DECISIONS OF SUPREME COURT*—Swisher
30 *MEDIEVAL TOWN*—Mundy and Riesenberg
31 *REVOLUTION AND REACTION 1848-1852*—Bruun
32 *CONTEMPORARY SOUTHEAST ASIA*—Buss
33 *HISTORIC DOCUMENTS OF W. W. I*—Snyder
34 *HISTORIC DOCUMENTS OF W. W. II*—Langsam*
35 *ROMAN MIND AT WORK*—MacKendrick
36 *SHORT HISTORY OF CANADA*—Masters
37 *WESTWARD MOVEMENT IN U.S.*—Billington
38 *DOCUMENTS IN MEDIEVAL HISTORY*—Downs
39 *BASIC HISTORY OF AMERICAN BUSINESS*—Rev. Ed.—Cochran
40 *DOCUMENTS IN CANADIAN HISTORY*—Talman
41 *FOUNDATIONS OF ISRAEL*—Janowsky
42 *MODERN CHINA*—Rowe
43 *BASIC HISTORY OF OLD SOUTH*—Stephenson
44 *THE BENELUX COUNTRIES*—Eyck
45 *MEXICO AND THE CARIBBEAN*—Rev. Ed.—Hanke
46 *SOUTH AMERICA*—Rev. Ed.—Hanke
47 *SOVIET FOREIGN POLICY, 1917-1941*—Kennan
48 *THE ERA OF REFORM, 1830-1860*—Commager
49 *EARLY CHRISTIANITY*—Bainton
50 *RISE AND FALL OF THE ROMANOVS*—Mazour
51 *CARDINAL DOCUMENTS IN BRITISH HISTORY*—Schuyler and Weston
52 *HABSBURG EMPIRE 1804-1918*—Kohn
53 *CAVOUR AND UNIFICATION OF ITALY*—Salvadori
54 *ERA OF CHARLEMAGNE*—Easton and Wieruszowski
55 *MAJOR DOCUMENTS IN AMERICAN ECONOMIC HISTORY, Vol. I*—Hacker
56 *MAJOR DOCUMENTS IN AMERICAN ECONOMIC HISTORY, Vol. II*—Hacker
57 *HISTORY OF THE CONFEDERACY*—Vandiver
58 *COLD WAR DIPLOMACY*—Graebner
59 *MOVEMENTS OF SOCIAL DISSENT IN MODERN EUROPE*—Schapiro
60 *MEDIEVAL COMMERCE*—Adelson
61 *THE PEOPLE'S REPUBLIC OF CHINA*—Buss
62 *WORLD COMMUNISM*—Hook
63 *ISLAM AND THE WEST*—Hitti

* Out of print; not available from Publisher.